Psychology

and

Religion

Psychology
and Religion

Edited by
David G. Benner

BAKER BOOK HOUSE
Grand Rapids, Michigan 49516

Library of Congress Cataloging-in-Publication Data

Psychology and religion / edited by David G. Benner.
    p.   cm.
   Includes index.
   ISBN 0-8010-0947-2
    1. Psychology—Religious aspects—Christianity. 2. Psychology,
Religious. 3. Christianity—Psychological aspects. I. Benner,
David G.
BF121.P8117 1987   88-3305
150—dc19   CIP

Contents

Part 2: Psychology in Christian Perspective

Part 3: Christian Psychology

Preface

The relationship between psychology and religion has often been fraught with tension and animosity. Psychologists have sometimes allowed their personal conflicts with religion to color their research and theorizing and religious persons have often permitted their anxieties about psychology's reductionistic methods to lead them to conclude that psychology is inherently hostile to religion.

Sigmund Freud's uncharitable views of religion are well known. However, it is not always equally well appreciated that the system of psychology which he founded, psychoanalysis, is neither hostile to, nor incompatible with, religion. Similarly, Albert Ellis has been singularly vocal in his opposition to religion of all sorts, but his rational-emotive therapy is not inherently antireligious. Many Christian therapists find both rational-emotive therapy and psychoanalysis quite acceptable foundations for their work.

Christians frequently regard psychology with great ambivalence. On the one hand, its subject matter fascinates them and they may feel themselves drawn to it. However, they approach it with considerable suspicion. Insights must therefore be carefully evaluated and taken one at a time. No system of knowledge should be adopted wholesale in an uncritical manner. Christians should attempt to bring their understanding of all of life, including themselves, into harmony with a Christian world- and life-view. However, too often suspicion and distrust block Christians from learning from psychology. This book should make clear both the profitability of a critical Christian evaluation of psychology as well as the significant contributions which psychology can in fact make to Christianity.

This volume is divided into three parts. Part 1, Psychology of Religion, consists of nineteen chapters addressing aspects of religious experience frequently studied by psychologists. After an initial chapter which provides an overview of the field of the psychology of religion, subsequent chapters present current research findings and a Christian perspective on various aspects of religious experience.

Part 2, Psychology in Christian Perspective, examines a number of aspects of psychology in the light of the Christian faith. These are topics which are not traditionally included within the psychology of religion but which are addressed by psychologists. The nineteen chapters in this section present issues and areas of research within psychology of interest and importance to Christians.

Part 3, Christian Psychology, includes fourteen chapters which deal with topics not usually addressed by secular psychologists but of particular concern to Christian psychologists who wish to develop a psychology which is distinctively Christian.

The chapters in this book were previously published in the *Baker Encyclopedia of Psychology* (Benner, 1985). The authors are eminently well qualified to write on the topics presented. Drawn from the ranks of both academic and practicing clinical psychologists and psychiatrists, the thirty-three contributors to this anthology include many who are currently giving leadership to efforts to relate the discipline and practice of psychology to the Christian faith. It is hoped, therefore, that this volume will be of assistance to those who wish to further understand this relationship.

Reference

Benner, D. G., ed. 1985. *Baker Encyclopedia of Psychology*. Grand Rapids: Baker Book House.

Contributors

Stanley N. Ballard, Th.M., Ph.D.
Chairman and Professor of
  Psychology
Cedarville College

James R. Beck, Ph.D.
Associate Professor of Psychology
  and Counseling
Denver Seminary

David G. Benner, Ph.D.
Professor of Psychology
Wheaton College

C. Markham Berry, M.D.
Department of Psychiatry
Emory University School of
  Medicine

William G. Bixler, Ph.D.
Oklahoma Christian Counseling
  Center
Oklahoma City

Jeffrey M. Brandsma, Ph.D.
Professor and Director of Clinical
  Psychology Internship

Department of Psychiatry
Medical College of Georgia

Richard E. Butman, Ph.D.
Assistant Professor of Psychology
Wheaton College

Dr. Clark D. Campbell, Ph.D.
Dammasch State Hospital
Wilsonville, Oregon

John D. Carter, Ph.D.
Professor of Psychology
Rosemead School of Psychology
Biola University

Mark P. Cosgrove, Ph.D.
Associate Professor of
  Psychology
Taylor University

J. Harold Ellens, Ph.D.
Executive Director
Christian Association for
  Psychological Studies
Farmington Hills, Michigan

Craig W. Ellison, Ph.D.
Professor of Psychology and Urban
 Studies
Alliance Theological Seminary
Nyack College

Ronald Enroth, Ph.D.
Professor of Sociology
Westmont College

C. Stephen Evans, Ph.D.
Associate Professor of Philosophy
 and Curator of the Hong
 Kierkegaard Library
St. Olaf College

John A. Hammes, Ph.D.
Professor of Psychology
University of Georgia

Elizabeth L. Hillstrom, Ph.D.
Associate Professor of Psychology
Wheaton College

Cedric B. Johnson, Ph.D.
Director
Bethesda Counseling Clinic
Santa Monica

Stanton L. Jones, Ph.D.
Associate Professor of Psychology
Wheaton College

Richard D. Kahoe, Ph.D.
Christian Haven Homes
Wheatfield, Indiana

William T. Kirwan, D.Min., Ph.D.
Psychiatric Associates
St. Louis

H. Newton Malony, Ph.D.
Professor of Psychology and Director
 of Programs in the Integration of
 Psychology and Theology
Graduate School of Psychology
Fuller Theological Seminary

George Matheson, Ph.D.
Chief of Psychology
Etobicoke General Hospital
Rexdale, Ontario

John McDonagh, Ph.D.
Private Practice
Huntington, New York

Rodney B. McKean, Ph.D.
First Alliance Church
Tucson

S. Bruce Narramore, Ph.D.
Professor and Dean
Rosemead School of Psychology
Biola University

Ronald H. Rottschafer, Ph.D.
Private Practice
Oak Brook, Illinois

Onas C. Scandrette, Ed.D.
Emeritus Professor of Psychology
Wheaton College

Joseph E. Talley, Ph.D.
Staff Psychologist
Counseling and Psychological
 Services
Clinical Associate
Department of Psychiatry
Duke University

Randie L. Timpe, Ph.D.
Chairperson and Professor of
 Psychology
Mt. Vernon Nazarene College

Bryan Van Dragt, Ph.D.
Private Practice
Gig Harbor, Washington

Henry A. Virkler, Ph.D.
Adjunct Faculty Member
Psychological Studies Institute
Georgia State University
Director of Counseling
 Services
Ministry Counseling Center
Atlanta

Paul C. Vitz, Ph.D.
Associate Professor of Psychology
New York University

William T. Weyerhaeuser, Ph.D.
Private Practice
Gig Harbor, Washington

Frances J. White, Ph.D.
Professor of Psychology
Wheaton College

Part 1

Psychology of Religion

1

Psychology of Religion: Overview
H. Newton Malony

The *psychology of religion* refers to the psychological study of religious issues, just as there might be the psychological study of social or family or developmental issues. Therefore, the psychology of religion includes efforts to understand, predict, and control the thoughts, words, feelings, and actions of persons when they are acting religiously. A fairly well accepted definition of acting religiously is that offered by James (1902/1961) in his Gifford Lectures: "Whatever men do in relation to that which they consider to be divine" (p. 42).

Psychological studies of religion have generally followed the distinction suggested by Berger (1974) in approaching religion either functionally or substantively. This distinction resembles somewhat the contrast made by James between roots and fruits. The functional approach to religion emphasizes the roots, or motivations, for religious behavior, while the substantive approach emphasizes the fruits, or the overt expressions, of such motivations. For example, Freud (1928) dealt entirely with the way religion served to assuage the neurotic individual's longing for a protective father figure (a functional approach), while Starbuck (1899) focused on the age and occasion of conversion (a substantive approach).

Although psychologists of religion have not shown a bias toward one approach or the other, at least two have expressed a preference for the substantive approach. James suggested that the fruits of religion were more important than the roots. He believed that it was more important to evaluate whether becoming religious resulted in greater mental health and personality integration than to study the motivations that led to religious behavior. His approach was an evaluation of the personal results of religion. James felt that there could be good and bad religion, depending on its effects. It was better to study substantive (overt) religion than to study functional (covert) religion because such an approach avoided labeling someone religious who would deny the ascription. For example, to say that all people are religious because all people ask questions about the meaning of life seems inappropriate, since some people would satisfy that question by attending professional football games while others would attend church. Lemert suggested that there is a need to find a definition of religion that could be agreed upon by everyone. He proposed that only those behaviors which reflect belief in a transempirical reality and which are expressed by participation in a recognizable social group should be called religious. Thus, the church on the corner would be religious while the Rotary Club would not.

Historical Developments

The early period

American psychologists became leaders in the psychology of religion movement during the period 1880–1925. After that time religion became a taboo topic and was not revived as a legitimate area for investigation until the 1960s. The reasons for this demise and rebirth of interest are varied.

Although the movement was given its major impetus by the publication in 1902 of James's classic *The Varieties of Religious Experience*, the last decade of the nineteenth century had seen not only the first published study of conversion (Leuba, 1896) but also the first textbook (Starbuck, 1899). The concern with conversion was to be a dominant theme for study. James, more a theoretician than an empirical researcher, depended heavily on Starbuck's surveys for material in *The Varieties*.

The stability of the psychology of religion movement was due in no small part to the leadership of G. Stanley Hall. He had initially trained for the ministry but shifted to philosophy and psychology. His interest in religious issues remained strong, however, and as early as the 1880s he lectured to educators in Boston on the moral and religious training of children and adolescents. Although he is chiefly remembered for the encouragement and support he gave to others, Hall wrote *Adolescence* (1904) and *Jesus the Christ, in the Light of Psychology* (1917). Both dealt with the motivations and psychodynamic rationale for religious conversion, a phenomenon thought to be characteristic of the teen-age years.

Hall taught at, and subsequently became president of, Clark University. Here he gathered a group of students who engaged vigorously in a program of research in the psychology of religion. Out of this "Clark school" came many of the studies that made the psychology of religion a highly respected part of American psychology during the first two decades of this century. That Hall became the first president of the American Psychological Association no doubt added to the legitimacy which the movement acquired. Both the *American Journal of Psychology* and the *Psychological Bulletin* printed many articles on the psychology of religion, and beginning in 1904 the *Bulletin* carried an annual review of the literature in the field. One of Hall's most important contributions, however, was the establishment of a journal devoted to the psychology of religion, the *American Journal of Religious Psychology and Education*. It continued periodic publication under the title *Journal of Religious Psychology* until 1915. Perhaps the irregular appearance of the journal plus its demise were omens of a declining interest as early as the second decade of this century.

Among the students of Hall, J. H. Leuba was the most prolific. As contrasted with Starbuck, who offered no rationale for religion beyond the storm and stress of the adolescent quest for meaning and identity, Leuba offered a physiological reductionistic alternative. He followed Freud and others in explaining away the validity of supernatural objects of worship (i.e., gods) and suggested they were only physiological epiphenomena.

The tenor of much of this study during the first part of the century was strictly positivistic in that it explicitly saw itself as engaged in applying scientific rigor to "the most complex, the most inaccessible and, of all, the most sacred domain—that of religion" (Starbuck, 1899, p. 1). However, the majority of the researchers were not antagonistic toward religion and, to the contrary, were concerned to contribute to the progress of religion. It was this applied concern that some have thought was partially instrumental in the loss of respect that the field was later to have in the wider psychological community.

1920–1960

There is little doubt that the 1920s saw a rapid demise of interest in the field. The annual reviews of the field in the *Psychological Bulletin* were not published between 1928 and 1932. They ceased altogether after a single review in 1933. This decline persisted until the 1960s, during which time the Society for the Scientific Study of Religion and the Christian Association for Psychological Studies were founded. Also the Catholic Psychological Association began meeting along with the American Psychological Association—an event that eventually led to the establishment of a division for the psychology of religion in the national association in the mid-1970s.

The reasons given for this hiatus of interest in the psychology of religion include: 1) an overly close alliance with theology and philosophy and with the goals of religious institutions; 2) the lack of an integrating theory around which to gather facts; 3) the overuse of the questionnaire as a method of data collection; 4) the rise of a behavioristic, positivistic world-view that led to an avoidance of subjective introspection; 5) the emphasis on psychoanalytic interpretations which came to supersede empirical approaches; 6) the lack of an impact on general psychology. Although the movement had defined itself as empirical and positivistic, subsequent advances in social psychology, for example, did not incorporate interest in religion; thus the field became neglected in the viewpoint of mainline psychology. Many of the issues of the psychology of religion were taken over by religious-education and pastoral-counseling movements—both of which began in the late 1920s.

One of the major influences on this change of interest may have been the lack of belief in the importance of religion by psychologists. In contrast to sociologists, who understand religion to be one of the major institutions of society and a necessary field of study, many psychologists have been heavily influenced by scientism and consider religion to be a vestige of premodern times that is unhealthful and will be outgrown with the passing of the years. Therefore, those who study religion or are religious have been discounted by many general psychologists.

Current status

The contemporary revival of interest in the psychology of religion was due in no small part to a revival of interest in religion in the culture at large. The 1950s were the time of a religious revival in the United States. The first modern text in the field, Clark's *The Psychology of Religion: An Introduction to Religious Experience and Behavior*

(1958), by its very title attests to a theme that has continued to occupy the interests of psychologists to the present; namely, the experience of being religious.

Another factor that has influenced the renewal of interest in the field has been the developing concern for the relation of religion and mental health. This was one of the concerns initiated by Freud's writings. It never fully disappeared from the scene, even though academic study of the psychology of religion did. Numerous writers in the field, beginning with Pfister and Boisen and continuing down to the present through Fromm, Menninger, and Ellis, have kept these issues alive.

Dittes (1968) noted several influences on the growth of the movement and commented on a lack of integrating theory for the field. His judgment was that this was a dangerous lack that might bring about another demise. Capps (1974) was more optimistic about the future. He felt that the new existentialist-humanist emphasis held much promise for a rediscovery of subjective introspection and individual experience. He further suggested that the greater willingness of psychologists of religion to deal with ontological questions, along with the opening up of the field to interdisciplinary study were encouraging developments.

Methods of Study

More than 20 different methods of study have been employed by psychologists of religion. Most of these involve self reports of one sort or another. Interviews, biographies, content analysis of diaries, and questionnaires have been used to investigate both functional dynamics and substantive behaviors. Although a number have investigated historical and cultural dimensions, psychologists of religion have typically focused on individual experience and behavior. Case studies were very common in some of the early work, and have again become a feature in recent investigations.

Much of the work has been correlational in format in that historical facts and verbal reports or answers have been related to certain types of religious behavior such as church attendance or devotional practice. Experimental studies in which the design involved the manipulation of an independent variable have been few. Several religious researchers have called for more of these types of investigations, but there is a continuing debate as to whether the phenomenon is of such a character to be amenable to experimental manipulation. As in numerous other areas of human behavior, religious behavior may be one of those areas which is destroyed when it is overcontrolled experimentally.

Some theorists are convinced that religion, at least in its substantive expressions, must remain a dependent and can never be treated as an independent variable. However, as Dittes (1968) noted, it is possible to treat such a religious behavior as church membership as either a dependent variable toward which one predicts on the basis of past cultural environments or as an independent variable on the basis of which one predicts future behavior such as opinions about nuclear war. Some may say that this is not true manipulation. However, it would be unethical to manipulate the social environment in order to see who would become religious, just as it would be unethical to withhold a known beneficial drug to see whether certain persons had natural immunity to a given illness.

Current Research

In the selected areas of interest discussed below, psychodynamics of religion and religious development are considered examples of a functional approach. Religious experience, religious orientation, and religious dimensions are substantive. These areas are presented as representative rather than exhaustive of the foci of psychology of religion.

Psychodynamics of religion

Without question the dominant force in psychodynamics has been psychoanalysis. Freud's writings reflect a persistent preoccupation with religious issues. They frequently include variations on his theme that religion is mass neurosis which, although preferable to individual neurosis, is based on a fixation at an immature level of development. He relates religious experience to a search for an exterior source of control for the unresolved ambivalence persons have toward parents to whom they ascribe unreasonable authority. Freud (1928) opined that religion should be superseded if not obliterated in order that mature development could progress.

From a more benign, less prejudgmental point of view, other authors have investigated the psychodynamics of religious experience. For example, Barkman (1968) suggested the possibility that verbal, emotional, social, and experiential personality types would be found more often in Reformed/Lutheran, Methodist, Anabaptist, and Catholic/Episcopalian religious groups because of the match between given types of religious expressions and these personality types. No validation of this has been attempted. Further, Benson and Spika

(1973) found that the more positive a person's self-esteem, the more likely he was to perceive God as loving, and vice versa, thus confirming a relationship between one's type of religious understanding and a predisposing personality dimension.

Religious development

In this area the research generally has affirmed religion and has had practical implications for religious education. Psychologists have been concerned with two issues: 1) How does religion relate to the developmental needs of persons from childhood through old age? 2) How does the content of religious beliefs change across the life span? Taking his cues from Piaget, Elkind (1970) proposed that the developing child's cognitive needs for conservation, representation, relations, and comprehension could be met through religion's offering of permanence in God, authority in Scripture, experience in worship, and meaning through providence, respectively. Building on contemporary humanistic psychology, Clippinger (1973) proposed a model for personhood that includes a deep-seated religious need. Similar to Jung's religious dynamism, this need must be met or personality is truncated and inadequately developed. Thus religion is presented as meeting an innate and instinctive urge in persons.

Changes in religious belief is the other developmental issue that has been addressed. For example, Goldman (1964) studied the changes that occur in religious belief among English children and adolescents. He noted a shift from concrete, to literal, to symbolic understandings of religious ideas. Feldman (1979) did extensive survey research on changes in religious belief and practice during the college years and found, as was expected, a trend toward liberalization and secularization in this age group. More recently Fowler (1981), working within Kohlberg's theories of moral development, has proposed a theory of faith development that involves the relating of cognitive structures, innate needs for meaning, and the interpretation of religious symbols. His multistage model resembles Goldman in his basic thesis that maturation involves an increasing tolerance for others' beliefs and a tendency to interpret religious ideas symbolically.

Religious experience

The role that conversion played in the field at the turn of the century has been taken over by religious experience. With the increasing interest in altered states of consciousness and transpersonal psychology, religious experience has become a popular focus of attention. Clark (1968) has been the dominant voice in this area, having written about the mystical dimensions of religious experience for the past two decades. It has been his contention that modern society with its pragmatic, technological, rationalistic emphases militates against religious experience, which he, along with other theorists, considers a basic human proclivity. He has therefore advocated the use of triggers such as meditative practices and even psychedelic drugs to induce the experience. While not necessarily agreeing with his willingness to use pharmacological substances for this purpose, many other scholars agree with his analysis and encourage persons to indulge this dimension of their personalities. Among research-oriented psychologists Hood (1976) has been most active in investigating the correlates of intense mystical experience. He has related it to the type of church background, ego strength, nature experiences, and mental health.

Through the years the focal religious experience that has occupied the attention of psychologists of religion has been conversion, and although other matters have assumed importance, there remains a persistent interest in this phenomenon as it applies to both Christianity and to newer religious movements in the United States. A recent publication (Johnson & Malony, 1982) summarizes the literature on Christian conversion, while an earlier volume (Needleman, 1978) attends to non-Christian movements.

Religious orientation

As originally conceived by Allport and Ross (1967), religious orientation has been the major theme in the psychology of religion for the last 15 years. Many investigations of this phenomenon have been undertaken. Originally conceived by Allport to explain the relationship between religiosity and prejudice, religion that is oriented intrinsically (toward inner, personal, private meaning) and religion that is extrinsically oriented (toward fellowship, pragmatic satisfaction, external value) have been contrasted in numerous studies. While Allport and his students found intrinsically oriented religion to be more idealistic and less related to ethnic prejudice, subsequent theorists have found less clear relationships between these orientations and other behaviors. Some have noted that the concepts behind the terms *intrinsic* and *extrinsic* are value loaded in favor of individualism—a characteristic not typically available to the average person. Others have concluded that the two orientations are not as clear conceptually as might be hoped. The research is ongoing and stimulating. Most recently an age-free form of the Extrinsic-Intrinsic Religious Orientation Scale has been designed to assess whether there is a tendency for persons to mature in one direction.

Religious dimensions

Finally, the last two decades have witnessed increasing attention paid to describing the several dimensions of religiousness. This line of research has attempted to develop taxonomies of how religious persons differ from one another. While it has been obvious that there are variations in beliefs among religious persons (e.g., fundamentalist, conservative, mainline, liberal), it has been less apparent that religious persons differ in religious knowledge, the importance of religion, openness to doubt, and participation. Among psychologists the most extensive research into these phenomena has been that of King and Hunt (1975). In a study involving a national sample they isolated a number of dimensions, including belief, devotional practices, church attendance, church activity, financial support, religious knowledge, rated importance of religion, intrinsic/extrinsic orientation, and attitude toward despair. Currently attempts are being made to see if this pattern can be replicated among racial and ethnic groups, since the original research was conducted among whites.

The religion of psychologists

One final aspect of research in psychology of religion should be noted; namely, studies of the religion of psychologists. Since all research in this century has indicated that psychologists are the least religious of all scientists, it has become of interest to see how, if at all, this pattern is changing in the present and what effect, if any, the religion of the psychologist has on the research that is done. In a recent study (Ragan, Malony, & Beit-Hallahmi, 1980) it was noted that while the previous pattern remains, an increasing number of psychologists are actively religious. And at least one theorist (Malony, 1972) has contended that only the religious psychologist knows the appropriate questions to ask of religion in psychological research.

References

Allport, G. W., & Ross, J. M. Personal religious orientation and prejudice. *Journal of Personality and Social Psychology*, 1967, *5*, 432–443.

Barkman, P. F. The relationship of personality modes to religious experience and behavior. *Journal of the American Scientific Affiliation*, 1968, *20*, 27–30.

Benson, P., & Spilka, B. God image as a function of self-image and locus of control. *Journal for the Scientific Study of Religion*, 1973, *12*, 297–310.

Berger, P. L. Some second thoughts on substantive versus functional definitions of religion. *Journal for the Scientific Study of Religion*, 1974, *13*, 125–133.

Capps, D. Contemporary psychology of religion: The task of theoretical reconstruction. *Social Research*, 1974, *41*, 362–383.

Clark, W. H. *The psychology of religion: An introduction to religious experience and behavior*. New York: Macmillan, 1958.

Clark, W. H. The psychology of religious experience. *Psychology Today*, 1968, *1*(9), 42–47, 68–69.

Clippinger, J. A. Toward a human psychology of personality. *Journal of Religion and Health*, 1973, *12*, 241–258.

Dittes, J. E. Psychology of religion. In N. Lindzey & E. Aronson (Eds.), *The handbook of social psychology* (2nd ed.). Reading, Mass: Addison-Wesley, 1968.

Elkind, D. The origins of religion in the child. *Review of Religious Research*, 1970, *12*, 35–42.

Feldman, K. A. Change and stability of religious orientations during college. *Review of Religious Research*, 1969, *11*, 40–60.

Fowler, J. W. *Stages of faith*. San Francisco: Harper & Row, 1981.

Freud, S. *The future of an illusion*. New York: Liveright, 1928.

Goldman, R. *Religious thinking from childhood to adolescence*. New York: Seabury, 1964.

Hall, G. S. *Adolescence* (2 vols.). New York: Arno Press, 1904.

Hall, G. S. *Jesus, the Christ, in the light of psychology* (2 vols.). New York: Doubleday, 1917.

Hood, R. W. Conceptual criticisms of regressive explanations of mysticism. *Review of Religious Research*, 1976, *17*, 179–188.

James, W. *The varieties of religious experience*. New York: Modern Library, 1961. (Originally published, 1902.)

Johnson, C. B., & Malony, H. N. *Christian conversion: Biblical and psychological perspectives*. Grand Rapids: Zondervan, 1982.

King, M. B., & Hunt, R. A. Measuring the religious variable: National replication. *Journal for the Scientific Study of Religion*, 1975, *14*, 13–22.

Lemert, C. C. Defining non-church religion. *Review of Religious Research*, 1975, *16*, 186–197.

Leuba, J. H. A study in the psychology of religious phenomena. *American Journal of Psychology*, 1896, *5*, 309–385.

Malony, H. N. The psychologist-Christian. *Journal of the American Scientific Affiliation*, 1972, *24*, 135–144.

Needleman, J. *Understanding the new religions*. New York: Seabury, 1978.

Ragan, C., Malony, H. N., & Beit-Hallahmi, B. Psychologists and religion: Professional factors and personal belief. *Review of Religious Research*, 1980, *21*, 208–217.

Starbuck, E. D. *Psychology of religion.* London: Walter Scott, 1899.

Additional Reading

Malony, H. N. (Ed.). *Current perspectives in the psychology of religion.* Grand Rapids: Eerdmans, 1977.

2

Conscience
S. Bruce Narramore

The term *conscience* refers to the set of personality processes involved in evaluating oneself by one's accepted ideals or standards. Beyond this broad definition, however, there is little agreement on the precise meaning and nature of conscience. Psychological theorists shape their understanding and definition of conscience to fit their theoretical framework. Fromm (1947), for example, spoke of an infantile, fear-based, authoritarian conscience and a more mature, rational, and sensitive humanistic conscience. Allport (1955) wrote of the generic conscience that enhances one's life, and Freud (1927) drew a general parallel between his concepts of the superego and conscience.

Theologians also differ in their understanding of conscience. Pierce (1955, p. 111), for example, sees conscience as God-given and the punitive functions of conscience as "the internal counterpart and complement of the wrath" of God. In contrast, Bavinck (1898) and Bonhoeffer (1959) view conscience as a result of the fall and as carrying out fallen humanity's attempt to "know good and evil" apart from God and to solve its moral dilemma on its own.

Conscience in the Bible

The Old Testament has no word fully equivalent to conscience. The Hebrew *lēb* (generally translated "heart"), however, is sometimes used to refer to the functions the New Testament calls conscience. Conscience (*syneidēsis*) is used 31 times in the New Testament, but nowhere is it clearly defined. Its functions include: 1) bearing witness or evaluating oneself in relation to a standard (Rom. 2:14–15); 2) assuring one of consistent, integrative living (2 Tim. 1:3); 3) motivating constructively (Rom. 13:5; Acts 24:16); 4) inhibiting unnecessarily (1 Cor. 8:4–8); and 5) producing feelings of guilt and self-condemnation (1 John 3:19–20).

The first three functions of conscience are God-given. As moral beings we are created with the capacity to observe ourselves and to live consistently and responsibly out of a motivation of love. At times, however, the conscience can also needlessly inhibit and become the source of self-punitive, destructive emotions of guilt. Although some assume these functions are also the work of God, Scripture indicates they are not. Paul speaks of those with a weak conscience that is overly restrictive (1 Cor. 8:7). And John indicates that condemnation is not God-given when he writes, "If our heart condemns us, God is greater than our heart" (1 John 3:20). The biblical doctrines of the atonement and justification make it clear that the believer's sins have already been paid for and that the Christian is no longer under condemnation (Rom. 8:1). Seen in this light the condemnation of a guilty conscience actually involves a denial of the efficacy of the atonement. It constitutes an additional, self-inflicted penalty or payment for one's sins.

Biblically conscience functions a great deal like the law. Prior to salvation it serves the useful purposes of showing us a standard to reach for, acting as a schoolmaster (Gal. 3:24), giving moral structure to society (Exod. 21:1–31:18), and showing us our failures and driving us to despair and consequently to God's grace (Rom. 5:20–21). After salvation, however, the Christian must learn to relate to conscience in an entirely different manner just as he does to the law. The attempt to merit acceptance or avoid punishment by living up to the demands of conscience can be as much a legalistic process as the attempt to merit God's approval by living up to the law. This effort to merit approval and avoid the condemnation of conscience must be replaced by a motivation of love growing out of the fact that Christ has fully taken our condemnation and that we are now acceptable through him.

The Development of Conscience

The processes we know as conscience develop out of the complex interaction between 1) one's God-given moral potential, which is rooted in the image of God and progressively unfolds with the development of one's cognitive capacities; 2) one's own desires and attempts to merit self-acceptance and avoid punishment; and 3) the impact of socializing agents, particularly parents. Although the Bible does not elaborate extensively on humanity's moral nature, it does describe us as moral beings, created in the image of God with the "law of God written in the heart" (Rom. 2:14–15). It is this fundamental moral nature that provides the ability for the individual to profit from the socializing process and to develop a set of moral values.

Beyond humanity's innate moral propensity and the law written on the heart, the unique shape of one's conscience is highly influenced by one's interaction with significant socialization agents. This takes place through the process of internalization. From early childhood children take in, or internalize, the ideals and expectations of parents and significant others because they fear parental punishment or rejection if they fall short and because they love and admire these significant adults. In the first five years of life parents are the main source of these expectations. As children grow older, they increasingly look to other authorities and to peers and broader social standards for the ideals they adopt.

As these ideals and expectations are internalized and merged with one's innate moral awareness and individual desires, they come together to form what is generally called the ideal self or the ego ideal. This set of ideals becomes the standard by which one judges himself or herself.

At the same time children are taking in their parents' values and standards they also internalize the corrective attitudes of significant others. When parents rely on angry, punitive corrections, children tend to take in these corrective attitudes as their own. As these punitive attitudes merge with the child's inherent sense of moral justice, they form the essential ingredients of punitive emotions of guilt generally called neurotic or false guilt. By contrast, when a child takes in predominantly loving disciplinary attitudes, those attitudes merge with the child's inherent moral sense and love to form a set of love-based corrective attitudes. These comprise the essence of godly sorrow, or what is sometimes referred to as true guilt.

With the completion of this process the development of the broad outlines of conscience is largely finished. Individuals have a set of standards, the perceptual ability to evaluate themselves (to bear witness), and two sets of corrective attitudes they can use to motivate themselves.

Pathologies of Conscience

Problems of conscience grow naturally out of disturbances in the function of conscience described above. Some people have problems with the functioning of conscience because they develop inadequate standards. They may have failed to internalize acceptable standards, or they may have repressed their inherent moral nature and developed antisocial or sociopathic personality styles because they have inappropriate values. Or they may have internalized rigid and narrow standards that inhibit unnecessarily, cause neurotic problems, and do not allow a creative and assertive style of life.

Others develop problems because of inappropriate corrective attitudes and emotions. Internalization of punitive corrective attitudes can result in the severe guilt emotions found in depressive and obsessive compulsive personalities, the two "guilt neuroses." The failure to internalize loving corrective attitudes can lead to a lack of concern for others and consequently antisocial behavior.

Psychotherapy of Problems of Conscience

An understanding of the processes involved in the development of conscience also provides direction for resolving problems of conscience. Effective therapy needs to give attention to the development and adequacy of both one's standards and one's corrective attitudes. People who have developed rigid, neurotic standards need to rework those. Those who have repressed or failed to internalize biblically and socially appropriate values need to develop those. And people who have developed self-punitive feelings need to internalize the fact that they are forgiven and accepted by God and can give up their own self-punishment. In each case this is most effectively carried out within the context of a meaningful personal relationship that provides an emotional bond to help effect deep changes in one's personal values rather than merely an intellectual change of standards.

References

Allport, G. *Becoming: Basic considerations for a psychology of personality.* New Haven: Yale University Press, 1955.

Bavinck, H. *Gereformerde dogmatiek* (Vol. 3). Kampen: J. H. Bos, 1898.

Bonhoeffer, D. *Creation and fall.* New York: Macmillan, 1959.

Freud, S. *The ego and the id.* London: Hogarth Press, 1927. (Originally published, 1923.)

Fromm, E. *Man for himself.* New York: Rinehart, 1947.

Pierce, C. A. *Conscience in the New Testament.* London: SCM, 1955.

Additional Reading

Narramore, B. *No condemnation: Rethinking guilt and motivation.* Grand Rapids: Zondervan, 1984.

3

Conversion
H. Newton Malony

Webster's dictionary suggests that the word *conversion* means to "turn around, transform, or change the characteristics of something." The word is sometimes used to refer to general personality or behavioral changes, such as those that result from education or psychotherapy. However, conversion refers most often to religious experiences in which attitudes or actions are dramatically altered, as when Paul was converted on the Damascus Road or, more recently, when Malcolm Muggeridge converted to Roman Catholicism.

The Paul and Muggeridge illustrations refer to the distinction between "inner" and "outer" conversion as suggested by some theorists. Often the joining of a given church or religious group (termed "outer" conversion) is mistaken for a radical change of perception and outlook (termed "inner" conversion). Although both may occur simultaneously, they are not necessarily synonymous. Gordon (1967) noted this fact in studying converts by marriage to the Jewish faith. Often these are cultural conversions rather than genuine transformations of outlook. Many persons attest that it was this outer conversion in which they participated when they joined the church in early adolescence and that this was followed by an inner conversion at a later time.

Whereas outer conversion refers to a formal action of identifying with a given faith, inner conversion refers to a newly acquired sense of inner security, unity, peace, and meaning such as is exemplified in Paul. James (1902) gave the classic definition of this experience: "To be converted, to be regenerate, to receive grace, to experience religion, to gain an assurance, are so many phrases which denote the process, gradual or sudden, by which a self hitherto divided, and consciously wrong, inferior and unhappy, becomes unified and consciously right, superior and happy, in consequence of its firmer hold on religious realities" (p. 157). James's definition has provided many of the themes which have been investigated by psychologists since the beginning of this century. These themes have included: 1) whether conversion is a process or an event; 2) the preconversion mental state; and 3) the nature of the inner change that occurs in conversion.

Conversion as Process or Event?

James considered conversion to be "a process, gradual or sudden," whereas many religionists have thought of it as a specific event occurring at a given point in time. In fact, many have used the word to apply only to those who can point to a time and place at which they were "born again" in a manner similar to that recommended to Nicodemus by Jesus (John 3:3) and exemplified by Paul (Acts 9). However, James contended that these events were part of a process and used the term *conversion* to apply both to those who could and those who could not point to a specific moment of decision.

Healthy and sick minded converts

James contended that the self-awareness of both sudden and gradual converts was preceded by a period of preparation whether the individuals were conscious of it or not. He paired up sudden conversions with "sick" minded and gradual conversions with "healthy" minded personalities. There was no bias toward the healthy minded in James's theory. In fact, he perceived them as weaker than their sick minded counterparts because they were unable to bear prolonged suffering in their minds and, consequently, had a tendency to deny conflict and to see things optimistically. Thus, they engaged in what the psychoanalysts call repression in an effort to avoid inner turmoil. This led the healthy minded to affirm a given type of religion, namely the idealistic, positive kind, and to be unaware of the time when they adopted such an outlook. James described these persons as "gradual" converts or as "once born" persons.

Sick minded individuals, on the other hand, had a stronger congenital temperament. These persons were, in fact, more realistic about themselves and about the world. They were able to perceive enigmas, injustices, hypocrisies, and evils. They agonized over problems in themselves in much the same fashion of which Paul spoke: "For I do not do the good I want, but the evil I do not want is what I do. . . . Wretched man that I am! Who will deliver me from this body of death?" (Rom. 7:19, 24). From a psychoanalytic point of view, they had enough ego strength to keep opposing impulses in consciousness. They were not neurotic in the sense that they remained aware of the conflict. The resolution of their dilemmas typically came suddenly and the immediate release that occurred prompted James to term these "twice born" persons.

James did not make the distinctions among levels of consciousness that were later clarified by analytic theorists. However, he did suggest that sick minded converts were more aware of their unconscious minds than were healthy minded persons. Nevertheless, there was a sense in which he considered the sick minded persons predisposed toward morbidity and an inability to trust either themselves or the universe. Whereas they were able to tolerate conflict better than healthy minded persons, they also tended to remain weak and fearful after the experience and to rely too intensely on divine power. This tendency toward self-depreciation and immature dependence was characteristic of much religious experience that Freud was later to criticize and denigrate.

Process of conversion

A model that encompasses both gradual and sudden conversions has been proposed by Tippett (1977). It includes both "periods" of time and "points" in time in alternating sequence. Initially there is a *period of growing awareness,* in which the individual becomes conscious of the possibilities of a given faith answer to problems of life but sees them as peripheral to his or her own concerns. This is tantamount to saying that the answers of faith which are later affirmed by the convert must first become a part of the mind at a subliminal level. This is usually the result of cultural contact with one or more religions.

This period of growing awareness is succeeded by a *point of realization,* at which time the potential convert becomes aware that the faith to which he or she will later accede is not merely an idea but a possibility. Tippett contends that there is such a moment even though persons may not be able to pinpoint it exactly. This is tantamount to saying that the cultural context which had been a backdrop for the thinking of the convert becomes somewhat more focal and results in fleeting ideas that the faith could have some personal meaning in the future.

This point of realization is succeeded by a *period of consideration* during which the individual wrestles with the dilemmas he is facing and also interacts with others who have found an answer to these same problems. The person becomes an active seeker during this period and places himself in settings where the faith which will later be affirmed is talked about and acted upon. As Tippett notes, the change which will later be made is never a change from *no* faith to a faith but a change from *this* faith to *that* faith. The ideas of faith come to the foreground in the mental life of the individual during this time. They compete with other options on an equal basis even though they do not dominate as they will in the future.

This period of consideration ends with a *point of encounter* for the gradual as well as the sudden convert, according to Tippett. Again, although the sudden convert may have a public event to which he can point, if the truth were known there is a day on which the gradual convert also felt sure of the faith which he espouses. However it comes about, it is at this point that most persons would say a conversion has occurred. Often this experience is accompanied by a sense that a problem has been solved and that peace and security have come. The supposed psychological processes that occur at this point will be discussed later in this chapter. Suffice it to say that a point at which the faith takes over and the individual decisively changes his or her outlook on life does happen and that many persons can indicate the time and place at which this occurs. This means that faith is no longer one among several options cognitively, but it takes over and dominates the other possibilities which the individual was considering as answers to dilemmas.

Although both Tippett and James consider conversion to be a process, Tippett proposes a sequence of events that occur after the point of encounter as well as before it. James also writes about these but calls them "saintliness" rather than conversion. This is an important distinction because Tippett is more aware of the absolute meaning of conversion as complete change of life. He is aware that this by no means occurs simply because a person has made a decision to accept a given faith, which is only the beginning of a change that will itself take time. The point of encounter may signify a "turning around" or a "stopping of going in one direction," but it does not signify that a person has reversed the past to the point where new life is a reality.

These considerations led Tippett to propose another period in the conversion process after the point of encounter. There is a *period of incorporation* during which the new convert is socialized into the new faith. For example, the public confession of faith, typical for the sudden convert, is often followed by a period of training and consultation during which the individual both reconsiders the meaning of the decision and learns more about the religion to which he or she desires to belong. This is followed by a "rite of passage" such as baptism and joining the church, which signifies that the person is now part of the faith in both its public and private dimensions. Furthermore, after a person has become a new member of the faith group, there are obligations and opportunities which are provided as means whereby the individual can grow in faith. This maturation process is sometimes ritualized into pressure to reach a new point of development and receive a "second blessing," which may express itself in such ways as speaking in tongues and healing powers. Tippett considers this process of growth in faith and practice to be an integral part of conversion. The new faith takes over the mental and physical life of the individual and becomes the dominant life force by which the person exists. Only when this is so can conversion be thought to have fully occurred.

Two contemporary communication theorists (Lofland & Stark, 1965) have translated Tippett's model into terms of traditional Christian categories, which include God's action, the role of the Christian evangelist, and the response of the convert. They begin with God's general revelation whereby persons are aware of a Supreme Being but have no effective knowledge of the gospel. This leads to the proclamation of Jesus as Savior, which is God's special revelation and which leads to an initial awareness of the Christian faith. As the proclaimer begins to influence and persuade the soon-to-be convert, a grasp of the fundamentals and implications of the gospel begins to grow. Soon the individual begins to have a positive attitude toward the gospel and toward the evangelist. This results in a decision to act, after which the convert repents and places his or her faith in Christ. God's role then becomes that of regeneration, and the convert both becomes and begins to become the new creature in Christ.

After this God's role becomes one of sanctification and the role of the evangelist one of support and cultivation. During this time and throughout the rest of life the convert evaluates his or her decision, is incorporated into the church, grows in Christian knowledge and behavior, begins to daily commune with God, identifies personal gifts of ministry, and begins to witness to others and to engage in social action. This total process is conversion in the same sense that it is for Tippett. It retains an acknowledgment that there is both a point in time at which a person changes direction and a period of time both preceding and succeeding this event wherein a person grows toward the full meaning of conversion.

The Preconversion Mental State

Several psychologists other than James have studied this phenomenon. At the turn of the century much attention was given to the experience of adolescence, which was thought to be accompanied by much stress and strain. Hall (1905) postulated in his theory of recapitulation that each individual went through the experience of the race and that adolescence was parallel to primitive society. Because conversion often occurs during this period, it was natural that it was conceived to be a distinctively adolescent phenomenon. Erikson later proposed adolescence to be a unique period of identity formation during which persons were especially open to a reconsideration of the meaning and purpose of life. Thus, it would seem natural that many conversions would occur in this period during which persons are struggling for independence and are looking for new authority in their lives.

Hall, one of the early pioneers in both developmental psychology and the psychology of religion, offered an apology for the Christian faith based on his understanding of the crucial nature of the adolescent experience (Hall, 1904). He suggested, along with many other theorists, that humans were created innocent and altruistic but became self-centered in the experience of growing up. During adolescence persons began to see both the limits and the possibilities of living selfishly, became torn but attracted by their egotistic tendencies. Their greed turned them against the altruism with which life began. No amount of reason or appeal to conscience changes persons from this greedy track, according to Hall. Only the Christian gospel with its story of a God who loved persons enough to die for them could break through this tough barrier and open persons up to the possibilities of loving again. Hall considered the gospel the most powerful psychological force in converting persons from a life of selfishness to the life of love for which they were created. He offered a psychodynamic explanation wherein the persuasive force of the gospel was powerful enough to interrupt all other mental forces in the conversion process during adolescence.

Whereas Hall conceived the process of Christian conversion as healthy and normal, Freud (1928) suggested that religious conversion is a sign of psychopathology. For Freud, affirming religous faith is a sign that one has resolved psychosexual conflicts inappropriately.

Although religion as a mass neurosis was better than individual neuroses, it was still abnormal and immature. Persons should face evil in themselves and in the world in a rational manner. They should solve problems with scientific pragmatism rather than dependent faith.

Salzman (1966), while agreeing with Freud in his basic model, suggested that there could be progressive as well as regressive conversions. Those that were progressive would result in courage and faithful action, while those that were regressive would result in self-doubt and dependency. Progressive conversions would seem to be more what Hall had in mind in his contention that the Christian faith made persons more loving.

In an alternate understanding of the place of psychopathology in conversion Boisen (1936) contended that there was a close affinity between mental illness and religious experience. He suggested that both the mentally ill and the sincerely religious were likely to be deeper thinkers than the average person. They experienced the crisis of life at its most intense and deepest level. He compared the fantasies of psychosis with the supernatural stories of faith and concluded that they were similar. He concluded that some persons came through these experiences with religious conversions while others went the way of mental illness. Thus, unlike Freud, he did not consider the experience itself as abnormal. Quite the contrary, it was a sign of greater depth of personality.

Changes Occurring Through Conversion

James felt that the event of conversion resulted in a shift of mental energy so that it was concentrated in one area of the mind and withdrawn from another. He felt this accounted for the intensity of the feelings and thoughts that accompanied the experience. He contended that there was no such thing as a unique religious emotion and that the feelings differed from normal experience in degree rather than in kind.

An alternative explanation for these phenomena was proposed by Sargent (1957), who compared conversion to brainwashing. Using the Pavlovian model of conditioning-crisis-breakdown-reorientation, he suggested that the individual is worked up into a hyperemotional state he termed *transmarginal inhibition*, during which the nerve endings become so exhausted that the individual borders on hysteria and becomes hypersuggestible. At this point the individual becomes more susceptible to ideas which he would resist in a normal mental state. This is coupled with a suppression of previously held beliefs. The new faith is acted upon in a dramatic manner and becomes the new conditioned stimulus for behavior.

Sargent's theory essentially equates the influence process which leads persons to conversion with those who manipulate others in a brainwashing fashion. He is thus negative in his evaluation and suggests that such influence processes have negative value for society in that they induce pathology and dependence. Although many would agree with his evaluation as it applied to some mass meetings, it should be noted that he makes no distinction between the process and the positive results that often occur in people's lives from such experiences.

From a more positive perspective Oden (1966) has equated healing in psychotherapy with the process of conversion. Oden contends that God's grace is always available to humans in that he unconditionally accepts them and has infinite positive regard toward them. Wherever persons experience this, either from a therapist or an evangelist, the result is the same. Persons cease being self-centered, self-protective, defensive, and easily led into wrongdoing. They begin to appreciate anew the purpose for which they were uniquely created and which they have been denying. They discover again the power which is given them to love and to live without pretense. They gain courage to risk themselves and to be loving. They have been converted.

On the question of the life changes resulting from conversion, once again James offered a model for evaluating as well as explaining these phenomena. He concluded that what conversion did was to integrate the personality around a dominant motive. He believed that conversion was the process whereby a divided self became unified. His dictum that religion should be judged by its fruits rather than its roots was a way of saying that if conversion resulted in a less conflicted, less indecisive, less troubled person, then it was valuable regardless of whether it occurred in a sick or a healthy mind. His *The Varieties of Religious Experience* is replete with accounts of lives in which this unification resulted from religious conversion. James was describing in behavioral terms the phenomenon referred to in Scripture as the "new creation" (2 Cor. 5:17). The gospel accounts of Zacchaeus, Nicodemus, and the woman at the well are prime biblical examples of James's description. Charles Colson is representative of many modern examples of lives that have been radically changed by conversion in the manner James depicted.

Ideally the person should feel inwardly less anxious, less confused, more in control, and more energized. The purpose and meaning of life should be more clear. Outwardly the person should become more unselfish, more loving, more just, and more merciful. However, research suggests that typically these life changes are far less radical than might be anticipated. If James was correct in suggesting that conversion should be evaluated in terms of the degree to which these changes occur, then far too many conversions fall short of the ideal. However, if Paul is correct in Romans, these changes are less impor-. tant than James might have presumed—at least from God's point of view. In fact, the juxtaposition of sin and grace in the Pauline model implies that salvation is less an achievement and more a gift and that righteousness, the biblical term for James's changes, is ascribed to the believer rather than a characteristic of her. Furthermore, from a psychological point of view the dilemma of achieving one's life goals of love and justice remains a problem even after conversion. These goals are better conceived as possible when they are understood as the gifts of grace rather than the expectations by which our salvation is proven.

More empirically, Gorsuch, a social psychologist, has concluded that we cannot expect change of mind, the typical kind of change that occurs in conversion, to generalize fully to other types of behavior such as overt actions of love and mercy (Gorsuch & Malony, 1976). Behavioral change will most likely generalize to other similar types of behavior and will less likely generalize to dissimilar kinds of acts. Thus, attitudes and thoughts and feelings would predictably change more than interpersonal behaviors. But, apart from whether change should or should not occur, from a strictly psychological point of view it would not be expected as much for some behaviors as for others.

One of the most recent reconceptualizations of the conversion experience has been that of Richardson (1979), who has proposed that we think less of conversion from a "preordained" than an "interactive" point of view. Taking the conversion of Paul as a focus, he suggested that the preordained model saw the event as planned by God in such a manner that it was *predispositional* from a psychological and *presituational* from a sociological perspective.

A corrective to these points of view might be to conceive of Paul's experience less as occuring on the Damascus Road than as *beginning* there and continuing for a prolonged period of seclusion in which he probably conversed with Jesus again and again. Again, Paul's experience was no surprise to him but instead came as the end result of long years of searching for the meaning of life. He knew the language of faith long before he met the Messiah on the road to Damascus. Paul's dramatic experience with Jesus was but the first of many times that Paul renewed his faith and grew in his understanding of the Good News which changed his life. And finally, in regard to behavioral changes which resulted from the experience, Paul reported "I die daily" (1 Cor. 15:31), as if to say his struggle with sin in his life was an ongoing struggle. He "grew in grace" throughout his life and in many new circumstances.

This interactive view of the changes that occur puts the experience of conversion in a sound sociopsychological as well as theological perspective. It preserves the power of God as well as the activity of persons in the conversion process. It allows for conceiving the behavior change in conversion more as a change of direction than a total change of life.

References

Boisen, A. *The exploration of the inner world.* Chicago: Willett, Clark, 1936.

Freud, S. *The future of an illusion.* New York: Liveright, 1928.

Gordon, A. *The nature of conversion.* Boston: Beacon Press, 1967.

Gorsuch, R. L., & Malony, H. N. *The nature of man.* Springfield, Ill.: Thomas, 1976.

Hall, G. *Adolescence.* New York: Appleton, 1905.

James, W. *The varieties of religious experience.* New York: Doubleday, 1902.

Lofland, J., & Stark, R. Becoming a world saver: A theory of conversion to a deviant perspective. *American Sociological Review,* 1965, *30,* 862–875.

Oden, T. C. *Kerygma and counseling.* Philadelphia: Westminster, 1966.

Richardson, J. T. *A new paradigm for conversion research.* Paper presented at the International Society for Political Psychology, Washington, D.C., May 1979.

Salzman, L. Types of religious conversion. *Pastoral Psychology,* September 1966, pp. 8–20.

Sargent, W. *Battle for the mind.* Garden City, N.Y.: Doubleday, 1957.

Tippett, A. Conversion as a dynamic process in Christian mission. *Missiology,* 1977, *5*(2), 203–221.

Additional Reading

Johnson, C., & Malony, H. N. *Christian conversion: Biblical and psychological perspectives.* Grand Rapids: Zondervan, 1982.

4

Cults
Ronald Enroth

Religious cults are not a new phenomenon on the human scene. Since 1965, however, there seems to have been an upsurge in the growth of new religious movements, aberrational Christian groups, and so-called mass therapies or self-improvement cults. Although most of these cultic movements have emerged in the West, many of them have been heavily influenced by an Eastern/mystical/occult world-view. This is true not only of the specifically religious movements but also of those groups which claim to be nonreligious in nature and whose stated objective is human transformation or the realization of human potential.

The definition of the term *cult* depends largely on the frame of reference of the definer. Most definitions stress the unconventional and non-normative dimensions of the word. There is usually negative connotation and stigma associated with its usage. Most cults are groups that are outside the mainstream of the prevailing, established religious tradition of any given society. Cult members view themselves as a minority group who share a common vision and who are dedicated to some person, ideology, or cause. Traditional churches are generally considered to be culture-accepting organizations whereas cults tend to avoid accommodation to the dominant social realities and are, in fact, culture rejecting. The degree to which they are separatist in orientation varies from group to group. They are often targets of suspicion and distrust.

A psychosocial approach to cults includes a consideration of group dynamics (especially leader-follower roles), recruitment and indoctrination practices, the assumption by a member of a new identity and its management by the group, and the various methods of ego destruction and thought control which characterize the more extreme cultic groups.

A theological approach to the identification of a cult focuses on the group's belief system and its relation to a standard of Christian orthodoxy. From this perspective a cult is a religious movement which has doctrines and/or practices that are in conflict with the teachings of biblical Christianity as represented by the major Catholic and Protestant denominations. Primary focus is on issues of truth and error as theologically defined.

Cult Membership: Predisposing Factors

Any serious consideration of cult dynamics must include an examination of the reasons why people are attracted to cults and what factors make some people more vulnerable to cultic involvement than others. While there is always a danger in generalizing, the existing literature—both popular and professional—suggests that certain patterns characterize the recruitment/joining process.

The target population for most recruitment efforts by the newer cults is the age bracket 18–28. Persons in this age grouping are frequently experiencing changes in their life situations and are in various stages of transition. They may be between high school and college, between college and career, or between love affairs. They may be the victims of other forms of situational contingencies that increase their vulnerability.

Cult recruits are usually normal people who are experiencing specific and transitory difficulties in life. They may be disenchanted with a sociopolitical cause, or suffering from academic frustration, or encountering career uncertainty or job dissatisfaction. There may be a recent history of disruption in relationships, such as a breakup with a boyfriend/girlfriend or spouse, or a troubling relationship with a parent.

Unlike the typical member profile of cults from the past, those who are joining the newer cults and self-improvement groups are more highly educated and tend to come from middle- and upper-middle-class surroundings. Few racial and ethnic minorities (with the exception of Jews) are found in the new cults. Rather than coming from the margins of society, the typical cult recruit today is from the white, affluent suburbs.

Prospective cult members are also individuals who can be characterized as seekers—people who are searching for religious experiences and for truth. Typically, the person who joins a cult has a very nominal religious background or no religious background at all. The fulfilling of perceived spiritual needs is an obvious component in the decision to explore alternative religious options. Those individuals who are attracted to aberrational Christian groups frequently are young Christians lacking in discernment skills or members of evangelical churches who become dissatisfied or disillusioned with their traditional church life.

There are also emotional and interpersonal factors which predispose some people to cult membership. Among the converts to cults are those individuals who show some evidence of developmental and emotional problems over a period of time. Frequently this type of recruit also has experienced some kind of disjuncture in family relations, such as conflict with parents.

Sometimes the decision to join a cult reflects a need to escape the family. Some clinicians who have worked with ex-cult members report a family background pattern that includes a passive father and a relatively domineering mother, or parents who are overly possessive and protective.

Cults appeal to persons who are experiencing a sense of personal inadequacy, loneliness, or disappointment with life in general. There are also those individuals who exhibit strong dependency needs and who are attracted to the more totalistic and communal groups. The cultic milieu thus becomes a haven of security where decision making is minimal and life's basic necessities are provided. Contact with the larger society is regulated and the demands of conventional existence can be bypassed or at least deferred.

Cults also appeal to people who have a strongly idealistic orientation. Such people are sincerely desirous of being a part of a group or organization which is focused on change—personal transformation or societal change. To join such a group is to affiliate with a cause, to become linked with a network of true believers who are determined to achieve their objectives. In the process any individual goals that may have been present merge with or are transcended by the goals of the group.

Commitment Mechanisms

Among the most significant psychological dynamics at work in the cultic milieu are the various commitment mechanisms which help bind members to the group and which militate against easy departure from the cult.

Most cultic organizations exercise control over members by requiring total loyalty to the group, its particular ideology, and its leadership. Unquestioning loyalty can result in forms of unhealthy commitment, in fanatical commitment. Often legitimate and acceptable biblical concepts such as loyalty and commitment are completely redefined and distorted to suit the needs of the leadership.

Another effective commitment mechanism involves the suspension of supportive ties with the member's precult life, a severing of ties with families, friends, and all other familiar social support networks. There is a dying to the past, a conscious distancing of oneself from the "outside" world and its attendant evils. There may well be a requirement to surrender one's personal and material resources to the group out of a sense of devotion to the cause.

Themes of sacrifice and investment pervade the cultic life style. There is frequently a willingness to forsake family, education, or career in order to advance the objectives of the group. Whether the decision to invest all of one's energy (and material resources) in the group is a decision freely entered into is a matter of controversy. Critics contend that informed consent is not always fully operative in totalistic cults and that considerable psychological and spiritual pressure is exerted on members to be committed to the group to a point beyond what is normative for conventional religious organizations. The demands for zealous commitment, as evidenced by interrupted life patterns, are a major focus of concern for parents and other observers critical of the manipulative aspects of cult existence.

A related pattern seen in many cults and aberrational Christian groups is the tendency to adopt a simple, often austere life style. While this is not an inherently negative characteristic, it is often accompanied by a whole syndrome of drastic life changes which, viewed as a whole, represent a radical and unconventional shift from the expectations of the larger society and give substance to the sometimes bizarre image of cultic groups. Various cultural insignia such as specialized clothing styles, speech patterns, cosmetics, and other identifying symbols help set off the group from more traditional religious groups.

Fervent commitment to the group is also enhanced by a deliberate devaluing of the individual in favor of the group. Drastic personality shifts are often observed in individuals who become involved with cults. The person tends to become more rigid and less autonomous. The individual personality is submerged in the group and a collective/ communal orientation predominates. Life's basic necessities as well as one's emotional needs are met within the group. The imagery of the family is evident and recognized. A new "spiritual" family often replaces the natural family. Cult leaders assume the role of surrogate parents.

Along with the adoption of a new life style and the acquisition of a new identity there is the assumption of a radically new world-view. Ideological conversion, however, usually is secondary to the gratification of basic human needs represented by the act of joining. In short, most individuals are attracted to cultic groups because of the need for acceptance, community, fellowship, a sense of belonging, and a need for purpose and direction rather than by the particular ideological propaganda of the group. Cults are successful because they meet human needs. Conversion to the ideological position of the group follows the decision to join, and the indoctrination process is often gradual.

The nature and scope of the indoctrination process varies from group to group. Some cults have rather elaborate theological systems; others are unsophisticated in this area. In any event, indoctrination is almost always wedded to elitist thinking: we alone possess the truth. Such thinking reinforces other aspects of cult life which emphasize an exclusiveness, a separateness, demarcating the group from unenlightened outsiders.

A crucial dimension of transformation and commitment is the process by which the human will is subverted. This mechanism is also related to a strong sense of group identification. It involves submission to the leadership and to the belief system of the group.

There is considerable debate among scholars and other observers as to whether the subjugation of the individual member's will to the requisites of the cult involves the loss (or diminishment) of personal autonomy. Cult critics maintain that, especially in the more totalistic groups, members' ability to think for themselves and to make independent decisions is impaired.

Cult defenders claim that allegations of brainwashing and thought control leveled at new religious movements are questionable and unfounded. Scholars are divided as to whether such charges are substantiated in the professional literature. Concepts of brainwashing and mind control are said to be vague and elusive. Some observers maintain that whatever manipulative techniques may be present in the controversial groups are simply extensions of basic principles of psychological conditioning and group dynamics. The changes that are often reported in the behavior of cult members are seen by these observers as the result of manipulated attitude adjustment rather than the effect of coercive persuasion.

Leadership Dynamics

Many feel that the most crucial factor in any approach to the psychology of cults is the role played by leaders. In the newer cultic movements as well as in the cults of the past there is always a single, living person (usually male) who is the founder/leader of the group and who occupies a position of respect and prominence within the organization. Almost without exception cult leaders are highly authoritarian and extract from their followers a loyalty and devotion that are probably due to a combination of awe, charisma, and psychospiritual intimidation.

Controversy surrounds the assorted gurus and self-appointed messiahs who represent the motivating force behind all cults. Existing evidence suggests that the leaders of most cults and aberrational Christian groups are strong-willed individualists. They frequently are ecclesiastical loners who find it difficult to conform to established, traditional religious systems and who therefore found groups that tend to be spiritually elitist and culture rejecting. Many of the leaders and their followers also tend to be very conservative in their sociopolitical leanings.

Similarly, there is some evidence to indicate that charismatic cult leaders are insecure individuals who need to exercise power over people and who find it easier to do so within a tightly structured environment. There is some debate as to whether their motives include any or all of the following: the exploitation of members for financial gain; political ambition; ego need for recognition and acceptance; genuine religious conviction that their own role is central to truth and the unfolding of history; the building of self-serving religious empires.

Cult critics claim that leaders use fear, intimidation, and guilt to control members' lives. In extreme cases physical punishment is employed as a sanction and control mechanism. The degree to which leaders are able to exercise control and directly impact individual members' lives varies from group to group.

There are those who argue that cult leaders exhibit varying degrees of psychopathology, particularly paranoia. The latter trait is linked with the frequent assertion by leaders that they and their movements are targets of attack and persecution by the media, parents, governmental agencies, and anticult activists.

In some cultic organizations the leader is granted special sexual access to the membership. Such access is either explicitly sanctioned by the group and its teachings or looked upon with indifference or resignation. Besides the sexual and material benefits that accrue to the role of leader, there are ego needs that are satisfied by virtue of the special status accorded leaders, not the least of which is the realization that one is recognized as a spiritual master, a religious pioneer, even a messianic figure. In most instances cult leaders sincerely believe in their spiritual mission. From their perspective, and certainly from the perspective of their loyal followers, they are not charlatans.

Postcult Adjustment

Most cults employ highly sophisticated techniques for inducing behavioral change and conversion to their ideological systems. The life situation of most cult members is all-encompassing and highly intense. It therefore follows that the period following separation from the cult is often traumatic and unsettling. Sensitivity to the special problems of former members is especially needed by helping professionals who might be called on for counseling.

The early transition period following the cult experience is frequently characterized by episodes of depression and feelings of confusion. There is often uncertainty and indecisiveness regarding the future and feelings of anger and embarassment about the past. Ex-members should be encouraged to sort things out regarding their cultic involvement. They need to understand their particular vulnerabilities and that they were not abnormal or "strange" because of their entry into a cult experience.

Depending on the particular person and specific cult involved, a considerable amount of time may be required for the process of resocialization following exit from an extremist cult. Opportunity should be made available for persons to rest, reflect on their experience, and reconnect with old friends as well as family members. Unresolved problems that may have precipitated entrance into the cult will have to be confronted.

Leaving a cult is like leaving the bosom of a family. Friends and meaningful experiences will be left behind. New friendships will have to be formed. Difficulties in decision making may be anticipated. Former cult members need to understand that family and friends will be watching them, looking for signals that might indicate a desire to slip back into the security of cult days. The cult veteran as well as relatives and friends will need encouragement and assistance in handling the difficult postcult period. Outsiders need to recognize that not all that happened in the cult was negative; former members may, in fact, want to recount some of their positive memories.

The reconstruction activity following the cult experience is incomplete if it fails to deal with the spiritual vacuum resulting from the exit from the group. The Christian counselor should be especially sensitive to the possibility of "spiritual burnout" that frequently characterizes the ex-member. A relationship of trust must be established in view of the likelihood of extreme distrust of religious authority of any kind. The individual therapist, like the Christian church at large, must be an agent of healing, restoration, and reconciliation.

Additional Readings

Appel, W. *Cults in America: Programmed for paradise*. New York: Holt, Rinehart & Winston, 1983.

Enroth, R. *Youth, brainwashing and the extremist cults*. Grand Rapids: Zondervan, 1977.

Enroth, R. *The lure of the cults*. Chappaqua, N.Y.: Christian Herald Books, 1979.

Enroth, R. (Ed.). *A guide to cults and new religions*. Downers Grove, Ill.: InterVarsity Press, 1983.

Stoner, C., & Parke, J. *All God's children*. Radnor, Pa.: Chilton, 1977.

5

Ecstatic Religious Experiences
Richard D. Kahoe

Ecstatic experiences play important roles in many Christian and non-Christian traditions. Other committed believers and religious subcultures find no need for such expressions.

Scope

Religious ecstasies (notably speaking in tongues, or glossolalia) are recorded in the New Testament, and some are reported throughout church history. The most consistent expressions, however, have been within the Pentecostal movement, beginning in the first decade of the twentieth century, with influences from southern black Christian traditions. Starting about 1960 ecstatic experiences, especially glossolalia, have found expression in Catholic and mainstream Protestant churches.

Perhaps the prototype of ecstatic religion is the possession trance in African animism, Haitian vodou (voodoo), and numerous other folk religions. Possession trance refers to an alteration of personality, consciousness, or will that is attributed to possession by an alien spirit, which might be the spirit of an animal or another person. In some primitive cultures possession trance is cultivated as an important part of the religious expression. Sometimes possession is seen as an experience to be avoided or terminated, as in Catholic exorcism rites. In some Pentecostal, charismatic, and black churches glossolalia, shouting, dancing, and fainting are interpreted as manifestations of possession by the Holy Spirit—that is, as possession trance. Others consider them gifts of the Spirit or simply "blessings." Almost invariably, though, such experiences are perceived as supernatural or beyond mere human will—in psychological terms, a trance or an altered or alternative state of consciousness.

Automatic writing, as claimed by some prophets and religious founders, has trancelike if not overtly ecstatic features. Much snake handling, fire handling, and fire walking are similarly trancelike and/or ecstatic. Some faith healing rituals and mystical experiences involve ecstacy and, especially in mysticism, altered states of consciousness, but they have significantly different religious functions and psychological causes or dynamics.

Functions

Considerable speculation and some firm evidence indicate that ecstatic religion functions in part as a compensation or outlet for frustrated or conflicting needs. Possession trance is more likely to occur in societies that have rigid, fixed status distinctions, including slavery. Trance behavior represents a "safety valve" for stresses caused by such social rigidities (Bourguignon, 1976). Pentecostalism has made its greatest inroads in American lower classes and African countries that have anxiety-producing status differences and class conflicts. Glossolalia is often associated with anxiety states and a need to discharge built-up tension, and is related to personality measures that give credence to this function (Smith, 1976).

A related function, beyond mere compensation, is actual personality integration. Do ecstatic experiences actually prove therapeutic to their anxious and frustrated subjects? Ritualized possession trance does not solve any of the social differences that spawn it, but it can give new structure and meaning to individual lives (Bourguignon, 1976). It is hard to separate the ecstatic expressions themselves from the belief and social support system of which they are a part. Most studies of glossolalia suggest that the total religious context, not just the ecstatic experience, is redemptive. Nonetheless, the emotional release and personal interpretations of ecstasies are part of the religious system that provides hope and meaning to many desperate lives.

Probably the most fundamental function of ecstatic religious experiences was suggested by James: "Beliefs are strengthened whenever automatisms corroborate them. Incursions from beyond the transmarginal have a peculiar power to increase conviction" (1902, p. 372). Speaking in tongues or other public display of "irrational" behavior irrevocably sets people apart from secular society, affirming their religious identities and belief systems. In the 1960s the disruption of traditional Roman Catholic practices by Vatican Council II changes and the secular drift of liberal Protestant denominations set the stage for the need to reaffirm spiritual identity and dependency. Visions, automatic writing, and other charismatic gifts have lent credence and impetus to the revelations of major religious leaders for centuries. Sometimes ecstasy functions as testimony to unbelievers of God's power. Appalachian Holiness fire handlers avow that their purpose is to convince sinners of God's power and produce repentance. Miracles in both Testaments frequently served these belief functions.

Dynamics of Ecstasy

To the uninitiated, religious ecstasies often look like psychiatric disorder—hysteria, schizophrenia, or even perhaps epilepsy. Consequently most serious psychological studies of the ecstasies have used personality measures like the Minnesota Multiphasic Personality Inventory (MMPI). The results have been minimal and sometimes inconsistent. Glossolalists (the most widely studied group) and snake handlers have usually shown fewer signs of pathology than nonecstatic religious groups. In general they show somewhat different personality patterns but no greater indication of personality disorder per se. Ecstasy practitioners tend to be less socially conforming and more pleasure oriented—that is, less inhibited and more expressive. Usually they show signs of lower autonomy and more dependence on other individuals, especially trusted religious leaders. They are more trusting in general. Hysteria—the MMPI scale indicating tendency to express inner conflicts through physical means—consistently has not been related to ecstatic behaviors. As a group glossolalists are apparently less intelligent and lower in educational levels than comparable nonglossolalists (Smith, 1976).

Glossolalists frequently have experienced some personal stress or crisis (e.g,. financial reversal, family or personal illness, marital discord) not long before they first spoke in tongues (Kildahl, 1972; Smith, 1976). A few studies have failed to find this effect. Perhaps it may be that in groups who use glossolalia in a more playful manner, for "ego enhancement," the gift is less likely to be related to stress, anxiety, or other psychiatric factors.

To a substantial extent religious ecstasy is more a matter of learning than of psychiatry. People who grow up in a culture or church where such experiences are routine are, in effect, imprinted to accept and enact such behaviors at an appropriate age and circumstance. Social learning has been explicitly observed for possession trance in Haitian vodou. Children who hear adults talk about the clan's favorite possessing spirits accept the spirits as virtually part of the extended family. Discussion and observation of the rites leading up to trance teach the children how to induce the trances and how to respond when in them (Bourguignon, 1976). Similar observations could surely be made in Pentecostal churches.

More individualized learning is sometimes observed. While glossolalia is not learned in the way one learns a foreign language, coaching has been noted at charismatic meetings—for example, "Come on now. Speak out. You're still begging. There you are. Keep talking. Come on. Hallelujah. He's praying a new language" (Samarin, 1969). Once an individual has experienced glossolalia, possession trance, or Pentecostal ecstatic expressions, these can be repeated with relative ease in the appropriately sanctioned religious setting.

Glossolalic utterances have frequently been claimed as real foreign tongues that the speaker has not learned. Scientifically verifiable, firsthand reports of such events have not been produced. Nor do glossolalic utterances show linguistic characteristics common to human languages.

Expression of trancelike religious ecstasies resembles hypnosis. Induction has been related to loud, rhythmic, repetitious, and/or stupefying music and other environmental and physical factors—a hot stuffy room high in carbon dioxide, social isolation, and fasting (Aylland, 1962).

Other unconscious factors undoubtedly play roles in glossolalia. Christian tongues speaking sometimes occurs spontaneously, without explicit social modeling or learning, but probably never without knowledge of such events in the New Testament record. Occurrence of glossolalia also in non-Christian religions and in psychosis suggests that the structure of the central nervous system enables nonrational use of language. The brain appears to have neurological structures that promote development of a natural language, given normal linguistic experience in a family or human community. Similarly various neural inhibitions, disinhibitions, and "switches" controlling them are consistent with current knowledge of the central nervous system. These brain mechanisms are probably involved in the practice of speaking in tongues.

Psychologists increasingly recognize various altered states of consciousness, and they frequently consider trancelike religious ecstasies from this perspective. Fire walking and handling fire in many religious traditions can involve a trance state or altered state of consciousness. Southern Appalachian Holiness fire handlers report an "anointing" that enables them to expose bodily parts to intense flames and heat for up to 15 seconds without pain or burning. The anointing is variously described by practitioners: "Just don't feel much at all. I get numb. Feels like my skin crawls." "A shield comes down over me. I know when it's around me. It's cold inside. My hands get numb and cold" (Kane, 1974, p. 119).

Hypnotic experiments spanning more than half a century demonstrate psychological control of heat pain. With few exceptions, hypnotic suggestion eliminates or minimizes the effects of heat stimuli applied to a limb. Similarly, given the suggestion that the experimenter's finger is a red-hot iron, a finger can produce pain and blisters like those normally produced by heat. When subjects are hypnotized to be insensitive to heat pain, their blood vessels constrict in the affected body parts, and they report numbness and coldness strikingly similar to reports of "anointed" Holiness fire handlers. Given either hypnosis or spiritual motivation, the central nervous system can control the effects of intense heat for as long as 15 seconds.

Every religious experience occurs in the context of an individual who is at once a physical, psychological, and social as well as spiritual being. Ecstatic religious experiences in particular serve a variety of functions, some primarily religious, some more psychological. Each such occurrence is grounded in a human personality with distinctive individual and cultural experiences, with neurological capabilities that are not fully understood. No single dynamic, cause, or factor explains any form of ecstatic religious experience. Even taken together they do not fully account for any individual's ecstatic behavior or feelings. Psychologists slowly and imperfectly seek better to understand and explain these factors and their interacting effects on human behavior. However, no psychological explanation, however complete, can "explain away" or determine the spiritual value of any religious experience.

References

Aylland, A., Jr. "Possession" in a revivalistic Negro church. *Journal for the Scientific Study of Religion*, 1962, *1*, 204–213.

Bourguignon, E. *Possession*. San Francisco: Chandler & Sharp, 1976.

James, W. *The varieties of religious experience*. Garden City, N.Y.: Image Books, 1978. (Originally published, 1902.)

Kane, S. M. Holiness fire handling in southern Appalachia. In J. D. Photiadis (Ed.), *Religion in Appalachia*. Morgantown: West Virginia University, 1974.

Kildahl, J. P. *The psychology of speaking in tongues*. New York: Harper & Row, 1972.

Samarin, W. J. Glossolalia as learned behavior. *Canadian Journal of Theology*, 1969, *15*, 60–64.

Smith, D. S. Glossolalia: The personality correlates of conventional and unconventional subgroups (Doctoral dissertation, Rosemead Graduate School of Psychology, 1976). (University Microfilms No. 77-21,537)

6

Faith
H. Newton Malony

Faith has been alternately defined as a set of beliefs or a set of actions. Of course, believing is itself an act, but the distinction between faith and work is as old as the New Testament Book of James, which seems to opt for one side of the dilemma in identifying faith as a set of beliefs over against faithful behavior (James 2:14ff.). However, it should be added that the writer of James was arguing for a combination of belief and practice, as suggested by the statements, "Be doers of the word, and not hearers only, deceiving yourselves" (1:22) and "faith by itself, if it has no works, is dead" (2:17).

This is a more balanced viewpoint than might be initially supposed, and it is consonant with the import of the 11th chapter of Hebrews, where faith is depicted as launching out into life on the basis of "the assurance of the things hoped for, the conviction of things not seen" (11:1). In the illustrations that follow, the writer of Hebrews mentions numerous biblical personages who "by faith" engaged in heroic, riskful action. The Thorndike-Barnhart dictionary affirms this combination of belief and action by defining faith as "believing without proof; trust."

It is this trust dimension, embedded in the Latin *credo*, that was the original connotation of the English word *believe*. The word *creed* came from the word for heart. To believe meant to set one's heart on. It had an active, behavioral component, similar to the implications of "entrustment" inherent in the Greek *pistis* used commonly in the New Testament to refer to faith.

Psychological Contributions

Early in this century Delacroix, a psychologist of religion, added a third dimension to the understanding of faith, namely culture or institutional religion. He termed this *authoritative faith* and distinguished it from *reasoning faith* (belief) and *trusting faith* (action). This third dimension provided for a person's accepting a given religious tradition as *the* faith for that person. Religious institutions in a culture provide this dimension with their creeds, rituals, and traditions. Delacroix's differentiation provided a basis for understanding people who identify themselves as members of the Christian faith, for example. He suggested that adjustment and conformity are the dynamic processes operating in this dimension of faith, just as reason and emotion are inherent in the other dimensions.

Most psychological understandings of faith have depended heavily on the proposal of the theologian Schleiermacher who, early in the nineteenth century, suggested faith was "a feeling of dependence" in which the individual had an intense experience of powerlessness coupled with an absolute reliance on the strength of a transcendent reality—that is, God. Kierkegaard continued this emphasis with his depiction of faith as based on a "sickness unto death" which propelled a person to make the "leap of faith."

In this century Leuba built on the ideas of Schleiermacher and Kierkegaard and detailed the components of what he termed the "faith state." Faith is always preceded by a period of self-dissatisfaction and a yearning for enlightenment. He compared this prefaith period to that of symptoms in a disease in which a person fears a breakdown. The higher state is envisioned but seems out of reach. The resolution of this turmoil becomes the dominant preoccupation of the individual's mental life. Leuba suggested that when faith arrives, it is characterized by two inner experiences. First, the person feels that nothing else matters now that faith has come. Second, the intensity of joy and peace which results from surrendering to God is greater than any before experienced. Leuba believed that faith is primarily an emotion and that it is these faith feelings which provide the certainty with which people assert the truthfulness of their beliefs.

Leuba's ideas are similar to the "shift of energy" theory proposed by James as an explanation for religious experience—which has been identified with faith by many theorists. James suggested that in religion the mind focused its energy on the experience and excluded much else that might be distracting or troubling it. This theory provided the basis for his assertion that religious experience could integrate a person and provide a central purpose for life.

The most recent theorizing about faith has been done by developmental psychologist/theologian Fowler, who has defined faith as the "making and maintaining of meaning in life" (1981). He follows H. R. Niebuhr and Tillich in asserting that faith is a universal human concern in that one of the unique aspects of being human is a need to find meaning. Thus faith is the experience of becoming "ultimately concerned" in the sense that faith is that which ties life together finally or ultimately.

Stages of Faith Development

Fowler has been primarily concerned with delineating the developmental stages by which faith develops. In this endeavor he has relied heavily on the thinking of Erikson, a neoanalytic ego psychologist who has written about the several stages of identity formation; Piaget, a cognitive psychologist who has written about the development of the mental structures that make thinking possible; and Kohlberg, a philosophical psychologist who has applied Piaget's theory to moral development.

Fowler proposes six stages of faith beyond infancy, which he describes as an "undifferentiated faith" period. He suggests that the theorists noted above contributed to his understanding of these stages by their emphasis on 1) how people know what they know (epistemology); 2) the structure, rather than the content, of faith; and 3) the interactional, as contrasted with the behavioral or the maturational, dimensions of development. As contrasted with these theorists, Fowler emphasizes a spiraling, as opposed to a hierarchical, model of development and perceives faith as dealing primarily with the logic of conviction, as opposed to the logic of rational certainty.

Following Erikson, Fowler sees infancy as a prefaith stage in which basic trust is the chief result of good parent-child interaction. The mutuality, hope, and love that emerge from such experiences provide the basis for faith in the later stages and can be distorted either by overindulgence, leading to narcissism, or negligence, leading to isolation and distrust.

Stage 1 typically occurs from ages 3–7 and is termed *intuitive-*

projective faith, in that the need for meaning is fashioned by fantasy-filled, imitative interactions with the overt faith of the primary adults in the child's life. Self-awareness comes into being during this time, and the child becomes aware for the first time of death, sex, and taboos that are central to cultural faith. The emergent strength of this stage is imagination, while the danger is that the child's mind will be filled with terror.

Stage 2 typically occurs at about 10 years of age and is termed *mythic-literal faith*, in that the need for meaning is fashioned by the child affirming for himself the stories, beliefs, and observances that indicate belonging to the community of faith with which he is soon to identify. The imagination of the previous stage is curbed and channeled into an almost literal acceptance of the symbols of the faith-culture in which he lives. The emergent strength of this stage is the ability to live through story and drama, which give coherence to experience, while there is danger in the overliteral acceptance of the factual truth of the stories.

Stage 3 is typical of the adolescent years and is termed *synthetic-conventional faith*, in that the need for meaning is fashioned by identification with others beyond the family and an affirmation of the interpersonal dimension of the faith experience. The literalness of the previous stage is replaced with the vitality of present experiences with others. The emergent strength of this stage is that the individual begins to form a personal story of faith identity, while the dangers lie in a possible overconformity to others' wishes and a too intense reliance on other persons who may betray such trust.

Stage 4 is typical of the adult years 20–30 and is termed *individuative-reflective faith*, in that the need for meaning is fashioned by the assumption of responsibility for fashioning one's own commitments, life style, beliefs, and attitudes. Although many persons remain at stage 3, those who move to stage 4 have to face the tension of individuality and the reality of personal feelings that may have been suppressed. The emergent strength of this stage lies in the critical capacity to reflect on identity (self) and on outlook (ideology), while there is the danger of becoming overconfident in one's ability to critically examine one's faith.

Stage 5 is typical of middle adulthood and is termed *conjunctive faith*, in that the need for meaning is fashioned by acquisition of the ability to do both/and rather than either/or thinking. In this stage, when it occurs, the individual becomes able to both trust others and the traditions they represent and to reflect in a critical manner on any and all conventions. Fowler calls this "dialogical" knowing. It involves a new reworking of one's past and an integration of convictions and feelings in a new unity. The emergent strength of this stage is the acquisition of ironic imagination in which one can be in, but not of, one's surroundings, while the danger is the possibility that one will become passive and inactive due to this newfound insight.

Stage 6, which does not usually appear before late adulthood—if it appears at all—is termed *universalizing faith*, in that the need for meaning is fashioned by an overcoming of the paradoxes of stage 5 and an active involvement in the imperatives of love and justice as an expression of faith. The emergent strength of this stage is the perception of the truths beneath the creeds of traditional religion and the willingness to become involved in bringing about the order to which these religions point—that is, the kingdom of God. The danger of this stage is possible disillusionment that may result when success does not come.

In all of the above stages there is the implicit assumption that faith is a universal necessity and that it can be more or less mature. Numerous investigations are presently being undertaken to assess whether Fowler's stages can be validated empirically.

Reference

Fowler, J. W. *Stages of faith*. San Francisco: Harper & Row, 1981.

7

Faith Healing
Bryan Van Dragt

In American culture faith healing is most commonly associated with miracles and religion. One imagines an emotionally charged gathering in which an enthusiastic, charismatic preacher exhorts members of the audience to trust in God, throw down their crutches, and "claim their cure." The "miracle services" led by Kathryn Kuhlman followed this pattern. Healing obtained in such a setting is usually attributed by the participants to a divine intervention which sets aside the natural laws governing the course of physical illness. The sufferer's belief or faith in God is seen as the key to this miraculous event.

In the popular and scientific literature the term *faith healing* is used in a variety of contexts. Psychic healing, chiropractic, folk medicine, and shamanism—as well as religious or sacramental healing—have all been referred to as faith healing. Some authors seem to use the term interchangeably with nonmedical treatment. Others use it in a pejorative fashion to connote quackery or primitive or unscientific technique.

Faith healing has, in fact, long been one of the more controversial topics in both the medical and religious communities. Nor has the debate over the validity of the phenomenon raged solely between the two camps, for each has been divided within its own ranks. The lines of argument have often been drawn quite absolutely, leading to incredible claims for the healing efficacy of religious faith on the one hand and, on the other, to blind rejection of genuine extramedical healing phenomena.

The resolution of at least some of this conflict has come in the research on psychosomatic relationships, which has made the concept of faith healing acceptable to the religious- and scientific-minded alike. Studies in such areas as biofeedback and meditation have demonstrated the mind's ability to influence bodily function. Among others, Simonton's cancer research suggests that visual imagery and positive changes in attitude can alter the course of illness, even to the point of total remission of cancer symptoms (Simonton, Matthews-Simonton, & Creighton, 1978). There is by now a host of research findings correlating changes in attitude, feeling, or belief with changes in the body, thus providing an empirical base for what has been observed phenomenologically for millennia: namely, that faith healing often "works."

However, what is known of psychosomatics fails to account for the rare but well-documented cases of instantaneous and total cure of diseases otherwise thought to be incurable and the rejuvenation of organ systems thought to be beyond repair (see Clapp, 1983).

Two concepts of faith healing will be addressed here. First, the term *faith healing* often refers to any process whereby positive physical change correlates with and is apparently caused or mediated by changes in the individual's values, attitudes, or beliefs. While virtually every healing is probably affected by the person's disposition toward it, faith healing in this first sense refers to healing in which the *primary* cause or mediating influence appears to be "faith," understood psychologically.

Note that this is a psychological rather than a religious or theological understanding of faith healing and that the content of one's beliefs may or may not relate to the divine. Faith healing in the psychological sense is differentiated from medical or surgical healing, in which the presumed cause is chemical or physical, and from psychic healing, in which the presumed cause is some power transmitted from or through the healer.

This first concept of faith healing is further differentiated from a second common usage, in which the term relates to "miraculous" healing, or healing occurring in contradiction to what is considered possible through medical/surgical or psychological intervention. Within the Christian religious community the presumed cause of such faith healing is God.

History

Healing by faith is an old tradition. In antiquity it often centered around religious ritual. The Greeks, for instance, believed that disease was the work of the gods and that cures required the intervention of other gods, such as Asclepius. Accordingly, people would journey far to one of his temples, there to sleep and, they hoped, to receive a healing vision of the god. Testimonial plaques left by some pilgrims attest to cures of blindness, lameness, paralysis, baldness, and a multitude of other ailments. Old Testament Hebrews also placed healing within the province of religion, believing that sickness was a result of sin, and therefore healing was a task reserved for the Levites and other religious figures.

Healing was an integral part of Jesus' ministry, and he also taught his followers to heal. Faith seems to have been a critical ingredient in at least some of these healings, in that Jesus often used the phrase, "Your faith has made you whole" (Mark 10:52). By contrast, on other occasions the utter disbelief of his audience apparently prevented healing from occurring (Mark 6:5–6).

Since the time of Christ there have been groups and individuals within the Christian church who have continued Jesus' emphasis on healing through faith. For example, since the mid-nineteenth century thousands of pilgrims yearly have journeyed to a shrine in Lourdes, France, in search of healing at the spring there. The shrine was constructed at the site of a young girl's vision of a woman calling herself the Immaculate Conception. The Roman Catholic Church has since carefully documented numerous cures (actually a very small fraction of the cures sought) obtained there which defy medical explanation.

Until recently, however, the church as a whole had largely departed from the ministry of healing. Kelsey (1973) traces this official departure to about the tenth century, when the service of unction for healing was gradually transformed into extreme unction, a rite of passage for the dying. Subsequently a whole theology arose to show why the "gift of healing" disappeared and is no longer a proper concern for Christianity. As Kelsey demonstrates, however, more recent theology and practice have reinstated healing by faith into the fabric of the church. Today it is practiced widely across the Christian denominations.

Psychological Approaches to Faith Healing

Psychological studies of faith healing have approached it from many directions, including the interpersonal, situational, psychophysiological, and intrapersonal dimensions of the phenomenon.

Social factors have been shown to have a powerful influence on healing, as is clearly demonstrated in research on the placebo effect in medicine. Placebo medications (usually saline or lactose), which have no specific chemical activity for the condition being treated, bring symptom relief in about a third of the cases in which they are used (Beecher, 1955). The "active ingredient" appears to be the patient's belief in the medication, which is affected in turn by the doctor-patient relationship (Shapiro, 1964). In general, the doctor who is warm, empathic, friendly, reassuring, and not conflicted about the patient or the treatment elicits positive placebo reactions, whereas the doctor who is angry, rejecting of the patient, or preoccupied with personal problems is more likely to elicit negative placebo reactions. Presumably any interpersonal variables affecting the doctor's ability to persuade the patient (see Frank, 1961) would be relevant here. The doctor's own belief in the medication's efficacy also affects the patient's response, since the placebo effect increases if the doctor is told that the agent is active and not a placebo.

Patient variables thought to influence faith, and thereby healing, have often been studied under the rubric of suggestibility, or susceptibility to interpersonal influence (Calestro, 1972). One broad area of research has tested hypotheses linking suggestibility to personality traits, various neurotic disorders, or other patient variables such as sex and age (Shapiro, 1964). Another line of research has studied the elements of communication that enhance attitude change. Compatibility of the patient's assumptive world or system of belief with that of the doctor or healer is one important factor here.

Still another relevant area of study is that of psychosomatic research, which addresses the broad question, "Under what conditions will what thoughts, feelings, beliefs, or attitudes produce what sorts of physiological changes and by what psychophysical mechanisms or pathways? For example, placebos have been hypothesized to act via the cerebral cortex, which activates elements of the endocrine system, thereby producing specific chemical changes in the body which promote healing.

Still, understanding the factors that enhance faith or the pathways by which it operates do not necessarily bring one to an understanding of faith itself.

Phenomenologically, we observe that one has faith that something is the case when it does not occur to one to doubt it. A nearly parallel expression is that faith is the lack of resistance to that which one hopes to receive. These expressions imply two things. First, faith has cognitive content. That is, there is some situation or event that is anticipated, based on a specific set of beliefs about the way things are—beliefs that may or may not have religious content. Second, faith involves an openness or a positive expectation that this event or situation will occur or is already occurring.

It is at this point that existential psychology further illuminates our understanding of faith. To the existentialist faith is more appropriately conceived as "faithing." That is, it is an act which one undertakes with the totality of one's being. Faith may be seen as the decision on the part of the self to open itself to the possibility of completion or growth. Such an act is the response of the person to life itself. It is the will to live—one's willingness to *be*. This act of opening oneself may be the key that unlocks the body's own healing resources. Indeed, faith healing is often seen simply as a facilitator of spontaneous remission.

A Transpersonal Approach to Faith Healing

There is quite possibly yet another aspect to faith healing; namely, a transpersonal dimension. One is forced into considering such a possibility by those cases of "miraculous" or instantaneous healing that apparently go beyond psychosomatics.

Viewed in this fashion faith is understood as that internal state of being "in which alone God can get near enough to man to do *his* work. The power of faith is, in one sense, nil. It is the state of personality in which God can exert *his* power" (Weatherhead, 1951, p. 431). In this religious concept of faith man may be conceived as essentially spirit and healing as resulting from his faithing response to, and joining with, Spirit, or God. Faith, then, is an existential openness, a "thirst and a desire that moves man toward the Absolute" (Panikkar, 1971, p. 223).

This view of faith does not supplant psychological approaches to faith healing, since the transpersonal dimension of faith is seen either as orthogonal to its psychosomatic dimension or as prior to it in the sense of being an ultimate cause, with the psychosomatic relationship being the proximate cause of the healing.

A Christian Critique

Misunderstanding of the nature and purpose of faith in healing has led to serious distortions within the church. While there is a relationship between health (conceived holistically rather than purely physically) and holiness (conceived as right relationship with God), some Christians believe that failure to be healed implies some fault on the sufferer's part (namely, a lack of religious faith) and consequently stigmatize those who are not cured. Others will die refusing medical or other physical assistance, believing that sickness is sent from God to punish sin and must therefore be endured unless and until one can "please" God with appropriate "faith."

Yet the concept of healing by faith is clearly rooted in the teachings of Jesus. Faith, whether considered in its psychological or religious aspect, is integral to healing. A balanced perspective on faith and healing would accept the help that psychology and medicine can afford, while at the same time being open to the possibility of miracles.

Whether such anomalous healing is the result of an unknown psychophysical mechanism, the direct intervention of the Deity, or something akin to the "inner shift" of which *A Course in Miracles* (Foundation for Inner Peace, 1975) speaks is yet unknown. The research problems inherent in any attempt to answer this question are enormous and probably insurmountable, although one may, of course, venture to discover the answer experientially.

References

Beecher, H. K. The powerful placebo. *Journal of the American Medical Association, 1955, 159,* 1602–1606.

Calestro, K. M. Psychotherapy, faith healing, and suggestion. *International Journal of Psychiatry,* 1972, *10* (2), 83–113.

Clapp, R. Faith healing: A look at what's happening. *Christianity Today,* 1983, 27(19), 12–17.

Foundation for Inner Peace. *A course in miracles* (3 vols.). Tiburon Calif.: Author, 1975.

Frank, J. D. *Persuasion and healing: A comparative study of psychotherapy.* Baltimore: Johns Hopkins Press, 1961.

Kelsey, M. T. *Healing and Christianity.* New York: Harper & Row, 1973.

Panikkar, R. Faith—A constitutive dimension of man. *Journal of Ecumenical Studies,* 1971, 8(2), 223–254.

Shapiro, A. K. Factors contributing to the placebo effect. *American Journal of Psychotherapy,* 1964, *18* (Supplement No. 1), 73–88.

Simonton, O. C., Matthews-Simonton, S., & Creighton, J. *Getting well again.* Los Angeles: J. P. Tarcher, 1978.

Weatherhead, L. D. *Psychology, religion, and healing.* Nashville: Abingdon, 1951.

Additional Reading

Frazier, C. A. (Ed.). *Faith healing: Finger of God or scientific curiosity?* Nashville: Thomas Nelson, 1973.

8

Guilt
S. Bruce Narramore

---

*G*uilt can be used either as a judicial term referring to violation of a law or to designate an emotion that follows judging oneself in violation of a standard. The first usage refers to an objective state or condition. When individuals break a civil law, they are objectively guilty whether they feel guilty or not. The second usage refers to a subjective experience. People may feel guilty even though they are not legally guilty.

Objective and subjective guilt can be further divided into two types. Objective guilt can refer to one's condition in relation to either a human law or to God. In reference to God all persons have been judged guilty (Isa. 53:6; Rom. 3:23), whereas only some people are guilty before human law. Subjective guilt can be divided into self-condemning emotions called neurotic guilt (false guilt, punitive guilt, or simply guilt feelings) and love-based corrective feelings variously called true guilt, ego guilt, existential guilt, or constructive sorrow.

Much confusion has been created by the failure to distinguish among these four types of guilt. Theologians have sometimes been alarmed by psychologists' efforts to eliminate neurotic guilt feelings because they were not aware that psychologists wanted to replace these punitive feelings with healthy love-based moral motivations. Similarly, some psychologists have viewed Christianity as a neurotic, guilt-inducing religion because of its stress on humanity's guilt before God. Not realizing the difference between objective and subjective guilt, they assumed that the concept of guilt before God meant that people should experience punitive feelings of guilt. Unfortunately, some Christians have also failed to differentiate between objective and subjective guilt and have assumed that since they are objectively guilty before God, they should experience feelings of guilt.

Guilt and Neurosis

An understanding of guilt feelings is central to the understanding of psychological maladjustment. Guilt is one of the major emotions (anxiety being the other) that sets in motion the various psychological defense mechanisms. Because anxiety and guilt are painful emotions, people attempt to repress the wishes and experiences surrounding them. This repression is one of the first steps in the formation of neurotic symptoms. It is also the main reason why many therapists promote a value-free approach to therapy in which they attempt to make no moral judgments of their clients. They believe any moral judgments in therapy will create further guilt feelings, motivate greater repression and rigidity, and move the client further into neurosis.

Development of Guilt Feelings

Punitive guilt emotions are usually referred to by psychologists simply as guilt. These feelings are based on feelings of self-punishment, self-rejection, and low self-esteem; they develop over a period of years within the context of the child's relationships with parents and significant others. Four dynamics appear to be central in their development: 1) the child's innate capacity for self-observation and judgment, 2) the taking in of the standards and expectations of others, 3) the taking in of the punishments and corrective attitudes of others, and 4) the child's anger over the frustration of his or her needs and wishes.

Although theorists vary in their understanding of the development of guilt feelings and other aspects of moral functioning, all agree that the child's innate potential for cognitive development is central to the process. Without the unfolding of these cognitive abilities children would be unable to accurately evaluate their actions and the consequences of them or to profit from the socialization process. It is this process that sets humanity's sense of right and wrong on a totally different level from animals. Animals have the capacity for some simple learning of right and wrong through rewards and punishments but not the capacity for self-observation that can result in true moral judgments.

Although most psychologists view the human potential for mature morality as simply the ability of an amoral individual to profit from socializing influences of parents and others, the scriptural assertion that we are created in God's image suggests that we are born with more than simply the capacity to profit from experience. It suggests that every person has at least some ability (or potential ability) to know whether his deeds are good or evil apart from (or in addition to) what he is taught. Paul's reference to the law written on the heart (Rom. 2:14–15) also suggests we are not born morally neutral but have some inherent sense of right and wrong.

The second factor in the development of guilt feelings is the child's taking in of the standards of parents and significant others. This process, called internalization, takes place as children begin to adopt parental and societal values. Since children admire and look up to their parents and because they fear punishment or rejection for disobedience, they gradually take their parents' standards as their own. These standards, when merged with the child's inherent moral capacity and own wishes and desires, form the core of the standard of conscience, or the child's ego ideal or ideal self. This set of ideals becomes the criterion by which the child judges his or her level of morality and accomplishment. After it is well established it will operate much as an internal law, and the child will tend to feel guilty any time its standards are violated.

At the same time children are taking in their parents' ideals and standards they also take in their corrective attitudes and actions. Consequently, if parental punishment is severely punitive or rejecting, children soon adopt these attitudes toward themselves and begin to mentally inflict similar punishments on themselves when they fall short of their ideals. These punitive and self-rejecting emotions form the core of neurotic guilt feelings.

The other contributor to the development of guilt feelings is the child's anger. When children become angry at parents and others, they naturally assume their parents are angry with them in return. Consequently, when parents punish children, children tend to see the parents as angrier than they really are. As children take in their parents' punitive attitudes, they take them in as they perceive them to be rather than as they are in reality. The strength of the child's punitive feelings of guilt, in other words, is not simply a reflection of the punitiveness of parental discipline. It is actually as strong as the combination of the parents' anger and the child's own anger. This is one reason why many people with loving parents still have serious problems with guilt.

Guilt in the Bible

Although the Bible has a great deal to say about humanity's objective guilt before God, it has surprisingly little to say about punitive feelings of guilt. In fact, not one of the three Greek words translated as *guilt* in the New Testament refers to the subjective experience of guilt feelings. They refer instead to our objective condition of guilt before God or to being under judgment or indebted to another person. This fact and the scriptural teaching on the atonement has led some (Bonhoeffer, 1955; Narramore, 1984; Thielicke, 1966) to conclude that guilt feelings are not a divinely ordained type of motivation. Since Christ has already paid for the believer's sins and made him acceptable to God, there are no grounds for continuing to punish and reject oneself by feelings of guilt (Rom. 8:1).

Since the believer's sins have been paid for by Christ, any further self-punishment can actually be seen as a form of self-atonement, which is ultimately based on a rejection of the efficacy of Christ's atoning death. From this perspective guilt feelings are seen as legalistic efforts to satisfy the demands of conscience apart from Christ. This perspective is supported not only by biblical teachings on justification and forgiveness but also by John's explicit statement that "we shall know by this that we are of the truth, and shall assure our heart before him, in whatever our heart condemns us; for God is greater than our heart, and knows all things" (1 John 3:19–20).

The Alternative to Guilt

While psychologists from a variety of theoretical perspectives point out the harm caused by punitive guilt emotions, most also see the need for an alternative form of motivation. Variously labeled *true guilt* (Tournier, 1962), *existential ego guilt* (Pattison, 1969), or *constructive sorrow* (Narramore, 1984), this type of motivation is set off from punitive guilt feelings in several ways. Whereas punitive guilt feelings are a self-centered form of punishment designed to atone for one's failures, constructive sorrow focuses on the damage done to others and the desire to make things right. Feelings of guilt are focused more on past failures, whereas constructive sorrow is oriented toward future changes. And feelings of guilt are based on anger, whereas constructive sorrow is motivated by love. Paul wrote of this type of motivation when he spoke of the sorrow that is according to the will of God "that produces repentance without regret in contrast to the sorrow of the world that produces death" (2 Cor. 7:8–10).

Much as punitive guilt feelings develop out of the child's innate capacity for moral functioning and internalized parental punitiveness, feelings of constructive sorrow grow out of one's innate moral capacities and the internalizing of loving parental corrections. When parents and significant others correct children with firm but loving and respectful discipline, children learn to respond to their failures not with punitive self-rejection but with a genuine desire to do better based on a concern for others and a desire for personal integrity. For Christians this constructive sorrow (or true guilt) is encouraged by God's loving care and provision. Before Paul wrote of a godly or constructive sorrow in 2 Corinthians 7:8–10, he reminded the Corinthians of a number of God's Old Testament promises (2 Cor. 6:16–18) and then wrote, "Therefore, having these promises, beloved, let us cleanse ourselves from all defilement of flesh and spirit, perfecting holiness in the fear of God" (2 Cor. 7:1). His appeal was not to avoid the pain of guilty condemnation, since that issue was already settled. Instead it was to respond in love to the work of God. It is this positive motivation that is the biblical alternative to guilt feelings.

References

Bonhoeffer, D. *Ethics*. New York: Macmillan, 1955.

Narramore, B. *The condemnation: Rethinking guilt and motivation*. Grand Rapids: Zondervan, 1984.

Pattison, E. Morality, guilt, and forgiveness in psychology. In E. Pattison (Ed.), *Clinical psychiatry and religion*. Boston: Little, Brown, 1969.

Thielicke, H. *Theological ethics* (2 vols.). Philadelphia: Fortress, 1966.

Tournier, P. *Guilt and grace*. New York: Harper & Row, 1962.

9

Hypnotic Aspects
of Spiritual Experience
George Matheson

Since its modern inception in the practices of Mesmer, hypnosis has frequently been associated with the spiritual and the occult. Because it appeared to be something magical, it was presumed to depend on unknown forces or powers. Since, on many occasions, hypnosis was employed to help people achieve things beyond the normal (e.g., avoid pain, sudden recovery of lost vision or sensation), it was seen as involving the supernatural. This association has unfortunately persisted despite the fact that the scientific foundations upon which the understanding of hypnosis is based have become firmer in the past two decades (Hilgard & Hilgard, 1975). The current conceptions of hypnosis remove the magical, occult characterization and allow hypnosis to provide another perspective on the understanding of religious experience (Matheson, 1979).

Hypnosis and Religious Events

Religious experiences are admittedly very personal and varied in their nature, but generally they are considered to be the effect of some being outside of the person or external to the self (Lindblom, 1962). However, religious experiences are usually the result of religious effects, the close observation of which reveals processes and phenomena equivalent in nature to those generally known as hypnotic. This is not to imply that all religious experiences are the result of hypnotic effects, nor is it intended to suggest that hypnosis is the sole contributing factor to any religious experience. Rather, the intention is to consider the role hypnotic experience plays in extending the religious experience beyond that of the rational.

Tappeiner (1977), in examining prophetical utterances, acknowledged the divine source of these prophecies but stressed that certain characteristics of the hypnagogic state—specifically vividness, originality, changefulness, and independence of conscious control—made it the most suitable channel for divine communication. Matheson (1979), in an examination of salvation, healing, and public prayer, also compared the systemic characteristics of these religious events to the formal and traditional styles of hypnosis. For example, the repetition, imagery, cadence, movement, and focus of the singing and the preaching induce a trancelike state in the listener which can then facilitate the spiritual response independently of mere rational thought. With these qualities, a religious experience is likely to have the subjective sense of having originated outside of the self.

The initial implications of this view of religious experiences as hypnotic phenomena are of two types: those that are complementary and those that clash with the implied religious intentions. This conceptualization supports a view of religious experience which is not merely rational in nature but which also integrally involves images and sensations. Thus, believing precedes knowing, as sensory experience precedes rational thought. Further, this view sheds light on theological conflicts that frequently have led to division. If the basis of faith resides in perceptual form, and if creed is a verbal description of this image, then attempts to debate doctrine without at least acknowledging and clarifying the perceptual models involved are destined to difficulty.

However, the effect of a hypnotic state can, at least in some people typically called high susceptibles, lead to behavioral responses that are not well grounded in the person. A response may be forthcoming but may extinguish over time, resulting in an apparent change in beliefs or loss of faith. In addition, the hypnotic process can be involved in the formation of various emotional states that can be pleasant and satisfying to the person. Associations between these pleasant affects and the producer of these feelings can then occur; if so, an intimate rapport develops in which the person is likely to respond to further suggestions, however incompatible they may be with the person's established personality. This effect is most noticeable in cults and sects established on very strict rules that are rigidly observed and enforced. Thus, the initial "good feeling" serves to create the fertile environment for later responses (Sargent, 1957; Stoner & Parke, 1977).

In summary, the traditional concept of hypnosis provides a means for examining many religious activities and the resulting religious experiences. The hypnotic process can lead to an expanded experience through imagery and sensation and does not restrict the event to a cognitive one. However, it also raises the risk that some may respond because of the pleasant affect and in a way not compatible with their existing selves. The above considerations briefly address the relationship of hypnotic processes to religious experiences. Religion is generally defined as any system of faith and worship of a supreme being, God. When compared with "spiritual," religion is generally seen as having an external focus on practice and form. In contrast, the essence of spiritual is that of soul or life, immaterial and yet at the center of one's being. The consideration of the relationship of hypnosis to spiritual experience involves an examination of the hypnotic facilitation of spiritual experience and the spiritual aspect of hypnotic experience.

The Spiritual and the Unconscious

As opposed to the religious, which usually finds its origin in the conscious and the deliberate, the spiritual is usually the gift of the unconscious. Religion is by nature something of form and structure, in which behavior is a product of tradition and deliberate intention, and content is thought and verbal recordings. In contrast, spiritual experiences seem to have their origin in darkness, breaking through into one's consciousness, often producing surprise and ecstasy.

As rich as the Age of Enlightenment was in its treasury of art and music, it also served to establish the preeminence of the conscious and the rational over that of the mystical, the imagined, and the unconscious. Consequently, that which could be decided or reasoned was valued and that which was dreamed or imagined was discredited. Concurrent with this thinking was the church's affirmation of Augustinian theology and the emergence of an approach to the Christian life that stressed the literal aspects of the Bible along with the logical understanding of one's faith. This emphasis promoted the rational and the conscious, and devalued the intuited and the unconscious. (This suspicious view of the unconscious was further enhanced by the Freudian concept of the unconscious as the seat of sexual and aggressive urges.) The emphasis on salvation as an act of personal decision and the continuing suppression of the inner world of feelngs and creativity in favor of the mental world of thought and volition have focused on a particular side of Christian truth and exaggerated it out of proportion.

However, this deemphasis on the unconscious has not always been present. Prior to the so-called Age of Enlightenment the unconscious was more typically seen as the creator, the motivator, and the source of spiritual experiences which achieved expression through the services of the conscious mind. The unconscious was understood as the source of spiritual experience: of visions, prophecies, "the still small voice." Such a view of unconscious functioning sees it not as a bound or closed system driven by previous experience and instinctive and antagonistic urges, but as an open system, receptive to creative and imaginary (nonrational) input. The unconscious processes serve to receive this input from within, from others, from the cosmos, and from God. Once received, the input is unconsciously perceived through a process of searching and organizing, and may then be made available to conscious awareness through a number of means including bodily sensations, dreams, daydreams, and behavior.

The visions of the Old and New Testaments all have elements of this creative unconscious. Ezekiel's wheels of fire and Jacob's ladder, as well as the dreams of Joseph and the revelations of John, are all consistent with the view of a receptive and perceptive unconscious. Similarly, Christ's teaching that we become as little children (implying, among other things, a reduction of the adult's rational thinking) and that we know in our hearts (in contrast to the knowing of the mind) are consistent with the role of the unconscious in the spiritual. Similarly Christ's use of parable, metaphor, and paradox also reflect his way of often bypassing the rational and analytical processes of consciousness in favor of communicating more directly with the unconscious mind. (See Sheperson, 1981, for a more detailed discussion of the place of unconscious hypnotic dynamics in Christ's communication patterns.)

Hypnosis and the Spiritual

Because hypnosis is an inborn ability and a naturally occurring process, it can be seen as relevant to the spiritual experience. Hypnosis is not to be considered as an invasive technique which imposes on human integrity and sanctity, but rather as an available resource for experience and growth. Once the spiritual can be seen as integrally involved in the receptive, perceptive, and creative processes of the unconscious, it can be seen as relevant to hypnosis. The spiritual is not a rational system of rules and thoughts but the intimate awareness and experience of the creation and the Creator.

Hypnosis, particularly as it is used to open up and expand experiences, can be a vehicle to approach the spiritual aspects of persons. Hypnosis can also be employed in such a way as to free up the sensory experience, to stimulate new perceptions, to activate unconscious searches, and to openly access unconscious phenomena. This experience of hypnosis is commonly achieved in self-hypnosis when the individual willingly and openly proceeds with images and techniques in order to facilitate new sensory occurrences such as visual images and altered physical perceptions. However, this same type of response may be evoked in heterohypnosis (i.e., with another person doing the hypnosis).

Self-hypnosis and heterohypnosis are both characterized by absorption and the fading of a general reality orientation. However, as Fromm, Brown, Hurt, Oberlander, Boxer, and Pfeifer (1981) noted, significant differences between these two types of hypnosis lie in areas of attention and ego receptivity. While concentrative attention and receptivity to stimuli coming from the hypnotist characterize heterohypnosis, expansive, free-floating attention and ego-receptivity to stimuli coming from within are characteristic of self-hypnosis. Many religious activities bear considerable similarity to the characteristics of heterohypnosis; there is increased absorption and narrowing of focused concentration and responsiveness to one external stimulus who may be the preacher, the healer, or the prophet. The result is an increase in responses consistent with what is suggested by the external source. In contrast, the spiritual experience is highly compatible with the nature of self-hypnosis in that the perceived events are expansive, freely changing or floating, and emerging from some place that seems to be within or independent of any objective, external source.

This does not reduce spirituality to some natural psychological process; rather, it aids in understanding the spiritual experience and even provides means to facilitate this part of one's life. Hypnosis, particularly in its self-experienced form, can be the process in which one achieves a state receptive to material from the unconscious. It may also be receptive to the intimate awareness and experience of the creation and the Creator. Such an understanding is foreign neither to the experiences described in Scripture nor to writings about prayer, contemplation, or spirituality.

The Bible and the Unconscious

The Bible contains many examples which attest to the creative role of the unconscious and the involvement of self-hypnotic activities in the experience of the Deity. The role of visions is prominent throughout Hebrew and Christian Scripture. "The word of the Lord came to Abram in a vision" telling him not to fear (Gen. 15:1). This was probably not an externally audible sound but one woven into a vision to which Abram could respond, suggesting that he was not asleep. Similarly, Samuel experienced the voice of the Lord calling him while he rested. Initially he responded as if it were the voice of Eli, but was then guided by his mentor (who apparently could not hear it) to attend to this voice as the voice of God (1 Sam. 3). Further examples exist throughout the Old and New Testaments, including Daniel, Joseph, Job, Elijah, Ezekiel, and the revelation of John.

Christ's examples of prayer are also indications of unconscious and hypnotic activities. Not only did he suggest a structure to prayer (Matt. 6:9–13), but he also went apart where he struggled with visions and experienced his praying physically. Paul addresses this nonrational, unconscious element of prayer when noting the basic inability of people to pray (Rom. 8:5–8, 26). This inability is not due to any psychological difficulties. Rather, it is because Christian prayer must begin by maintaining the fundamental mystery of God, and consequently not knowing how we ought to pray (Rom. 8:26) is paradoxically the condition that makes all true prayer possible. It is the focusing of both conscious and unconscious mental processes on God that results in expressions of "unutterable groanings."

Here the parallel to self-hypnotic techniques can be seen most closely, for the self-hypnotic abilities allow nonrational, nonverbal attention to symbols and mysteries. These can be perceived and experienced outside of consciousness but may culminate in images, words, or voices reappearing in the arena of consciousness. A structured technique for the utilization of unconscious resources in self-hypnosis is to ask oneself one important or focused question before commencing self-hypnosis. This is assumed to direct the unconscious search processes, perhaps resulting in a hypnotic response or an "answer" sometime later (Erickson & Rossi, 1976).

Implications and Conclusions

A theology which overcomes the Augustinian dualism and declares all of creation to be of God, to be experienced and enjoyed, can accept hypnosis as a part of that creation, a naturally occurring phenomenon which is neither inherently evil or good. The value of hypnosis is that it provides a means of achieving a special state in which the person can go beyond the bounds of usual rational thinking to affect both mental and physical processes. Sensations and experiences which were previously considered to be beyond access can be influenced, and unconscious processes and responses can be stimulated.

Self-hypnosis is particularly effective, since the resulting trance state is expansive, free-floating, and internally responsive in nature. Consequently, this state is a desirable means for individuals to approach and utilize their own unconscious resources.

According to Jung (1936) the unconscious psyche contains both a personal part, which holds an assembly of past, repressed content, and a collective or universal part, the product of heredity and creation. This latter part contains the archetypes or models for development and can be seen as that aspect of the person which is initially subject to synchronistic influence and communication with God. Thus, the activity of the unconscious can be experienced as the "still, small voice," or the awareness of God within, and can be the source of our spiritual experience. Similarly, the contemplative experience can be viewed as the achievement of a self-hypnotic state which is furthered by an activation of the unconscious in ways that defy verbal description, and yet have a real and appreciable effect on the individual.

Self-hypnosis is a learnable process that is generally available to anyone; it can be the means for the achievement of trance, the transcendence of the rational, and the entrance into the mystical. Such experience taps into the spiritual and unconscious resources of the individual and also into that part of the psyche that is open to the influence of God and the cosmos. Hypnosis has in reality always been integral to the experience of spirituality; its use can enhance spiritual growth.

References

Erickson, M. H., & Rossi, E. L. Two-level communication and the microdynamics of trance and suggestion. *American Journal of Clinical Hypnosis*, 1976, *18*(3), 153–171.

Fromm, E., Brown, D. P., Hurt, S. W., Oberlander, J. Z., Boxer, A. M., & Pfeifer, G. The phenomena and characteristics of self-hypnosis. *International Journal of Clinical and Experimental Hypnosis*, 1981, *29*(3), 189–246.

Hilgard, E. R., & Hilgard, J. R. *Hypnosis in the relief of pain*. Los Altos, Calif.: William Kaufman, 1975.

Jung, C. G. The concept of the collective unconscious. In C. G. Jung, *The archetypes and the collective unconscious*. Princeton, N.J.: Princeton University Press, 1936.

Lindblom, J. *Prophecy in ancient Israel.* Philadelphia: Fortress, 1962.

Matheson, G. Hypnotic aspects of religious experience. *Journal of Psychology and Theology,* 1979, 7, 13–21.

Sargent, W. *Battle for the mind: The physiology of conversion and brainwashing.* Garden City, N.Y.: Doubleday, 1957.

Shepperson, V. L. Paradox, parables, and change. *Journal of Psychology and Theology,* 1981, 9, 3–11.

Stoner, C., & Parke, J. *All God's children: The cult experience—salvation or slavery?* Radnor, Pa.: Chilton, 1977.

Tappeiner, D. A. A psychological paradigm of the interpretation of the charismatic phenomenon of prophecy. *Journal of Psychology and Theology,* 1977, 5(1), 23–29.

10

Mass Evangelism
Craig W. Ellison

The use of communications media to convey the gospel of Jesus Christ to large numbers of people in efforts to persuade them to become Christians is usually described as mass evangelism. The media include television, radio, movies, and newspapers. Mass evangelism is comparatively indiscriminate in its targeting, although selective viewing and the advent of public television have resulted in some narrowing of the audience.

Although there have been some positive results from the use of mass communications, the failure of the church to understand the strengths and weaknesses of these approaches often results in haphazard evangelism strategy that is costly and relatively ineffective.

In general, mass communication rarely brings about major attitude change (Klapper, 1967). People are most likely to expose themselves to presentations with which they agree and to avoid those messages that challenge their beliefs. This is especially true for those attitudes that are central to a person's identity and are expressive of his or her fundamental values. Changing a central belief has repercussions throughout a person's belief system. Such changes create uncertainty and anxiety until the implications of a new set of core beliefs can be perceived and worked through in the self-image, decisions, and behaviors of the person. As a result, people usually ignore, distort, or forget messages that threaten a centrally important belief.

The implications of this for mass evangelism are significant. The likelihood that those who are uninterested in Christianity, for whatever reason, will choose to be exposed to evangelistic messages is minimal. Second, the probability of causing a major change in the core values of the viewer is small. Those who are not antagonistic to Christianity in general but do not wish to respond positively to appeals for fundamental change will tend to avoid evangelistic programs that are highly persuasion oriented. If their lack of response is due to ego-defensive reasons, some research suggests a boomerang effect may occur in response to persuasive attempts (Katz, 1960). If a communicator is unaware of the recipient's attitudinal base, he may unwittingly stimulate resistance to subsequent presentation of the gospel. Further, the fact that emotional arousal is normally crucial for radical change to occur militates against mass conversions. These factors suggest that the format and content of mass evangelistic appeals need to include channels of persuasion beyond the purely cognitive, and that the content needs to be focused primarily toward those who are interested in Christianity and open to the possibility of change.

The increased use of music and drama as means of connection with the emotional roots of religious belief increases the likelihood that viewers will listen and the possibility that conversion will occur among the interested. The development of content designed to identify with the life context of typical viewers who are interested in Christianity and showing how commitment to Christianity helps meet their needs would be more effective than appeals for change that are abstract and theological. Since mass communication is relatively unsuccessful in effecting a major change in the unsaved person's attitudinal core, it would be better to direct the bulk of mass communication efforts to building bridges of relevancy and aiming toward modification of existing attitudes. Such modification would "soften" a person's attitude for future conversion.

This is not to say that people cannot be converted through mass evangelistic appeals. However, awareness of the fact that spiritual decision making is a process (Engel, 1975) and that those most likely to be saved normally have at least a positive attitude toward the gospel is important for effective programming strategy. Regarding those who are more neutral or uninterested in Christianity, attitude modification and exposure to basic, positive aspects of the Judeo-Christian faith should be the goal.

In cultures where the masses are relatively unaware of the basics of Christianity and have no opinion about it, research suggests that mass communication can be used successfully to bring about radical conversions. This is due to the fact that mass communication has been found to be highly effective in creating attitudes about topics on which a person had no previous opinion (Klapper, 1967). Although the potential for foreign missions may be significant, the actual response of a person to persuasion attempts will depend upon his felt need, the extent to which the message addresses that need, whether the change required is seen as antagonistic to other cultural mores, and whether the mode of communication connects with the person's primary channel of receptivity (abstract vs. concrete thinking; emotions vs. cognition; aural vs. visual). While making certain that biblical principles are not compromised, missionaries should make every effort to adapt the message of Christ to those values and beliefs that are prevalent in a particular culture.

The fact that mass communication serves as an agent of reinforcement for the attitudes, opinions, and behavioral tendencies that viewers already possess further suggests an important role for mass communications in evangelism follow-up. Programs designed to identify with and nurture the spiritual development of new believers could be highly effective.

References

Engel, J. F. World evangelization: A myth, a dream, or a reality? *Spectrum*, 1975, *1*, 4–6.

Katz, D. The functional approach to the study of attitudes. *Public Opinion Quarterly*, 1960, *24*, 163–204.

Klapper, J. T. Mass communication, attitude stability, and change. In C. W. Sherif & M. Sherif (Eds.), *Attitude, ego-involvement, and change*. New York: Wiley, 1967.

11

Meditation
Mark P. Cosgrove

The practice of meditation can include a variety of efforts to produce an altered state of consciousness. It has become very popular in recent years in the Western world with the introduction of Eastern meditative practices such as Zen Buddhism, yoga, and similar disciplines. The reason for this increased interest in meditation may be the growing search in our fast-paced society for peace, spiritual truth, and an expanded awareness.

While there are many Eastern meditative techniques, all seem to share the common view that human beings live their lives at a low level of conscious experience, and that true enlightenment and peace will only come as conscious experience is elevated. A variety of techniques can be used to accomplish this end, including sensory deprivation, biofeedback, and hallucinogenic drugs, but the technique preferred by many is some sort of meditative exercise. All these techniques seek to suppress or alter ordinary sensory experience. Ornstein (1977) describes meditation as a technique for "turning down the brilliance of the day, so that ever-present and subtle sources of energy can be perceived within" (p. 159). It constitutes a deliberate attempt to inhibit the usual mode of consciousness and to cultivate an alternate mode.

The exact methods in such mind-altering meditation can involve a wide variety of practices, including bizarre dancing, gazing at an object, focusing on one's breathing, or concentrating on a meaningless phrase. The knowledge gained in such meditation is intuitive and experiential rather than rational. The experience is ineffable—that is, defies being put into words—and is often called the mystic experience.

Transcendental Meditation

A clearer picture of meditation can be gained by examining more closely one particular type: Transcendental Meditation. TM, as it is popularly abbreviated, is a commercialized form of meditation taught in the United States by Maharishi Mahesh Yogi. It is also called the Science of Creative Intelligence. Transcendental Meditation became popular in the United States in the 1970s when the Maharishi discovered that Americans would seek to learn his techniques if they were taught devoid of spiritual and religious ideas.

In Transcendental Meditation a mantra, or a sound repeated continuously, is used to increase a person's deep relaxation and refined specialized awareness. The Maharishi's theory behind the choice of a mantra for a person is that each person meditates best with a sound that fits the vibrations that constitute his personality. After a mantra is chosen, the recommended steps in meditation include: 1) sit quietly in a comfortable position; 2) close the eyes; 3) relax all the body's muscles; 4) concentrate on the act of breathing or on the mantra and banish all other thinking; 5) practice these steps twice daily.

Meditators practicing these steps report feelings of peace, well-being, and a deep sense of relaxation. The person is both highly wakeful and relaxed. Experienced transcendental meditators learn to experience a loss of sense of self and a union with things around them. Objects begin to feel as if they are a part of the meditator rather than "out there." It is this oneness experience that is the ultimate goal of the meditation experience. Psychotherapists who use meditation in therapy seek to produce these same results in their clients. They hope that regular meditation will bring a calming peace to the one troubled emotionally, and that the oneness feeling will allow people to better understand and relate to self, others, and the world around them.

The mind-altering experiences of this type of meditation seem to relate to the sensory reduction practices used. With the eyes closed and attention focused on a mantra, the meditator seeks to decrease the amount of incoming sensory information. Eastern meditators have argued that the human brain as a sensory reducer screens out valuable information about the greater realities of the universe. According to this view, what a person eventually experiences is only a fractional part of the total picture of reality, and a misleading picture at that. According to the Eastern meditator's world-view, which is panpsychism (all things are one mind or force), the ordinary person has an erroneous experience of physical reality and personal identity. The person who does not meditate, they feel, is not in touch with the greater reality of the immaterial essence of the universe and a nonpersonal identification with all things. The meditative techniques of closing the eyes and narrowing concentration (and experience) to a single sound or feeling serve to allow the greater nonpersonal, nonrational reality to be experienced.

Physiological Research

In a study of the physiological changes during meditation it was found that heart rate slows, respiration is reduced, less oxygen is consumed, and the meditator's brain waves show a marked increase in alpha frequencies (Wallace & Bensen, 1972). These bodily changes are the opposite of what occurs in the body when a person is subjected to stress. Therefore, it is possible that meditative techniques such as Transcendental Meditation can be a useful means of dealing with the stresses of modern life. The brain-wave changes in meditation are also similar to what occurs in the technique of biofeedback, which is also used to ease some symptoms of stress. In biofeedback the person learns to control brain waves and autonomic responses because he receives feedback on these states; therefore, it seems likely that the experienced meditator is learning to tune in to his internal bodily states and brain waves in order to control them.

Somewhat countering the claims of Eastern meditators, it has been demonstrated that the physical benefits of meditation are similar no matter what is used for a mantra. It may be that meditation produces an innate relaxation response in the body, a response that counters the body's autonomic stress response. Doubts about this form of meditation being a unique state of consciousness also surfaced when Pagano, Rose, Stivers, and Warrenburg (1976) found that electroencephalograph readings differed from one day to the next. Other research has countered the spiritual enlightenment claims of Eastern meditation by showing that the meditative state is more similar to a resting state than a unique state of consciousness (Michaels, Huber, & McCann, 1976). It was found that the biochemical states of meditators are highly similar to control data from subjects who merely rested. Therefore, it may be summarized that Eastern forms of meditation may produce a sense of peace and relaxation, if practiced regularly, but there is little evidence to support claims for spiritual enlightenment.

Christian Meditation

Meditation can also be practiced as a part of the Christian life of worship, but it is only remotely similar to Eastern meditation. Christian mystics, most of whom regularly experienced meditative states, have adorned church history down to current times, including Augustine, Theresa, Francis of Assisi, George Fox, John Wesley, and Brother Lawrence.

These Christian mystics well understood that human life is meant to be a personal relationship with a personal God, and that Christ is the only way into spiritual knowledge and life. The meditative experience in this context is the act of listening to God, communicating with him, and experiencing a love relationship with him. When Christians have a blissful, peaceful experience in the act of meditation, they are not experiencing a cosmic consciousness so much as they are learning to shut out the chatter of a noisy world that can interfere with focusing attention on God. This is not to say that the mystic is more Christian than one who has not had this experience. All Christians experience a relationship with God to a greater or lesser degree and are, therefore, mystical. The differences in the depth of that experience are probably related more to psychological temperament and God's calling than to a person's degree of commitment to God.

The Christian mystic may indeed practice some of the same techniques as the Eastern mystic in order to further his closeness to God. These techniques could involve fasting or focusing one's attention on an attribute of God or a Bible verse. However, the experience gained from these meditative exercises is not the central facet of Christian meditation.

The Eastern meditator seeks to shatter the feelings of self and personhood and to merge with the cosmic consciousness of the universe. The Christian meditator, on the other hand, sees his personhood as a creation of God and not an erroneous experience. A Christian seeks to lose not self, but self-centeredness. The Christian meditator's goal is not to annihilate human nature but to master it with Christ's help.

The Eastern mystic seeks to become one with the universe because all of the universe is god. The Christian understands that God is a person and humans have become estranged from him. The Christian seeks to draw closer to God while in this life on earth through meditative worship.

The Eastern mystic seeks to become detached from the world and shuns both its pleasures and its evils. In Eastern mysticism there is a longing to be released from the burdens and pains of this life, and to enter into the effortless, blissful state of nirvana. The Christian meditator may also shun some of the pleasures of life and will certainly shun its sins, but for a different reason. The Eastern mystic uses virtue as a tool to achieve a higher cosmic consciousness. The Christian, knowing that unconfessed sins estrange us from both God and man, has as a goal to live in obedience to God. The Christian believes that a practical asceticism may aid in withdrawing from the confusion of life that often dampens the contemplation of spiritual matters. Christians may detach themselves from some of things of this life, but only as a method of redirecting life toward a richer attachment to God and to other human beings. Therefore, the insights gained in Christian meditation ought to be practical. Christian meditators seek to clear their minds and meditate as a communion with God. Christian meditation, therefore, represents an expansion of the human personality toward the experience of a relationship with God for which they were created.

References

Michaels, R. R., Huber, M. J., & McCann, D. S. Evaluation of transcendental meditation as a method of reducing stress. *Science*, 1976, *192* (4245), 1242–1244.

Ornstein, R. E. *The psychology of consciousness* (2nd ed.). New York: Harcourt Brace Jovanovich, 1977.

Pagano, R. R., Rose, R. M., Stivers, R. M., & Warrenburg, S. Sleep during transcendental meditation. *Science*, 1976, *191* (4224), 308–309.

Wallace, R., & Bensen, H. The physiology of meditation. *Scientific American*, 1972, *226* (2), 84–90.

Additional Readings

Campbell, C. The facts on transcendental meditation. *Psychology Today*, 1974, *7* (11), 37–46.

Foster, R. J. *Celebration of discipline.* San Francisco: Harper & Row, 1978.

McNamara, W. Psychology and the Christian mystical tradition. In C. T. Tart (Ed.), *Transpersonal psychologies.* New York: Harper & Row, 1975.

12

Moral Development
Rodney B. McKean

$\mathbf{M}$ost often associated with the work of Kohlberg (1971, 1981), moral development theory describes the development of moral judgment. Kohlberg's theory is based on the cognitive development theory of Piaget which emphasizes cognitive structures that help explain the reasoning process a person uses to make sense of his experience and environment. Kohlberg has used Piaget's concept of structure to make a distinction between content and structure in a moral judgment.

The content of a moral judgment is the normative statement of what is right or wrong. "It is wrong to steal" is the content of a moral judgment. The structure of a moral judgment refers to the cognitive structure one uses to make sense of the world in order to reach the content (i.e., that it is wrong to steal). Thus one person might decide that it is wrong to steal because he is using preoperational reasoning and makes moral decisions on the basis of the size and severity of physical consequences. Another person might decide that it is wrong to steal because her cognitive reasoning is oriented to concrete answers to social situations, and she believes that it is best to obey concrete rules.

Kohlberg suggests that changes in one's cognitive structural reasons for specific moral judgments are a function of normal cognitive development as explained by Piaget. Thus, for Kohlberg, the term *moral development* refers to development within a system of stages of cognitive structure. His research indicates that a system of cognitive structural stages of moral judgment consists of six separate stages, with two stages each representing three of Piaget's stages of cognitive development.

Level I: Preconventional Morality

Kohlberg's first two stages of moral development are characteristic of Piaget's stage of preoperational thinking. Using preoperational thinking a person tends to focus more on the physical appearance of objects and events rather than on logical and verbal explanations. Preoperational thinking tends to be fantasy based and nonlogical; thus moral judgments of this type would also appear nonlogical to adult thinking. In Level I cognitive judgments about right and wrong tend to be based more on the nature of the physical consequences resulting from a certain action rather than on the conventionality or ethical appropriateness of the action.

Stage 1: Punishment, avoidance

In the first stage of moral development one usually defines what is right or wrong on the basis of the severity of the punishment associated with the action. Power and size are often the bases on which authority and rightness are attributed to a person or an idea. A person would also consider an action that caused more physical damage to be more wrong than one that caused less, regardless of the ethical intentions of the person who caused the damage. Often persons in this stage do not even realize that they have done something wrong until they sense the punishment coming. A person using this kind of thinking may say that it is wrong to steal "because I will get put in jail," or "because my parents will spank me."

Stage 2: Reciprocal hedonism

In the second stage of moral development a person usually defines right and wrong on the basis of benefit or reward. In this stage the benefit or reward is usually perceived only in physical terms (candy, money, sex). This kind of thinking is represented by the statement, "you scratch my back, and I'll scratch yours." Whereas in stage 1 morality was defined in terms of the "badness" of an act, in stage 2 it is defined in terms of the "goodness" of an act. Also in stage 1, the relative goodness of the act is determined by the relative physical size of the reward or benefit. A person using this kind of thinking might say that it is wrong to steal "because I get to do special things when I have been good."

Level II: Conventional Morality

Kohlberg's third and fourth stages of moral development are based on Piaget's concrete operational stage of thinking. In this stage one can use adultlike logic for solving problems, but only in a concrete black-and-white, right-and-wrong way. Thus, in Level II cognitive judgments about right and wrong are based largely on concrete codes of morality or social conventions.

Stage 3: Interpersonal concordance

Though similar to stage 2 in terms of seeking a benefit or reward as the basis for judging a particular action to be correct, stage 3 shifts the emphasis from a physical benefit to an affectional or interpersonal benefit. Kohlberg described this as a "good-boy, nice-girl" stage. The primary motivation for moral behavior seems to be approval or acceptance by some respected authority. From the perception of this stage that authority could be a parent, a peer group, an ethnic tradition, a church, a nationality, or even God. The main objective is to live up to an external standard of goodness. A person using stage 3 thinking might say that it is wrong to steal "because good girls don't steal," or "good Christians don't steal."

Stage 4: Maintenance of social order

In the fourth stage of cognitive moral development a person usually makes judgments about right and wrong on the basis of keeping a sense of order in society, a particular institution, or the world. The main emphasis of this perception of morality is on maintaining the status quo. It is often represented by the statement, "If we let you have this exception, we'll have to let everyone have it." It is characterized by a fear of setting new precedents. There is also the perception that moral conventions are good for all and that they keep order although in particular instances they may seem unfair. The concern is usually for the good of the majority of people. A person using stage 4 thinking might say that it is wrong to steal "because we just can't have everybody going around stealing all the time."

Level III: Postconventional Morality

Kohlberg's fifth and sixth stages of moral development are based on Piaget's formal operational stage of thinking. Formal operations is the most abstract form of reasoning. Using formal operational reasoning a person can easily consider more than one viewpoint at a time. He can look beyond what he is presently aware of, either physically or in terms of social conventions, and speculate about new and hypothetical solutions to given problems. Thus, in level 3 cognitive judgments about right and wrong tend to involve ethical principles about universal human rights and ethical standards rather than concerns about physical consequences or conventional rules.

Stage 5: Social contract

Whereas in stage 4 rules are understood as providing for social order, in stage 5 rules are agreed upon by a group of people in order to protect the rights and welfare of those people. This type of thinking about morality is represented by the Constitution and Bill of Rights of the United States. In stage 5 structural reasoning rules exist to serve ethical rights of individuals, and rules can be changed collectively by those individuals when they seem to be no longer effective. In stage 4 reasoning, decisions about maintaining order seem always to favor the majority. In stage 5 reasoning, decisions about ethical rights tend to be made with concern for the minority. A person using stage 5 structural reasoning might say that it is wrong to steal "because it would violate someone's right of ownership."

Stage 6: Universal ethical principles

The sixth stage of cognitive reasoning about morality is the most abstract of all. It is not connected either with conventional rules and consequences or with social agreements. Decisions about right and wrong are based on self-chosen ethical principles that are perceived by the person to be universal. Kant's categorical imperative well represents this stage of reasoning. This kind of reasoning requires that a person be able cognitively to take an objective third-person perspective on a given situation or issue. He should be able to come to a conclusion without regard for any particular person's interests but with regard to an ethical principle that is deemed universal. Kohlberg suggests that the kind of ethical principles involved in stage 6 reasoning include love, justice, truthfulness, and welfare rather than conventional rules or civil and ethical rights. A person using stage 6 moral judgment might say that it is wrong to steal "because it is unjust for me to advance my welfare at someone else's expense."

Summary

Kohlberg's theory of psychological stages of moral judgment is a specific theory of cognitive structural development resulting from the research of Piaget. It is not a comprehensive theory of how people do in fact act in moral situations at any point in their lives. Many psychologists and educators have speculated that the link between moral judgment and moral actions has something to do with ego strength, will power, emotional stability, or a combination of any of these. However, at this time Kohlberg's theory is the most comprehensive existing psychological theory of moral development.

Moral Education

The concept of moral development has been an important part of education for centuries. In Scripture education focused primarily on religious and moral education. Much of the writing of Plato and Aristotle on education made significant reference to moral education. The development of theology as an academic discipline in the Middle Ages brought a renewed emphasis on moral education. In later centuries Kant, Dewey, Durkeim, and other leading scholars from many disciplines have written about moral education.

The major task of moral education is to determine what values should be taught and the most effective way to teach them so that people will really act upon them. Some educators have focused on the values and character traits to be taught, and then assumed some sort of teaching or instructional procedure without much thought. Others focus more specifically on ethical arguments and rules, and then teach them as they would any other set of facts or line of thinking. Still others put their attention on the actual behavior of people and recommend instructional procedures that either reinforce acceptable behavior or socialize people into habits and customs of socially moral actions. These are only some of the typical solutions to the task of moral education.

The major task and its typical solutions reveal some basic issues involved in thinking about moral education: 1) *The nature of values:* Are values things? thoughts? beliefs? Are they a set code? Are they abstract principles? Are moral values universal? cultural? religious? political/economic? 2) *The appropriateness of teaching values:* Should we impose values on others? Should we just let people figure out their own values? 3) *The nature of morality:* What part do logical/rational thinking skills play? What part does knowledge play? What part do emotions play? Where does intentionality come in? Where do the physical acts and consequences come into play? What influence do normal developmental processes have (do we judge morality to be the same for people of all different ages)? 4) *The process of learning values:* Do people learn values by verbal/direct instruction? By practicing them under social control? By discovering them through experience?

Resolving these issues requires combinations of insights and perceptions from various scholarly disciplines. Psychology contributes by offering ideas about how a person comes to possess a certain set of values. There seem to be three major psychological schools of thought which influence ideas about moral education. These will be referred to as association learning, self-actualization, and interactional development.

Schools of psychology that emphasize *association learning* view the learner as someone who is less mature or initiated than the surrounding society, especially the teacher. The learner's role is to receive from the teacher the knowledge, values, or skills that are deemed by the teacher to be useful in making the learner more mature. Within this school of thought values are typically understood to exist objectively, and they usually exist as propositional verbal statements to be believed or repeated. Values then are something belonging to the environment, and it is the student's task to come to accept or internalize those external values.

Educational programs based on this psychological view of values and morality usually predefine correct values; these are either verbally transmitted from the teacher to the learner, or the learner's behavior is controlled or reinforced until it approximates the kind of behavior prescribed by the defined code of values. Such approaches to moral education often seem to make little distinction between moral/ethical values, social/cultural values, and traits of personality and character.

Schools of psychology that emphasize *self-actualization* and personal meaning tend to view values as mental constructs created by the individual to guide the behavior of the individual. They are not viewed as existing outside of the learner, but are seen to exist subjectively as a result of the learner's thoughts about his or her own experience. Thus, the learner is viewed as the most active agent in the moral/value learning process. The teacher may be viewed as a guide into experience or as a guardian to protect the right of the individual to come to personal choices about what values to believe and act on. The task of moral education is to help people feel more confident about their moral choices and behavior rather than to help people conform to external standards about such choices and behavior. Thus, the teacher is often viewed, not as more mature or knowledgeable than the learner, but as another person in the process of discovering personal values.

Schools of psychological thought which emphasize *interactional development* and construction learning tend to view the learner as an organism actively attempting to adapt to the environment. Learning is viewed as constructing knowledge (subjectively) by interacting with the concrete (objective) reality of the environment in order to solve problems. Thus, values are viewed as conclusions reached by the organism about the most healthy way to be and act in the environment. The learner is viewed as very active in the learning process by recognizing problems and testing various hypotheses until he comes to a conclusion about what makes most sense. The environment plays a crucial role in helping the learner distinguish between real and perceived problems, identify various potential solutions to the problems, and validate the conclusions reached. The term *interaction* then refers to a very real interaction between the organism and the environment—or the learner and the teacher.

Moral education programs that employ these views work on trying to resolve real-life moral cases or hypothetical case studies rather than on transmitting a predefined set of values. It is believed that learners learn best when they are trying to solve moral problems that they are actually facing. Thus, this kind of moral education does not usually consist of a prepackaged curriculum but of a caring relationship between the teacher and learner where problem solving can occur. It is not inappropriate for the teacher to suggest personal or external values as possible solutions for the moral problem being explored. However, the role of the teacher remains that of a co-explorer, not someone who hands ready-made conclusions to the learner.

Along with psychology other academic disciplines also offer ideas that are useful to moral education. Sociology puts an emphasis on social values and the social networks that transmit those values. It has contributed to moral education by defining the socialization process and the impact of imitation of significant models. Philosophy has suggested how to define the moral/ethical content of moral education. Philosophers have also suggested that moral education ought to teach logic as it applies to moral, social, and civic issues. Theology has suggested ways to define the content of moral education. This content has ranged from prescribed codes to rather abstract guiding principles.

It has been suggested that most real moral learning occurs as the result of the "hidden curriculum." The hidden curriculum is understood as the things we do and the ways we treat people, which in turn have a strong impact on the kinds of moral values people learn. Some believe that democratic social institutions are the most healthy kind of environment for moral education. Others feel the interdependent relational atmosphere usually associated with families is the most powerful force for moral education. There seems to be some consensus that typical hierarchical schooling structures that emphasize conformity to external values and deemphasize the involvement of people in developing their own values will have little impact on teaching people to participate in democratic societies or solve emerging moral problems.

If the contributions from psychology and other scholarly disciplines are combined, the options for moral education can be analyzed in terms of both content and methodology. The optional content foci seem to be 1) absolute moral values; 2) social or socially prescribed moral values; 3) individualistic-relativistic values; 4) logical reasoning skills; or 5) the valuing process. The optional methodological foci seem to be 1) indoctrination; 2) verbal propositional instruction; 3) values clarification; or 4) logical problem-solving case studies and moral dilemmas.

Recently moral education in American public schools has most often incorporated the values clarification and case studies approaches. This has been in an attempt to avoid the problem of indoctrination in a pluralistic society. Following World War II moral education was usually a neglected aspect of public schooling, but it received new emphasis as a result of the social protest over industrialistic/materialistic society, the Vietnam War, and Watergate. Prior to that time moral education usually consisted of direct content-centered propositional instruction and character building. This was also the primary approach to moral education in Christian ministry—and still is, though there have been recent emphases on personal internalization and problem solving paralleling these emphases in public schooling.

References

Kohlberg, L. Stages of moral development as a basis for moral education. In C. M. Beck, B. S. Crittenden, & E. V. Sullivan (Eds.), *Moral education: Interdisciplinary approaches.* New York: Newman Press, 1971.

Kohlberg, L. *The philosophy of moral development.* San Francisco: Harper & Row, 1981.

Additional Readings

Hall, R. T., & Davis, J. U. *Moral education in theory and practice.* Buffalo: Prometheus Books, 1975.

Purpel, D., & Ryan, K. *Moral education . . . it comes with the territory.* Berkeley, Calif.: McCutchan Publishing, 1976.

13

Near-Death Experiences
John McDonagh

Most modern psychologists would probably reject the notion that the human personality survives bodily death, and would likewise reject the idea that a "spirit world" exists. Even if some of these thinkers should acknowledge such possibilities among their personal beliefs, they would most likely rule the study of the psyche after death out of bounds for psychology because such phenomena are considered to be nonobservable. However, since the mid-1970s this whole set of assumptions is being questioned seriously by a group of investigators of the near-death experience.

Basically the near-death experience is a series of phenomena experienced by individuals who were clinically dead for short periods of time (usually 10 or 15 minutes, though sometimes longer). These near-death survivors report extraordinary experiences which, although somewhat variable, are remarkably homogeneous considering the diversity of the individuals studied. The classic description of the near-death experience is outlined by Moody (1975a). First, the person sometimes reports hearing himself pronounced dead by his doctor. He then hears a loud ringing or buzzing and feels himself moving through a dark tunnel. He then may suddenly find himself outside his physical body; he may see his own body as though he were a spectator, and may watch as resuscitation attempts are made.

If the near-death experience progresses further, the individual may find others coming to meet and help him. He sees spirits of relatives and friends who have died, and what many describe as a "loving warm spirit" of a kind never encountered before. This spirit asks him nonverbally to evaluate his life and helps by showing him a panoramic, instantaneous playback of the major events in his life. A later stage of the experience may involve approaching some kind of barrier, which apparently represents the limit between earthly life and the next life. The individual finds that it is not time for his death and he must return to earth. But he does not want to return because of the overwhelming, intense feelings of joy, love, and peace (Moody, 1975a).

The basic elements making up the near-death experience were found by researchers independently of Moody (Grof & Grof, 1980; Rawlings, 1978; Ring, 1980; and Sabom, 1982). This research is the focus of most controversy. The first controversy involves the explanation of the near-death experience. Some researchers have attempted to explain it as resulting from psychological defense mechanisms (Siegel, 1980). Such an interpretation would argue that a dying person, either consciously or unconsciously wishing to deny his or her imminent death, becomes psychologically detached. The experiences that ensue are then viewed as resulting from a depersonalization process. However, Ring (1980) cites cases in which the near-death survivors report seeing dead relatives and/or friends who were not known to be dead at the time of the experience, while no survivor has ever reported seeing a human spirit concurrently alive on earth. Such a phenomenon is not adequately explained by depersonalization or any psychological defense mechanism.

Another set of interpretations focuses on medical rather than psychological factors. These include effects presumed to result from anesthetics or other drugs. However, many near-death survivors did not have any anesthetic or other drug at the time, and those who did tend to report less intense near-death experiences (Ring, 1980). Noyes and Kletti (1972) have offered an explanation of the panoramic playback of one's past as resulting from a seizurelike neural firing pattern in the temporal lobe. Moody (1975a) observes that such temporal lobe firing does not usually result in memory images played back in an orderly fashion, nor are such flashbacks seen at once in a unifying vision. Also, seizure victims typically do not remember their flashbacks after regaining consciousness. Cerebral anoxia is another medical hypothesis that has been offered. However, some individuals have a near-death experience in which no apparent clinical death took place, yet they have essentially the same experiences as those in which there was such a death (Moody, 1975b). Other medical or physiological explanations include the possible release of endorphins (the body's own opiate), which could account for the release from physical pain and the feelings of peace.

Of great significance also are the aftereffects of the near-death experience. Survivors often report a changed world-view and a change in their value systems. Ring (1980) sees these phenomena as being related to getting in touch with the "higher self" or "true self" described in various religious traditions. McDonagh (1982) views such changes as being related to a death of the ego and a rebirth of a new self, and points to a similarity between the near-death experience and conversion or "born-again" Christian experience.

Investigators of this phenomenon are careful to point out that their research does not prove in any strict scientific or philosophical sense the existence of an afterlife, nor does it specify indisputably the nature of an afterlife. However, even with this qualification it does seem to represent an important development. The survival of the human personality after death is being taken as a serious possibility, and has at least gained the status of a plausible scientific hypothesis—something that would have been dismissed by many as an intellectual absurdity only a generation ago.

References

Grof, S., & Grof. C. *Beyond death*. New York: Thames & Hudson, 1980.

McDonagh, J. *Christian psychology: Towards a new synthesis*. New York: Crossroad, 1982.

Moody, R. *Life after life*. Atlanta: Mockingbird Books, 1975.(a)

Moody, R. *Reflections on "life after life."* Carmel, N.Y.: Guideposts, 1975. (b)

Noyes, R., & Kletti, R. The experience of dying from falls. Omega, 1972, *3*, 45–52.

Rawlings, M. *Beyond death's door*. Nashville: Nelson, 1978.

Ring, K. *Life at death*. New York: Coward, McCann & Geoghegan, 1980.

Sabom, M. B. *Recollections of death: A medical investigation*. New York: Simon & Schuster, 1982.

Siegel, R. K. The psychology of life after death. *American Psychologist*, 1980, *35*, 911–931.

14

Parapsychology
Richard D. Kahoe

Parapsychology is the study of psychic phenomena, *psychic* referring to either the events or the persons who seem to possess inexplicable abilities to perceive or influence events. *Psi* refers to hypothetical energy forces assumed to mediate psychic phenomena. The subject of parapsychology elicits responses ranging from fervent belief to rabid rejection, from lay persons, religious believers, psychologists, and other scientists alike.

The Scope of Study

In formal study parapsychology encompasses three varieties of extrasensory perception (ESP) and psychokinesis (PK). Telepathy is the ability to read another's thoughts; clairvoyance implies knowledge of inanimate objects or events without use of the known senses; and precognitition is knowledge of events before they occur. Psychokinesis is the ability to move or otherwise control an inanimate object or event without known physical energies.

These presumed phenomena are defined negatively: they cannot be explained by scientific laws, principles, or energies. The knowledge, perceptions, or behavior also must not be a product of unconscious mental (brain) processes, employing sensory cues, past or present, however subtle. Parapsychology assumes that the mind is an "unextended substance," not merely a product of the brain, and therefore involves energy separable from the physical body.

Reports and Research

Parapsychology arose from common life situations. Countless stories tell of uncanny premonitions, precognitive dreams, hauntings, and fortunetelling that defy explanation. Around this kind of observation many belief systems have developed—spiritualist churches, palmistry, astrology, I Ching, out-of-body experiences (OBEs), and near-death visions. Poltergeists (noisy spirits) break dishes and furniture, and propel objects through the air or off shelves. Mystics claim to levitate—rise bodily into the air—by purely mental powers. Healers perform "psychic surgery," removing apparently malignant tissue from a patient with bare hands, leaving no incision. Dowsers "witch" for water or minerals; performers inexplicably bend keys or spoons; Kirlian photography reveals unearthly "auras" around human fingertips and other objects.

Such reports are widely critiqued by scientists (Hansel, 1966), magicians (Christopher, 1970), and other skeptics. Careful investigation of reports usually reveals critical errors of fact. Poltergeists are usually associated with youths playing tricks on gullible adults. Fortunetellers vary from outright frauds to astute observers who lead their clients to reveal what they want to hear. Astrological and other predictions, when carefully checked and tabulated, have negligible validity. Psychic surgeons and metal benders do not withstand the scrutiny of trained magicians. Even prominent parapsychologists see Kirlian photographs as chemoelectrical artifacts. Of course not every case is discredited, and some must be counted as coincidences. But even a few unexplained reports encourage many people to believe that psi really exists.

Some surveys of psychic phenomena include what might better be called pseudo-psychic events—phenomena without clearly mechanistic explanations, including possession, automatic writing and other automatisms, fire walking, faith healing, hypnosis, and biofeedback. The latter two have been accepted into psychology's domain of fact, and, but for its association with religion, faith healing would probably hold such status. The first three phenomena can be explained by suggestion, learning, and unconscious processes.

Formal investigation of parapsychology began with the founding of the Society for Psychical Research at Cambridge University, England, in 1882 and a similar American society a few years later. In 1920 psychologist William McDougall, then president of the British Society for Psychical Research, went to Harvard University and began a study of psychic phenomena. Botanist Joseph B. Rhine joined McDougall as a research assistant in 1926 and followed him to Duke University the next year. Rhine and his wife, Louisa, founded the Duke Parapsychology Laboratory, which has conducted the most consistent psychical research. During an initial period of disappointing work psychologist K. E. Zener designed ESP (or Zener) cards that were used in many later studies. A deck of the famous cards included five sets of five bold symbols: plus sign, three parallel wavy lines, and outlines of circle, square, and star. The telepathy procedure usually involved one sender, who thought of five Zener symbols in a run, with the subject or receiver making five guesses.

More encouraging results began appearing in the winter of 1931–32 and were published in 1934 and 1935. Statistical probabilities against the Rhines's research being mere chance are astronomical, and most parapsychologists consider the experimental controls to have been tight. However, Hansel (1966) identified a number of weaknesses, including evidence for recognizing the ESP cards from their backs and/or edges. Rhine's best subject, Hubert Pearce, no longer showed clairvoyance when the deck of cards was moved 8–12 feet away. When ESP card guesses were typically checked after every five cards, subjects could rationally infer the last five cards in the deck. Rhine himself was aware of this problem, noting high scores on the last trials with this procedure.

More recent studies control for the Rhines's apparent defects, but they still draw frequent, very damaging criticisms. Contemporary research includes the use of sophisticated electronic gadgets and new ventures outside the laboratory. From early psychokinesis research with hand-thrown dice the Rhines progressed to dice mechanically thrown down a corrogated, inclined plane. Now instead of affecting the throw of dice a subject may attempt to alter the outcome of an electronic random number generator. Another psychokinesis subject reportedly was able to raise or lower temperatures on a highly accurate thermister, on a random schedule. Some psychics are said to impress photographic film with images that have no known physical source.

In the Ganzfeld procedure a telepathy subject relaxes in a sound-proof room, eyes covered with split table tennis balls. Meanwhile a sender, some distance away, looks at a picture or series of color transparencies and mentally transmits the images to the sensory-deprived receiver. Astonishing claims have been made for this procedure. In remote viewing telepathy a psychic (supervised in a laboratory) describes the journey taken by experimenters who leave the laboratory, randomly select a route or destination, and drive for a half-hour or so. Independent judges attempt to match the psychic's report with descriptions or pictures of the route actually driven. Brain waves of some psychics have been monitored to study optimum mental conditions for the expression of psi. Animals and plants have also been studied for evidence of psi. Even convinced parapsychologists admit that no current research procedure consistently yields positive results.

Research Conclusions

After more than 50 years of research, what facts, laws, or principles of parapsychology have been established? Not many, and none assuredly. Most research merely demonstrates that something can occur beyond statistical odds. One review (Bowles & Hynds, 1978) concluded that everybody potentially has psychic abilities, though some are exceptionally sensitive. Nothing can be affirmed about the relation of psi to intelligence or personality. Some studies relate success in psychic tasks to friendly, outgoing personalities, good visual imagery, and the subject's belief in psi. Some find that hypnosis, dreaming, relaxation, and meditation enhance psychic abilities. Partners with good rapport frequently make better telepathy subjects. Telepathic communication with animals is equivocal, and plant psi has not been replicated beyond a few spectacular reports.

What can psi communicate? If all reports are accepted, practically anything. All sorts of symbols, perceptions, and knowledge have supposedly been received by the various forms of extrasensory perception, and an almost endless list of events have reportedly been affected by psychokinesis. When does the supposed psi force operate? Time presents no barriers. In some Ganzfeld trials the receiver begins to describe pictures before the sender has looked at any. If the pictures match, precognition rather than telepathy has occurred. Many other situations cannot unambiguously be identified among the four prime forms of parapsychology. If the experimenter knows a fact before a clairvoyant subject does, a correct explanation might be telepathy. When the experimenter or a machine selects items to be guessed in telepathy or clairvoyance, the subject might have exercised psychokinesis over the choices. Such ambiguities led Rhine to disregard the separate categories of extrasensory perception.

Where can psi occur? Again, anywhere. In real life and in laboratories and across virtually any distance. If psi were some as-yet-unknown energy, it would violate the scientifically established inverse square law for the propagation of energy (Reber, 1982). The apparent limitlessness of psi may impress the believer as pervasiveness, but it rouses doubts among skeptics. All natural phenomena are affected or limited by definable parameters; without such limits scientifically oriented observers tend to dismiss parapsychology as illusory, or to investigate the source of the illusions.

Parapsychology critics continue to attack methodologies and reporting of psychic demonstrations. A typical, widely reported case involves platform psychic Uri Geller. A secondary source tells: "Geller was asked to guess which face of a die was up in an opaque box shaken by the experimenter. Geller, who was not permitted to touch the box, was told he could decline to guess when he felt uncertain. The die was shaken ten times, and Geller chose to respond eight of those times. Each time that he chose to respond he was correct, giving a result at odds of 17,500,000 to 1" (Bowles & Hynds, 1978, p. 66). The original report cited the statistical odds at about 1,000,000 to 1. Gardner reports that one of the experimenters said Geller "was allowed to place his hands on the box in a 'dowsing fashion'" (1982, p. 34). Further inquiry revealed that the tests actually took place over a three- to seven-day period; records reportedly were kept but were not provided when Geller requested them. A film was made of one of the trials (on which Geller chose not to guess), and reports of videotapes were never confirmed by actual film documents. One magician thought cheating could have occurred in several ways, but without seeing the records or films he could not confirm his suspicions.

Contradictory reporting, methodological looseness, and withholding of primary experimental records are typical of much parapsychology research. Defenders of the psychic realm accurately retort that few other research areas attract this kind of critical analysis. No known data could convince most skeptics of the existence of psi, nor is any critique of the work sufficiently cogent to persuade a believer that it is all artifact.

Reber (1982) cites three canons of science that parapsychology violates, thus prejudicing scientists against the field. 1) Whereas nature is reliable, psychic phenomena are elusive, frequently disappearing under the closest controls. 2) While science is coherent, psi violates the inverse square law for transmission of energy, and precognition itself violates at least three scientific laws: the principle that cause precedes effect, the linearity of time, and the first law of thermodynamics (that anything without substance can have no impact on a material substance). 3) Scientific explanations are mechanistic, but parapsychology has not proposed any mechanism whereby psi might operate—without violating other scientific canons. Admittedly science is conservative with regard to new facts and systems, but it has accepted biofeedback principles, and is prone to accept acupuncture as a physiological reality.

Since parapsychology meets none of the three canons, it is not accepted by most scientists. Some phenomena now classed with parapsychology probably will find acceptance within psychology. The regularity of near-death visions points toward unconscious and/or brain mechanisms as an explanation; out-of-body experiences may engage similar mechanisms. Some "mind reading" by stage magicians avowedly employs such key sensitivity to cues from the audience as almost to constitute an altered state of consciousness. Heightened psychic powers associated with hypnosis, relaxation, and meditation may result from sensitization to physical and/or social cues that have eluded experimental control. The unconscious mind and subtle neurological structures hold unplumbed secrets that probably operate in many parapsychology experiments.

Belief and Christian Faith

The psychology of belief offers a different explanation for parapsychology. Adherents tend also to accept unlikely, extrascientific phenomena such as the Bigfoot legends, the Loch Ness monster, UFOs, and Bermuda triangle mysteries. Little research has studied the functions and causes of such belief systems, but many people seem strongly inclined to believe in the psychic. Psychologists arranged for a magic demonstration in several California university classes, explicitly warning students that the performer "does not really have psychic abilities, and what you'll be seeing are really only tricks" (Benassi, Singer, & Reynolds, 1980, p. 338). When questioned about the performance, 58% of the students called it psychic, and only 33% considered it mere magic.

Religious believers tend to believe the nonmaterial claims of parapsychology also, sometimes even citing them as objective evidence for God and the spirit realm. Rhine left ministerial study because psychology provided no basis for free will; he hoped parapsychology would give evidence for a transcendent aspect of human nature. On the other hand, some Christians reject the psychic realm as blasphemy (Bowles & Hynds, 1978). The Jewish prophetic tradition had roots in the clairvoyant seer (1 Sam. 9:6–9). Jesus himself, being also the omniscient God, seems frequently to have had clairvoyant or telepathic insights into people's lives (Matt. 9:4; John 1:48; 4:17–18).

The miracles have psychokinetic implications. However, the practice of sorcery—seeking answers or affecting events by psychic means—was condemned in Old and New Testaments (Lev. 20:6; Deut. 18:10–11; Acts 19:18–19).

Pursuit of the psychic poses dangers for Christians. While psychic evidences may reinforce belief in the nonmaterial, actively "seeking a sign" implies that religious faith needs outside support. Parapsychology claims a degree of technology and truth held by science itself. If psychic claims are eventually falsified by empirical research, religious faith that depends on them will be unnecessarily undermined. On the other hand, if nonmaterial psi were accorded scientific status, religion might be reduced to technology, not a matter of faith. More significantly, focus on the psychic (whether miracle or illusion) courts triviality in religion. When people revel in the marvelous, they may abandon "the search for truth by other more orthodox and more strenuous and more profitable means, calling for a measure of self-discipline" (Moore, 1977, p. 116).

Even though we may remain skeptical about psi, Christians might be humbly open to the claims of parapsychology. After all, our relationship with God implies direct knowledge through nonsensory means; our claim for prayer power implies faith in spiritual effects on the real world (the first law of thermodynamics notwithstanding). However, attempts to prove the nonmaterial or resting our faith on statistical experiments is a poor substitute for faith in God through Christ Jesus.

References

Benassi, V. A., Singer, B., & Reynolds, C. B. Occult belief: Seeing is believing. *Journal for the Scientific Study of Religion*, 1980, *19*, 337–349.

Bowles, N., & Hynds, F. *Psi search*. San Francisco: Harper & Row, 1978.

Christopher, M. *ESP, seers & psychics*. New York: Crowell, 1970.

Gardner, M. How not to test a psychic: The great SRI die mystery. *The Skeptical Inquirer*, Winter 1982–83, 7(2), 33–39.

Hansel, C. E. M. *ESP: A scientific evaluation*. New York: Scribners, 1966.

Moore, E. G. *Try the spirits: Christianity and psychical research*. New York: Oxford University Press, 1977.

Reber, A. S. On the paranormal: In defense of skepticism. *The Skeptical Inquirer*, Winter 1982–83, 7(2), 55–64.

15

Psychological Roots of Religion
Clark D. Campbell and Cedric B. Johnson

The biblical and historical roots of religion have been studied for centuries, but only relatively recently have the psychological roots of religion been investigated. The sources of religious need in personality and the needs that are met by religion are two topics that developed out of this investigation. In many ways these two topics are like different sides of the same coin. They are inextricably connected, yet can be approached from different viewpoints. Most of the literature available on these topics is theoretical rather than empirical in nature, and therefore theories rather than experimental data will be presented.

Sources of Religious Need in Personality

One may appropriately ask, "Is there a religious need in personality?" One way to approach this question is to survey personality theories to see how they treat religion. Nearly all personality theories address religion as a normal or abnormal need and offer psychological explanations for it. Another approach is to consider the desire for religious experience within cultures. The desire for religious experience, which is both cross-generational and cross-cultural, yields evidence for a religious need in personality.

A theoretician's definition of religion and personality is foundational to his or her discussion of the source of religious needs in personality. Five broad theoretical categories of religious needs in personality are outlined below, each having a particular view of religion and personality.

Innate or instinctual

The psychological view that religious needs are innate or instinctual has received little support. Although this position was commonly held at the turn of the century, few contemporary psychologists hold it at present. The position was challenged by James, who believed that religion was not an instinct but rather a complex mixture of a multitude of feelings, acts, attitudes, and values. James's (1961) view was readily accepted and soon eclipsed the "innate religion" view.

A result of personality development

Freud (1928) was probably the greatest proponent of the view that religious needs grow out of personality developmental processes. One of his basic assumptions was that religion is nothing other than psychological processes projected into the outer world. These processes were generated by personality development that occurred in four stages: oral, anal, phallic, and genital. The cornerstone of personality development is the resolution of the Oedipus complex, which occurs in the phallic stage. Basically, the Oedipus complex is a child's desire to kill the same sex parent so that he can fulfill his sexual fantasies with the opposite sex parent. The psychoanalytic cure for neuroses, of which religious desire was one, is to resolve the Oedipus complex and the underlying libidinal conflict.

According to Freud religious practice was the culturally accepted way of expressing one's guilt over an unresolved Oedipus complex. God was nothing more than an exalted father figure. Freud believed that religion was an illusion whose future was limited by the rise of modern-day science, which would disprove the myth of religion.

Erikson (1950) also has a developmental perspective on religious needs and personality development, but it is different from Freud's perspective. He believes that personality develops through eight stages that encompass the entire life cycle. Each stage presents a conflict to the individual, such as trust versus distrust or intimacy versus isolation. Personality is developed as an individual resolves these conflicts. According to Erikson religion has developed out of people's need to find reassurance and consolation in times of regression to an earlier stage of development. Thus, religious needs in personality grow out of one's need for reassurance in times of heightened conflict. Both Freud and Erikson view the source of religion as coming from a personality development process.

A result of moral development

Others have identified the source of religious needs to be the result of moral development. Kohlberg (1981) has postulated a process of six stages of moral development. The first stage is the obedience and punishment orientation. The motive behind a person's moral behavior in this stage is to avoid punishment and achieve gratification. The sixth stage is called universal ethical principles orientation and is characterized by moral behavior based on the highest values of human life. Kohlberg has demonstrated that people tend to move through these stages, but that most people become fixated at a particular stage. Very few ever attain stage six. He has also demonstrated that his theory is cross-cultural.

Moral stages are determined by the way a person resolves moral dilemmas and explains metaphysical phenomena. From this perspective religious needs are founded in one's moral development and are a systematic expression of one's moral developmental stage. A person's religious needs are contingent on his or her moral development, and the religious needs change in accordance with changes in moral development.

Existential phenomena

Religious needs can also be seen as coming from one's search for meaning, an encounter with the infinite, or an encounter with finitude. Frankl (1962) correlates religious needs with a person's desire to find meaning in a seemingly meaningless existence. A person seeking to make sense of nonsense in the metaphysical arena asks questions about the meaning of life, destiny, and values. A confrontation with these questions is seen as the source of religious need.

A person's encounters with the infinite or with his or her finitude are other existential sources of religion. As a person begins to explore the universe he quickly encounters its infinite nature, and some see this encounter with infinity as giving rise to religious thoughts. As soon as people encounter infinity, however, they are generally struck by their own finitude. Some, including Paul Tillich, believe that it is a person's encounter with finitude that leads him into religious thought.

Interpersonal phenomena

Several theorists hold that the source of religion is within the relational nature of man. Buber (1937) is one who takes this position, arguing that it is the relational aspect of human nature, the need to relate to an Other, that gives rise to religion. Religion, from this perspective, is found in the community that comes from the human desire to relate.

Needs That Are Met by Religion

Maslow (1962) formulated a hierarchical theory of human needs. Within his theory the six levels are physiological, safety, love and belonging, esteem, self-actualization, and transcendence needs. People cannot meet their higher needs until their lower needs are met. However, as soon as a person's lower needs are met, he strives to meet the higher ones.

Many of the needs met by religion can be viewed in terms of this theoretical model. Most religions offer some social welfare programs to help people meet their physiological needs for food and health. Religions also offer people love and a sense of belonging. Organized religions have long offered persons membership in a group; however, newer religions and cults now achieve this in various ways of peer pressure and harassment. Individuals find their need for esteem met in religion also. Most religious groups have parishioners from a range of socioeconomic classes, and individuals have the opportunity to relate to members of the same class as well as other classes. The ability to relate with others and utilize what psychologists call "social comparison" gives individuals a sense of self-esteem.

According to Maslow only a few people ever fulfill their needs for self-actualization and transcendence. Self-actualization is one's ability to fully realize his or her potential, particularly the ability to love and be loved. Transcendence is basically the spiritual search in life that goes beyond identity, individuality, and self-actualization. Most religions offer individuals opportunities for fulfillment in these areas. Of course, different religions vary in the degree to which they will tolerate divergent thinking, which is also part of this need.

Religion also offers fulfillment for other human needs. Intrapersonally it offers a person meaning in life, a sense of oneness with the universe, and a set of values. Interpersonally religion offers a person a sense of community with others and the fulfillment of relationship needs in areas such as authority, leadership, submission, servanthood, and altruism.

Integration and Conclusion

The response of the religious community to the behavioral sciences' explanation of the psychological roots of religion has covered the spectrum from ignorance, to acceptance, to outright rejection. Freud's reductionism, which views religion as the resolution of the Oedipus complex, has usually been rejected as speculative. However, his perspective that unconscious forces play a part in religious behavior has been accepted by many Christians. Distorted views of God as a punitive or judgmental father have been traced to events in the early development of the person when he related to earthly parents who were harsh or judgmental. Freud's chief weakness was that he never considered the psychological sources of healthy religion that led the person to work and love well. In contrast, Erikson has proven helpful in the identification of life crises, which often accompany significant religious experiences such as conversion. However, Erikson also assumes that religion is a sign of regression in development and therefore represents immaturity. Thus, his theory of religious sources is not totally acceptable to most Christians.

The findings of Kohlberg have been embraced by a wide range of religious people as a biblically viable explanation of moral development. His theories are based on Piaget's concepts of cognitive development. Religious education has been the beneficiary of the correlation of moral development with cognitive developmental stages. For example, since it is not likely that a preadolescent will think abstractly, his need is for a concrete statement or experience of religion.

The existential and interpersonal statements of religious need probably are the most similar to those of the Bible. Encounters with one's finitude and with the infinite God are the heart of biblical expression, especially in the psalms. The great lack in existential psychology as it seeks to define religion is in the relationship to the redemptive event of Christ. The Christian position is that one simply cannot establish a meaningful contact with God apart from Christ.

Many religious writers have identified with the human needs as defined by Maslow. The chief deficit of his theory, however, is its inherent self-centeredness. There is little focus on the human needs to give, to be a servant, or to generally promote the welfare of others, which are emphasized in Christianity. The self-actualized person and the sanctified person may appear the same behaviorally, but the motivation of the heart may differ.

Biblical data indicate that all people have a religious need (Rom. 1–3) and that this need is stimulated by both internal factors (e.g., conscience; Rom. 2:14–15) and external factors (e.g., general revelation; Rom. 1:20). Undoubtedly this religious need stems from the fact that all people are created in the image of God and therefore seek a relationship with the Creator (Gen. 1:27). Although we seek God as our Creator, he is the one who moved to restore a relationship with humanity through Jesus Christ (Rom. 3). Likewise he has instructed people individually and corporately (i.e., the church) to maintain relationships (1 John 4:7–21) and meet the needs of others (James 1:27).

Whether there is a one-to-one correspondence between these religious needs and those mentioned by psychological theories is open to question in many instances. More work needs to be done in defining the psychological base for religion. More work also needs to be done in defining a biblical theory of personality and human need. To date the emphasis has been on ontic qualities such as the heart, soul, mind, and body in the definition of the image of God in a person. The alternative that the image is relational and functional, defined in terms of how people give and receive love and engage in productive work may be a more fruitful source of exploration for a biblical psychology.

References

Buber, M. *I and thou*. New York: Scribners, 1937.

Erikson, E. H. *Childhood and society*. New York: Norton, 1950.

Frankl, V. E. *Man's search for meaning*. Boston: Beacon Press, 1962.

Freud, S. *The future of an illusion*. New York: Liveright, 1928.

James, W. *The varieties of religious experience*. New York: Macmillan, 1961.

Kohlberg, L. *The philosophy of moral development*. San Francisco: Harper & Row, 1981.

Maslow, A. H. *Toward a psychology of being*. Princeton, N.J.: Van Nostrand, 1962.

Additional Readings

Fleck, J. R., & Carter, J. D. (Eds.). *Psychology and Christianity: Integrative readings*. Nashville: Abingdon, 1981.

Malony, H. N. (Ed.). *Current perspectives in the psychology of religion*. Grand Rapids: Eerdmans, 1977.

16

Religious Concept Development
Stanley N. Ballard

The investigation of the growth of religious understanding deals with the changes in meaning attributed to religion in the course of individual development. For the purpose of this chapter, religion will be defined as one's thoughts in connection with God and his activities in the universe. A concept is an idea a person holds to, usually based on both knowledge and experience. One's concepts may change with exposure to new knowledge and experience.

In recent years a great deal of attention has been given to the role of cognition (intellect) as a central variable in all phases of development. Human thought is seen as an emerging, changing function that affects all aspects of personality functioning and growth. This means that the development of religious concepts presupposes cognitive development.

Present interest in cognitive development has been stimulated largely by the work of Piaget (1952). Piaget's work may be classified as an age-stage theory. His hypothesis was that a child's cognitive development proceeds through sequential stages that are progressively more mature and better defined. These stages are usually associated with particular ages. For Piaget cognitive development is accumulative. What is learned at one stage of development can be learned only if there have never been the necessary prerequisite learnings during earlier stages. Piaget's four stages of intellectual development are the sensorimotor stage (birth to about 2 years), the preoperative stage (2 to 7 years), the concrete operations stage (7 to 11 years), and the formal operations stage (11 years and older). Most research in the development of religious concepts has focused on the last three stages. This emphasis does not imply, however, that religious conceptual development is totally nil during the first two years of life.

The most salient characteristics of the preoperational child's intellectual functioning are the use of newly acquired internal mental representations of external objects and the related language abilities. The internal object representations (symbols) allow for thinking. Preoperational thinking, however, is egocentric and inflexible. It is difficult for the child to understand that other people might think differently from himself or to distinguish between "real" and "pretend."

The concrete operations stage involves concrete thinking. The child now becomes less egocentric and comes to understand certain principles or relationships between ideas. However, thinking is rooted in concrete events and objects. The final step of cognitive development, formal operations, involves abstract thinking. The individual with these skills can entertain concepts with which he has had no experience.

Overview of Research Findings

Although studies regarding the growth of religious understanding are not numerous by today's research standards, a number of investigations in this area have accumulated. General patterns of religious concept formation have been demonstrated. There appears to be a good fit between the Piagetian stages of cognitive development and the development of religious concepts and religious maturity.

Harms (1944) presented empirical evidence for age changes in the concept of God. Harms asked his subjects (ages 3–18) to draw how God looked when they pictured him in their mind, or to imagine the appearance of the highest being they thought to exist. Adolescents, who apparently objected to imagining God as such, were given the opportunity of drawing what to them represented religion or the highest ideal expressed in religion. Harms arrived at three broad classes of drawings that were related to age and reflected what he assumed to be universal stages of religious development. The three stages identified by Harms seem to correspond closely to the prelogical, egocentric thinking of Piaget's preoperational child; the concrete, logical thinking of the concrete operational child; and the abstract thinking of the formal operational child.

Deconchy (1965) employed a word-association procedure to study the development of ideas about God in 4,733 children ranging from 7 to 16 years of age. The task was to write five word associations to six inductor words, one of which was *God*. The associations to the indicator word *God* were grouped into 29 categories and along three age-related dimensions: attributivity, personalization, and interiorization.

The 7–10-year-old child thinks of God chiefly in terms of his attributes: 1) objective attributes such as greatness, omniscience, and omnipresence; 2) subjective attributes (qualities) such as goodness and justice; and 3) affective attributes such as strength and beauty. The theme of this age group seems to be God's transcendence. Deconchy called this stage attributivity. Personalization refers to the 13–14-year-old stage, when the child thinks of God as a person. The themes of fatherhood, redeemer, master, and sovereignty predominate. The final stage, interiorization, describes the 14–16-year-olds. These individuals think of God in terms of subjective abstract themes such as love, trust, doubt, and fear. The three stages mark the transition for the child from the God of his thoughts (attributivity) to the God of his life (interiorization).

Deconchy did not test younger children corresponding to Piaget's preoperational stage, and so was unable to identify a stage of religious development parallel to that stage. The stage of attributivity, with its emphasis on the attributes of God, would seem to parallel Piaget's concrete operational stage; the stage of interiorization, with its emphasis on subjective, abstract themes concerning God, appears to parallel formal operational thinking. The middle stage of personalization serves as a transition between the concrete stage of attributivity and the abstract stage of interiorization. The God themes of this middle stage are similar to both the affective attributes of attributivity and the internal qualities of interiorization.

Elkind (1961) defined religious identity in terms of spontaneous meanings children attach to their religious denomination. In three separate studies he investigated the growth of religious identity among Jewish (1961), Catholic (1962), and Congregational Protestant (1963) children. Elkind believed it was possible to distinguish three fairly distinct stages in the attainment of religious identity which held true of Jewish, Catholic, and Protestant children. He referred to these stages as global (5–7 years), concrete (7–9 years), and abstract (10–12 years). These three stages appear to parallel closely Piaget's preoperational, concrete operational, and formal operational stages.

Long, Elkind, and Spilka (1967) used an interview procedure in studying children's understanding of prayer. One hundred sixty boys and girls between the ages of 5 and 12 were interviewed. A set of semistructured questions was employed in order to explore developmental changes in the concept of prayer. The results suggested three major developmental stages in the child's understanding of the prayer concept. These stages were designed as global undifferentiated (5–7 years), concrete differentiated (7–9 years) and abstract differentiated (10–12 years). Again these three stages appear to closely parallel Piaget's preoperational, concrete operational, and formal operational stages.

Goldman (1964) studied religious thinking in 200 white Protestant children in England (10 boys and 10 girls at every age level from 6 through 16). He constructed a picture and story religious test, which consisted of three pictures (a family entering church, a boy or a girl at prayer, and a boy or girl looking at a mutilated Bible) and three Bible stories (Moses and the burning bush, the crossing of the Red Sea, and the temptation of Jesus). Each child was individually interviewed; following the presentation of each picture or story, the child was asked a standardized set of questions about the material. From his analysis of these data Goldman then proceeded to identify three stages in the development of religious thinking that closely parallel the three Piagetian stages. Goldman labeled these stages preoperational intuitive thought (7/8 years mental age), concrete operational thought (7/8–13/14 years mental age), and formal (abstract) operational thought (13/14 years mental age).

All of these research findings clearly fit quite well into a three-stage Piagetian development. The progression is from the prelogical, global, egocentric, perception-bound thinking of Piaget's preoperational child; to the concrete, logical, reversible thinking of the concrete operational child; and finally to the abstract, theoretical, propositional thinking of the formal operational child.

The Teaching of Religious Concepts

Piaget believed that the intellectual content a child can interact with at any level of development depends upon his understanding of the world around him. Thus Piaget was concerned with specifying just what understandings the child has at each stage of development because these understandings limit the intellectual content that can be mastered at any level.

The pressing question for Christian education is whether or not Piaget's stages can be applied to the development of spiritual concepts in the life of the child. Christian educators Joy (1975) and Wakefield (1975) are two contemporary writers who have seen the relevance of Piaget's work for the development of mature biblical concepts in the home and church. While much biblical content is difficult and beyond the grasp of young children, these authors argue that Christian education curriculum should be built around the developmental stages identified in the above research.

Preoperational stage (2–7 years)

Parents and educators must not expect too much of children at this age. The child does have difficulty in developing and relating biblical concepts. He utilizes percepts and images, but his thinking is fragmentary and discrete. He tries to understand biblical material, but his intellectual powers are not sufficiently developed to piece all the information together.

The biblical information that is given must be accurate and must be broken down to the preoperational child's level of comprehension. However, even during this stage the child is building a world-view. It is, therefore, an excellent time to create an awareness of God. Young children gain a preconceptual awareness of the nature of God by observing others who express the love of God through their behavior. The modeling behavior of both parents and Christian educators is crucial at this time.

Content is very important, but for the preoperational child the methodology of content presentation is also important. Teaching must not rely solely on verbal explanations. The Bible must be related to the firsthand experiences of the child. Deuteronomy 6:1–9 is instructive at this point. The teaching here is that childhood education is to be comprehensive in scope, making virtually all of life a school. It indicates that children are to be immersed in a total curriculum of experience and that God is to be related to the totality of experience.

Recognizing the above principles, Goldman (1965) recommends spiritual content that is related to the experience and spontaneous questions of children in this age group. The concept of God is to be simply and frequently expressed in connection with the everyday experiences of the child and his spontaneous questions. These expressions should emphasize the concepts of a God who loves and cares for us, and a God who has provided for us in this earthly home and who is always with us. In the home the aware parent can capitalize quite easily on this approach. In the church teachers may accomplish the same ends by establishing various learning centers in the classrooms that deal in simple fashion with the questions and needs of the child.

Beers (1975) is convinced that the preoperational child can learn certain theological concepts dealing with God, Jesus, the Bible, home and parents, and church and Sunday school. For example, he feels that the preoperational child can learn that God loves him, God provides sun and rain, God made the world, God made him, and that he should please and obey God. This approach is feasible if one remembers the cognitive characteristics of the preoperational child.

Memorization of specific scriptural content is also a viable possibility with this age group. Such themes as the child's behavior ("Love one another," John 4:7); creation ("God created the heaven and the earth," Gen. 1:1); the Lord's attitude to us ("He careth for you," 1 Peter 5:7); and our attitude to the Lord ("I will love thee, O Lord," Ps. 18:1) would be specific examples. Again, these memorizations are to be related to the everyday experiences of the child.

Since children in this age group enjoy fantasy, play, and motoric involvement, the utilization of story playing offers a great opportunity to teach specific Bible content. When children can dramatize a story in simple form, they can more readily understand the story cognitively. The event becomes more real in story play. The drama does not need to be practiced but can be spontaneous. Possibilities for story playing are illustrated by the following: how Joshua conquered the land of Canaan (Josh. 9:1–11:23); the great ship that saved eight people (Gen. 6:1–9:17); and Palm Sunday (Matt. 21:1–11).

Concrete operational stage (7–11 years)

In this stage the child is becoming more able to put facts together, to generalize and classify his experiences, and to reverse his thinking processes. Limitations, however, still accompany the advancement of this period. When a child is asked to use verbal propositions rather than objects, he must consider one statement at a time in reasoning the proposition through. His generalizing cannot go beyond particular situations or examples. His intellectual abilities are restricted to physical actions that he can internalize. His skill at grouping common relationships is a significant factor during this period.

When teaching content to the concrete operational child, one must remember that the child is concerned with concrete people, actions, and situations. Because this is true, factual information can be presented. Facts pertaining to the sources and people of the Christian faith would be appropriate at this time. Possible content might be drawn from the following: the life of Jesus; what is the Bible (Bible background facts); the story of a beautiful garden; creation (Gen. 1:1–

3:24); the baby who was found in a river (Exod. 1:1–2:10); Gideon and his brave 300 (Judges 6:1–8:28); the shepherd boy's fight with the giant (1 Sam. 17:1–54); Daniel in the den of lions (Dan. 6); the manger at Bethlehem (Luke 2:1–20); the earliest missionaries (Acts 11:19–30; 13:1–14:28); Stephen with the shining face (Acts 6:1–8:3).

In teaching these concepts the emphasis is upon the children doing things, finding out, experimenting, and thinking creatively.

Formal operational stage (11 years and older)

At this stage the individual develops the mental ability for mature conceptual thinking. There is present the capacity to think in abstract terms, utilizing the world of propositions. Problems can be approached in a systematic manner and solved by using logical procedures that are expressed in abstract form. In this stage the person is concerned with the theoretical, the remote, and the future.

It is important to link content in some way with the real life experiences and needs of individuals in this stage—for example, the opposite sex, problems of science, life ambitions, happiness, the place of God in one's life. Biblical content must be correlated to issues of life.

Many biblical themes can be explored at this time: the inspiration of the Bible; parables; the attributes of God; Satan, his personality and power; the creation and fall of humankind; sin, its character and universality; the second coming of Christ; the study of any individual book of the Bible; the purpose of life as seen in the Scriptures; who am I according to the Bible; and the biblical concept of marriage.

Conclusion

The task of facilitating the development of mature spiritual concepts is obviously very complex. However, four factors appear to stand out. First, Bible-centered content must be present, but at the same time the methodology of presentation is crucial. Second, parents and educators must model the content they are attempting to teach. Third, that which is taught should be part of the child's real world in that the content is related to his present needs and experiences. Words are to be matched with experience and experience with words. Finally, scriptural material must be taught in a manner that is appropriate to the level of cognitive development of the child.

References

Beers, V. G. Teaching theological concepts to children. In R. B. Zuck & R. E. Clark (Eds.), *Childhood education in the church.* Chicago: Moody Press, 1975.

Deconchy, J. P. The idea of God: Its emergence between 7 and 16 years. In A. Godin (Ed.), *From religious experience to a religious attitude.* Chicago: Loyola University Press, 1965.

Elkind, D. The child's conception of his religious denomination I: The Jewish child. *Journal of Genetic Psychology,* 1961, *99,* 209–225.

Elkind, D. The child's conception of his religious denomination II: The Catholic child. *Journal of Genetic Psychology,* 1962, *101,* 185–195.

Elkind, D. The child's conception of his religious denomination III: The Protestant child. *Journal of Genetic Psychology,* 1963, *103,* 291–304.

Goldman, R. *Religious thinking from childhood to adolescence.* New York: Seabury, 1964.

Goldman, R. *Readiness for religion.* London: Routledge and K. Paul, 1965.

Harms, E. The development of religious experience in children. *American Journal of Sociology,* 1944, *50,* 112–122.

Joy, D. M. Why teach children. In R. B. Zuck & R. E. Clark (Eds.), *Childhood education in the church.* Chicago: Moody Press, 1975.

Long, D., Elkind, D., & Spilka, B. The child's conception of prayer. *Journal for the Scientific Study of Religion,* 1967, *6,* 101–109.

Piaget, J. *The origins of intelligence in children.* New York: International Universities Press, 1952.

Wakefield, N. Children and their theological concepts. In R. B. Zuck & R. E. Clark (Eds.), *Childhood education in the church.* Chicago: Moody Press, 1975.

17

Religious Health and Pathology
Frances J. White

Religion can be the most potent health-inducing, health-maintaining force or the most insidious health-depleting, health-preventing influence in a person's life. An important difference between the manifestations of healthy and unhealthy religion appears to lie in the way individuals appropriate their religious beliefs (James, 1902).

In their classic study Allport and Ross (1967) divided religious orientations into intrinsic and extrinsic. People who are intrinsically religious internalize their religious values, making them an integral part of their whole being and way of life. They are committed to transcending self-centeredness. Conversely, extrinsically oriented religious individuals employ their religion as a means to achieve their own ends. They are more absorbed in self-interests, looking to secular sources for power. This description of intrinsic and extrinsic religious expressions makes it evident that the individual who is intrinsically religious expresses his or her faith in healthier ways. Although Allport and Ross did not associate these modes with any particular religion, their parallel to the biblical concept of living one's life to glorify either God or oneself makes them relevant to a discussion of healthy or unhealthy Christianity.

Healthy Christianity tends to be positively correlated with psychological health. This is an expected relationship in view of the fact that an individual's responses to life are determined by the hereditary and environmental circumstances that shape them. The resulting personality structure influences the way a person responds to religion. Likewise, the quality of a person's religion affects his or her response to life's circumstances. This interrelationship of mental and religious health implies that Christians who have had positive background experiences may be more prone to healthier religious attitudes and behaviors than those who have experienced deleterious circumstances. It could also be true that a non-Christian with healthy background experiences might be healthier psychologically than a Christian exposed to less favorable situations.

Several qualifying factors are involved in evaluating the quality of religious health. The first involves the cultural concepts of health. Since society's values reflect the influence of generations of sin, and since a consensus of the values is generally used as the criterion to evaluate psychological health, it is conceivable that the attributes of mental health will be viewed differently in certain aspects by Christians. This is particularly true in societies where Christian values are either decreasing in acceptance or else have not infiltrated the worldview of the people. For Christians the concept of health would transcend the culture in whatever ways it conflicts with biblical norms.

Another consideration is that Christians, in their relationship to the Lord, have resources available to facilitate their growth in the direction of a more intrinsic religious orientation. This increases the possibility that their religion will enable them to overcome the less healthy effects of their background and thereby develop in more positive directions. Involved in their growth is the gradual awareness of the wholeness they actually possess through their commitment to Jesus Christ. This process of sanctification can lead them to a fuller realization of what it means to be all that God intended them to be.

A major consideration for the Christian is that religious health in its fullest sense has its roots in the restoration of the wholeness present in the creation. What constitutes health is within the nature of human beings, marred by the fall but restored and empowered through a relationship with Jesus Christ. Therefore, examples of the characteristics of healthy and unhealthy Christianity are discussed under selected rubrics of universal themes of human functioning that emanate from the very nature of man. Each is expressed as a set of polarities.

Several factors determine the point on the spectrum between the polarities that indicates maximum health. The first is the appropriate balance between the polarities. This vital equilibrium is present in individuals who accept and integrate into their total being the many aspects of their creatureliness. The second is that individuals necessarily fluctuate along the spectrum according to their need to adjust to the changing developmental and situational circumstances of life. For example, between the dependent-independent polarities a child or an invalid would be more dependent, whereas an adolescent would be moving toward the independent end. These differences that place individuals at different points along the spectrum demonstrate the broad possible range of health. A final necessary consideration is that at either extreme there is a precariously fine line between health and pathology. For example, along the self-sacrificing/self-accepting spectrum, self-sacrificing can enhance health, or, carried too far and not balanced by self-appreciation, could become a masochistic tendency. This delicate balance is also an example of the constant tension Christians experience between their finiteness that glorifies God and their sinfulness that serves self.

Characteristics of Healthy Religion

The following five sets of polarities of human functioning suggest some insights about healthy and unhealthy religion.

Dependency-independency

Healthy religion fosters a harmonious balance between these two dimensions in a way that permits interdependency through developing and maintaining one's individual identity, and yet experiencing a sense of oneness with others. Overdependency can result in enmeshed relationships that deprive persons of growth in their own uniqueness. Differences tend to be seen as disloyalty. Guilt messages often are communicated to anyone either expressing something new or questioning aspects of the old. An exclusive attitude that results in isolation from other groups is apt to develop. Healthy, realistic changes are hindered. Those who are dissatisfied find that to leave the group they must rebel or make a traumatic cutoff, neither of which permits healthy separation. On the other hand, too much independence inhibits mutual support, loyalty, and a sense of belonging and commitment.

A criterion to evaluate health in this area is the degree to which the dynamics of the religious group permits open channels to form that enable its members to develop their own potential, both within and outside the group, as well as mutually contribute to and benefit from strengths of the total membership.

Control-freedom

A synthesis of these two polarities encourages spontaneity, creativity, and self-direction tempered by inner discipline and external restraints. Healthy Christian communities provide the freedom from a nonjudgmental environment where their members sense an acceptance of the full range of emotions and ideas. There is therefore opportunity to try things on for fit and receive constructive feedback based on biblical principles. The paradoxical burden of each individual's freedom to depend wholly on God while accepting the responsibility of his own decisions is mitigated by group support.

Overstepping the freedom end results in lack of a sense of responsibility toward oneself and others. Accountability that permits helpful restraints tends to be lacking. Persons may feel leaderless and often powerless. On the other hand, overstepping the control end can lead to authoritarianism, legalism, and a constriction of affect, cognitions, or behaviors. Suppressed anger is often prevalent. A judgmental atmosphere develops, and a suspicious rather than a trusting attitude toward the world is more probable.

A criterion to check out health is the extent to which the structure of the group facilitates the possibility for its adherents to experience the quality of leadership and participation that results in a mutual openness, caring, and trust.

Self-denial—self-acceptance

An integration of these polarities results in adequate self-esteem. Recognition and acceptance of strengths and limitations are promoted by the religious community. The unconditional acceptance Christians have in Jesus Christ is stressed as the basis for self-worth. A distinction is made between true guilt, stemming from violation of scriptural moral principles, and false guilt, emanating from absolutized environmentally inculcated feelings. The latter feelings, often transformed into moral beliefs, are checked against Scripture and either relinquished or confessed. The forgiveness in Jesus Christ is presented not only as the source of release from sin but also as the channel through which even the consequences of failures when confessed are used for the growth of the individual and the glory of God.

A Christian fellowship that disproportionately stresses self-denial is often preoccupied with sin to the point of fostering masochism, sadism, workaholics, or self-deprecating individuals. Overstepping the opposite extreme leads to an inadequate sense of guilt and too much self-interest, often expressed in grandiosity, pride, and exaggerated demands for one's rights at the expense of others.

An indication of balance between the two extremes is the amount of energy available and used in a relaxed as opposed to an obsessive-compulsive way in order to minister to others. At the same time a personal satisfaction is evident whether at work or at play.

Stability-change

A healthy religious group, sensing the amount of change it can tolerate over a period of time, establishes an equilibrium between the amount of constancy it maintains and change it introduces. Periods of change that permit growth are alternated with times of stability wherein the group can assimilate and accommodate into its structure what is deemed worthy of internalization. The more settled periods also provide a rest from the ambiguities, risks, and anxieties that are normal accompaniments of change.

Extremes on the stability end result in a stagnation that hampers necessary adjustments to a changing society. The religious group is therefore hindered from exerting an influence on the direction and consequences of new developments. The seclusion that results from blocking new elements from entering the system smothers any sparks of renewal and regeneration. Apathy tends to develop from a lack of new challenges and stimulations. Too much change, however, can lead to a diminishing appreciation of the immutability of scriptural truths. Members may experience a decreasing sense of belonging. Adequately secure moorings that provide predictability are more easily undermined. Sufficient time for an in-depth evaluation of what to keep, modify, or change is less possible. Hyperactivity and confusion can result.

A key to a harmonious balance of change and stability is the degree to which a religious group tests its practices, old and new, against the realities of both society and Scripture. An additional test is the amount of order and calm confidence that reigns in contrast to disorganization, agitation, and anxiety.

Finiteness-transcendence

Christians find a consolation of this aspect of their being through a relationship with the Godhead. The fact that human beings were created as finite creatures by a sovereign God implies that they need their limitations to fulfill fully their purpose of glorifying God. Nonetheless, infused in their nature is the need to reach out beyond themselves to a superior Being.

Religions based on anthropocentricism leave their followers susceptible to the paralysis of the despair that results from the inevitability of death. An inclination to hedonistic tendencies is more probable. The lack of ultimate significance could push persons to find meaning in less worthy directions—for example, drugs, sexual aberrations, driven ambition, undue competitiveness, deification of man. Values become more relative. There is a failure to appropriate spiritual resources. Contrariwise, religious groups that minimize the finite aspects of humans and overemphasize the transcendent often are not as ready to realize their given opportunities and responsibilities. They are more apt to avoid taking responsibility, preferring to see the members of the Godhead as magicians who enable them to bypass the pain of growth toward maturity. Their concept of God, man, and the universe, therefore, is limited. Their excessive otherworldliness generally detracts from their influence on society.

Religious persons' wholesome acceptance of their finitude in the light of God's sovereign purpose for all of creation is evidenced by their reactions to life's events. They more realistically accept in themselves and others the normalcy of their humanness (e.g., hurt, downcast feelings in the face of a loss). Simultaneously they manifest in themselves, and encourage in others, an underlying hope and sense of purpose in all happenings.

The healthy Christian

Balance on any one of these polarities, or on any other additional single theme of human functioning, does not guarantee religious health. Rather, the dimensions of human beings created in God's image are so intricately interrelated that a harmonious integrated balance of all aspects of humanness is necessary. The promotion of such an ideal state of existence is possible only to the extent that the individuals constituting the religious group have experienced the restoration of the image of God in them through an acceptance of the redemptive work of Jesus Christ and the empowering of the Holy Spirit.

A word of caution is in order here. A personal relationship with God does not inevitably result in the realization of perfect harmony within oneself or with others. The apperception of God's healing is a lifelong process for the Christian that may not include a diminution of all the tangible effects of an imperfect world. However, Christian conversion does provide the inner strength, known by the intrinsically religious person, that infuses all life with meaning. There is the assurance that God's sovereignty works through the Christian's humanness. A religion imbued with this quality of transcendence of self-centeredness offers its members the necessary prerequisites to develop those characteristics that spell health.

References

Allport, G. W., & Ross, J. M. Personal religious orientation and prejudice. *Journal of Personality and Social Psychology,* 1967, 5, 432–443.

James. W. *The varieties of religious experience.* New York: Longman, Green, 1902.

Additional Readings

Oates, W. E. *When religion gets sick.* Philadelphia: Westminster, 1970.

Peck, M. S. *The road less traveled.* New York: Simon & Schuster, 1978.

Roberts, R. *Spirituality and human emotions.* Grand Rapids: Eerdmans, 1982.

18

Religious Orientation
Randie L. Timpe

Religious persons differ considerably in the depth, sentiments, and expressions of their religiousness. Religion may serve an instrumental function for those who *use* religion in the pursuit of personal ends or an integral function for those who *live* religion. These two function preferences illustrate varieties in religious orientations in which basic personality and temperamental processes influence religious behavior.

That an individual's religiousness has its foundation in a personality substratum has been a prominent theme among psychologists (e.g., Allport, 1937; Oates, 1973). Freud speculated that religion originated in the tribe's worship of a totem (an animal or plant that was normally taboo in the clan). The taboo was symbolic of a prohibition against incest within the clan, the source of which lay in sexual cathexes of the Oedipus complex. Fear and guilt initiated a ban on incest and on marriage within the clan. In a seasonal act of sublimation the totem was sacrificially or ritualistically eaten as a symbolic substitution for the father's murder, the murder stemming from thwarted oedipal desires and hostility from the father's ban. Oedipal dynamics form the basis of organized religion; the doctrine of God is but a rearranged doctrine of the father (Freud, 1918).

Similar psychological accounts of the individual's religion are to be found in James's *The Varieties of Religious Experience* and Erikson's *Young Man Luther.* Allport's (1950) fivefold account of origins includes organic needs, temperament and mental capacity, psychogenic interests and values, a desire for rational explanation, and response to surrounding culture. It seems apparent that an individual's religion grows out of personal needs and motives, especially those having some existential significance to the person (Oates, 1973).

The individual's religion is expressed in several ways (Smart, 1976). Ritual is the outer expression coordinated with an inner intention. The mythological dimension embodies the stories that are believed within the religion. The mythical and symbolic elements are formalized by theologians into doctrine. Inherent within religion lie the ethical prescriptions that govern the behavior of the individual. The social dimension represents those communal and organizational aspects supposed to be significant to the group of adherents. The ritualistic, mythological, doctrinal, ethical, and social aspects are external evidences of religion's existence. The experiential dimension comprises the subjective, internal, and invisible world in which the individual communes and worships. Variety in religious experience incorporates a confluence of diversity in content and variation in elemental strength.

Psychologists over the years have been intrigued with the interaction of sentimental and temperamental variables with religiousness. The literature on religious orientation owes much of its origin to the research finding that racial prejudice increases as religiousness increases. Further investigation revealed a more complex relationship in which racial prejudice was a curvilinear function of religiousness (Allport & Ross, 1967). When religiousness was measured by a self report of the frequency of church attendance (a standard measure of religiousness), individuals who reported attending church from once a month to once weekly were more prejudiced than individuals who did not attend at all. Those attending 11 times a month or more were less prejudiced than the nonattenders. It was this consistent finding that Allport and Ross sought to explain. They hypothesized that the motivation of different religious orientations was operating. The two poles of the religious orientation concept were the extrinsically oriented individual, whose religion serves self, and the intrinsically motivated person, whose self serves religion (Allport, 1960).

More specifically, Allport and Ross (1967) considered the motivation and uses each type makes of religion. "Persons with [extrinsic] orientation may find religion useful in a variety of ways—to provide security and solace, sociability and distraction, status and self-justification. The embraced creed is lightly held or else selectively shaped to fit more primary needs. . . . Persons with [intrinsic] orientation find their master motive in religion. Other needs, strong as they may be, are regarded as of less ultimate significance, and they are, so far as possible, brought into harmony with the religious beliefs and prescriptions" (p. 436).

Allport and Ross accounted for the relation between religiousness and prejudice by means of religious orientation. Extrinsically oriented individuals who attended church only occasionally were the highly prejudiced. The very frequent attenders were more likely to be intrinsic, and thus less racially prejudiced. To control for social desirability Allport and Ross used both intrinsic and extrinsic items with which the individual could disagree or agree on the religious orientation scale. In addition to consistently extrinsic and consistently intrinsic individuals, they found individuals who were indiscriminately proreligious and others who were indiscriminately antireligious. The indiscriminately proreligious individuals were found to be highly prejudiced, more so than even the extrinsically oriented.

Hunt and King (1971) reviewed the empirical and conceptual literature on the intrinsic-extrinsic concept. Rather than being bipolarities on a unidimensional continuum, it was found to be a multidimensional construct, something that was anticipated by Allport and Ross (1967). Item analysis and factor analysis revealed two components in the extrinsic orientation: an instrumental one and a selfish one. Intrinsic religion was more personal and more relevant to all of life, and was associated with such religious practice components as church attendance and reading religious literature. Allport and Ross (1967) had intimated that the extrinsic-intrinsic concept was, in fact, a complex of personality and cognitive variables; Hunt and King (1971) explicitly evaluated the construct as a pervasive personality and motivational process that could explain "secular" behavior as well as "religious" action. It is not surprising that extrinsic orientation correlated with aspects of authoritarianism (Adorno, Frenkel-Brunswick, Levinson, & Sanford, 1950), prejudice (Allport, 1954), closed-mindedness (Rokeach, 1960), and external locus of control.

What evolved to become a personality variable began for Allport (1950, 1954) as two types of religion. Interiorized religion became the intrinsic orientation; institutionalized religion became the extrinsic orientation. A related and parallel concept, suggested by Dittes (1971), is the church-sect typology. Two problems identified with each of these conceptual sets are conceptual sloppiness (i.e., imprecision of definition and theoretical mechanism) and value judgments (i.e., the purity of religion in the orientation and in the sect).

The church-sect distinction is usually credited to Troeltsch. The sect typified a primitive, pure state of religion initially independent of culture and society. But with growth and through time the culture imposed itself and compromised the purity of the sect. The church accommodated itself to culture, with increased insensitivity to social issues, by adopting the administrative structure and governance polity of secular institutions but with a greater eye toward social interaction and social norms. In doing so, the religious body moved from an intrinsic commitment to communal purity to an extrinsic association serving other than purely religious purposes.

In summary, the sociopsychological analysis of religious orientation posits the etiology of divergent religious life styles in underlying personality and motivational variations, and considers the style of one's religious expression to be founded on the personality substratum. When considered alongside sociological and cultural processes, the religious orientation approach expresses varieties in religious expression such as asceticism, monasticism, and mysticism, as well as the once-born versus the twice-born typology of James (1902). The need for inner assurance and solace and the need for participation in external rituals arise from fundamental differences in human personality.

References

Adorno, T. W., Frenkel-Brunswick, E., Levinson, D. J., & Sanford, R. N. *The authoritarian personality.* New York: Harper & Row, 1950.

Allport, G. W. *Personality: A psychological interpretation.* New York: Holt, 1937.

Allport, G. W. *The individual and his religion.* New York: Macmillan, 1950.

Allport, G. W. *The nature of prejudice.* Reading, Mass.: Addison-Wesley, 1954.

Allport, G. W. *Personality and social encounter.* Boston: Beacon Press, 1960.

Allport, G. W., & Ross, J. M. Personal religious orientation and prejudice. *Journal of Personality and Social Psychology,* 1967, *5,* 432–443.

Dittes, J. E. Typing the typologies: Some parallels in the career of church-sect and extrinsic-intrinsic. *Journal for the Scientific Study of Religion,* 1971, *10,* 375–383.

Freud, S. *Totem and taboo.* New York: Moffat, Yard, 1918.

James, W. *The varieties of religious experience.* New York: Longmans, Green, 1902.

Hunt, R. A., & King, M. B. The intrinsic-extrinsic concept: A review and evaluation. *Journal for the Scientific Study of Religion,* 1971, *10,* 339–356.

Oates, W. E. *The psychology of religion.* Waco, Tex.: Word Books, 1973.

Rokeach, M. *The open and closed mind.* New York: Basic Books, 1960.

Smart, N. *The religious experience of mankind* (2nd ed.). New York: Scribners, 1976.

19

Ritual
J. Harold Ellens

Ritual may be defined as a pattern of repetitious behavior in an established routine, intended consciously or subconsciously for efficient achievement of personal fulfillment or anxiety reduction and for manipulative control with regard to some significant aspect of one's internal or external world. The objectives and the routine patterns designed to meet them may be physical, psychological, social, or spiritual. Indeed, they may include several of these facets of human experience simultaneously (Taylor & Thompson, 1972). Ritual is readily evident in at least three spheres of human function: worship, relationships, and work. In each of these areas ritual may be either pathological or healthy.

Worship is the area of human behavior in which the role of ritual has been most obvious throughout human history (Westerhof & Willimon, 1980). This is probably due to the fact that humans universally experience relatively high levels of anxiety about spirituality, as we do about sexuality. Both are rooted in personality and character close to the center of our sense of identity. Both are forces driving toward relationship, which has its own inherent anxiety. Moreover, in religious and spiritual matters humans perceive themselves dealing with sacred, transcendent, divine relationship. Historically the sense of the sacred has carried with it an understandable sense of awesome encounter with the world of the unknown and eternal. Such encounter has usually produced a sense of anxiety or even dread. Only in the Judeo-Christian religion of unconditional grace is our encounter with God a source of relief, assurance, joy, and health.

The high anxiety function of religion has caused humans to experience a high level of need to conduct religious matters with great care. That carefulness tends to lead to the creation of carefully controlled procedures for religious behavior: orthodox theology, rigid codes of ethical-moral conduct, and ritualization of the worship process (MacGregor, 1974). These controlled systems function as anxiety-reducing mechanisms in religions where the radical and redemptive nature of God's grace is not perceived or is not really trusted. As such ritualized religion becomes more and more tightly controlled for the purpose of managing the ever increasing religious anxiety, and the rituals tend to become increasingly compulsive and ultimately obsessive (Loder, 1966).

Ritual can also play a very constructive role in religion. It is helpful for Christians to adopt a generally agreed-upon perspective in theology, a functionally effective code of conduct, and a patterned worship process. Ritual in worship adds dignity and aesthetic quality to communal behavior and gives programmatic focus to the experiences of prayer, praise, and religious pronouncement.

Unfortunately there remains in all religion a tendency to cabalistic ritual in worship. Cabalistic worship is that in which the ritual has become an end in itself and has lost its rational connection between the procedure and the objective it was originally designed to achieve: personal fulfillment or anxiety reduction. Cabalistic ritual is always imbued with some significant degree of compulsivity. It is pathological in that it callouses both the soul and psyche by decreasing the sensitivity of the human spirit to the genuine meaning of worship. It has the same effect upon the psyche as a constant chafing has upon one's hand. It desensitizes that organ and creates a defensive and protective callus at the place where the rub is. True worship always moves through ritual to encounter with God in his grandeur.

Ritual also plays an important role in the patterning of human relationships. Emerson thought that politeness was the ritual of society as prayers and praises are the ritual of the worshiping church. Since effective interpersonal relationships depend essentially upon trust, friendship requires that the agenda of mutual expectations be clearly and openly shared. The number and variety of individual differences, therefore, tends to enhance the desirability of predictable patterns and styles of interpersonal behavior. Thus the rituals of friendship arise and make the processes of friendship gratifying, comfortable, and edifying. Friendships, like personalities, can get sick. When they do, the rituals, or predictable behavior patterning, become compulsively oriented toward manipulative control by one or both of the persons in the relationship. The objective in that case is anxiety reduction by excessive dominance of one by the other. When that compulsivity is challenged or its goal achievement frustrated, it tends toward obsessiveness unless the wholesome objective of mutual fulfillment and gratification for all participants in the relationship can be brought back into focus.

It is clear that ritual also plays an important role in work behavior. Routines can enhance efficiency, particularly in our mass-production society. However, they can also sometimes obstruct job efficiency and must then be seen as pathological. Obsessive checking and rechecking of one's work exemplifies this.

The psychopathology most closely associated with pathological ritual is the obsessive-compulsive disorder. Obsessiveness and compulsivity are always fueled by insecurity and driven by the need for anxiety reduction through certainty or control. So an obsessive-compulsive personality may be manifested in the need to check and recheck a door lock or gas jet or in the repeated ritual of washing one's hands. Since these rituals enacted to achieve certainty and control do not result in significant change in the original insecurity, they tend to increase in intensity and in obsessional quality and move toward the pseudo-omnipotent dynamics of magic. The rational link between the cause of the original insecurity and the function of the ritual is then no longer discernible. The process becomes a self-reinfecting exaggeration of the insecurity; that is, the insecurity fuels the obsessive ritual, which does not increase security by anxiety reduction. Fear therefore increases, and the intensity of the ritual is heightened to compensate for the increased anxiety.

Ritualistic behavior of this sort is clearly pathological whether it appears in work, worship, or relationships. The criteria for pathological ritual would seem to be the presence of any of the following conditions: 1) the relationship between the ritual and its objective is lost or nonfunctional; 2) the behavior obstructs the functioning of the life of the person or community; or 3) the enactment of the ritual increasingly fails in its objective of reducing anxiety and therefore escalates in frequency. In extreme cases only the self-limiting experiences of physical and psychic exhaustion or the limits of formal external constraint can control the infinite "wildfire" effect of the expansion of the self-defeating ritualistic behavior (Salzman, 1980).

It is evident, therefore, that ritual may be constructive or destructive, depending on its nature and function. All wholesome idealism requires routines to lead humanity to civilization and aesthetic self-actualization. Efficiency in productivity requires precision and its inherent patterning. Communal life requires coordination, schedule, and ritualization if it is to achieve success, mutual trust, comfort, and gratification. Instruction in the faith requires the routines of catechesis if it is to achieve its growth-enhancing objectives. All of these tend to institutionalize themselves in constructive ritual. All are impaired by pathological ritual.

References

Loder, J. E. *Religious pathology and Christian faith.* Philadelphia: Westminster, 1966.

MacGregor, G. *The rhythm of God.* New York: Seabury, 1974.

Salzman, L. *Treatment of the obsessive personality.* New York: Aronson, 1980.

Taylor, J. C., & Thompson, G. R. *Ritual, realism, and revolt.* New York: Scribners, 1972.

Westerhof, J. H., & Willimon, W. H. *Liturgy and learning through the life cycle.* New York: Seabury, 1980.

Part 2

Psychology in Christian Perspective

20

Ambiguity
Onas C. Scandrette

$\mathbf{A}$n ambiguous situation may be defined as one that is unclear because of a lack of meaningful cues. Intolerance of ambiguity is the tendency to perceive (or interpret) ambiguous situations as sources of threat. There are basically three types of situations that may fit this definition: 1) a novel situation in which familiar cues are totally lacking; 2) a complex situation in which many disparate cues must be organized; and 3) a contradictory situation where existing cues suggest mutually exclusive solutions.

More than 30 years ago Adorno, Frenkel-Brunswick, Levinson, and Sanford (1950) found that authoritarian personalities had more difficulty in coping with ambiguity than did people in general. Since that time hundreds of studies of intolerance of ambiguity have been conducted by means of questionnaires, interviews, projective tests, systematic observation, and experimental research. Several tests of tolerance-intolerance of ambiguity have been developed, the most frequently used being that of Budner (1962). The focus of most of the research studies has been the attempt to determine how intolerance of ambiguity relates to other personality characteristics. It has been found to be positively related to rigidity, closed-mindedness, dogmatism, anxiety, repression, religious fundamentalism, conformity, prejudice, racism, negative attitudes toward employment of the handicapped, negative attitudes toward homosexuals, dislike for abstract art, lack of curiosity, low creativity, and aesthetic insensitivity.

Although the dynamics of intolerance of ambiguity are not altogether clear, Frenkel-Brunswick hypothesized that this trait is the result of repression and projection. When a person represses an unacceptable emotion, he tends to project this emotion to others. Stimuli which fail to support his perception (are ambiguous with respect to his projection) are threatening. Frenkel-Brunswick (1949) documented a strong correlation between intolerance for ambiguity and hostility, power orientation, externalization, and rigid stereotyping.

Budner (1978) believes that the confusion about tolerance-intolerance of ambiguity results from the fact that research has largely taken the form of correlations between specific variables rather than longitudinal studies of the development of individual predispositions. In one longitudinal experimental study (Harrington, Block, & Block, 1978) measures of intolerance of ambiguity were obtained on the same group of subjects at three, four, five, and seven years of age. Information about parents and parent-child interactions was also obtained. Reliable independent ratings of intolerance of ambiguity were obtained from nursery school teachers. Subjects who were intolerant of ambiguity were hesitant to enter, narrow in deploying attention within, and premature in imposing structure upon three ambiguous experimental situations. Early intolerance of ambiguity in boys was related to later intolerance of ambiguity, general anxiety, structure-seeking behaviors, and less effective cognitive functioning at age seven. Fathers of boys intolerant of ambiguity described themselves as relatively distant and authoritarian. In a standardized teaching situation fathers of boys intolerant of ambiguity tended to be impatient, critical, and less resourceful when interacting with their sons. Early intolerance of ambiguity in girls related to later stable peer relationships in which girls played nonassertive roles. Mothers of girls who were intolerant of ambiguity described themselves as nurturant, and in the teaching situation were emotionally supportive and task structuring.

In summary, the most readily observable attitudinal and behavioral characteristics of people who are intolerant of ambiguity are 1) low self-regard, 2) inability to understand the feelings of others, 3) strong ethnocentrism, 4) strong needs to receive support from authority figures, 5) tendency to see issues as black or white, 6) preference for the known and routine, 7) tendency to jump to conclusions without adequate data, 8) acceptance of what they have been taught, regardless of inconsistencies, 9) repression of impulses, and 10) rigidity in thinking.

Research findings on intolerance of ambiguity have implications for Christian leaders. In the first place, many Christians have been reared in the kind of homes from which persons intolerant of ambiguity come. In the second place, there are many ambiguities within Christian theology and life. Hard-to-understand passages of Scripture, differing theological viewpoints, and conflicting views with regard to the proper life style for the Christian all demand high tolerance for ambiguity.

Persons who are intolerant of ambiguity are emotionally insecure. Consequently, anything that will make the individual feel more secure will increase his ability to cope with ambiguity. Obviously, the more a person can feel forgiven, accepted, and loved by God, the more secure he will feel. However, unless the individual can experience the love of Christian people, he will find it difficult to believe in and accept God's love.

Doubt may be regarded as a form of intolerance of ambiguity since the doubter is threatened by cues which seem contradictory and suggest mutually exclusive responses. An important factor in resolving doubt is an atmosphere of openness and honesty. Where this is lacking, doubters are afraid to voice their doubts for fear of being condemned or ostracized. Many college students who are exposed to ideas which challenge their faith hesitate to discuss their doubts with parents, pastor, or members of their church for fear of censure. Christians who have repressed their own doubts instead of resolving them often are shocked when young people raise the same questions. When young people raise disturbing questions with their elders, they are sometimes rebuked for entertaining sinful thoughts, given proof texts, or prayed for. Too infrequently are they listened to with understanding and love. The person who is bothered by ambiguities with regard to his faith must be given the assurance that it is not sinful to have sincere doubts. Christ's attitude toward the sincere doubter is instructive. Although Christ harshly condemned the insincere scribes, Pharisees, and Sadducees who asked questions in an attempt to trap him, his treatment of the sincere questioner was quite different.

When John the Baptist, who was then in prison, sent two of his disciples to inquire of Christ, "Art thou he that should come or do we look for another?" one might have expected Christ to be justifiably exasperated. Instead, he answered, "Go and shew John again these things which ye do hear and see; the blind receive their sight, and the lame walk, the lepers are healed, and the deaf hear, the dead are raised up, and the poor have the gospel preached to them" (Matt. 11:4–5).

Thomas had not been present when the risen Christ appeared to the other disciples and showed them his hands and side. When the other disciples told Thomas that they had seen the Lord, Thomas doubted their report, saying, "Except I shall see in his hands the print of the nails and thrust my hand into his side, I will not believe" (John 20:25). Eight days later Christ appeared to the disciples again, but this time Thomas was with them. Instead of upbraiding Thomas for his lack of faith, Christ invited Thomas to examine his hands and side.

Doubts can often be resolved in intimate dialogue with fellow believers. Scripture exhorts us to "confess our faults one to another" (James 5:16), "bear one another's burdens" (Gal. 6:2), and "rejoice with those who do rejoice and weep with those who weep" (Rom. 12:15). Leslie (1971) has shown that encounter-like groups within the church setting can be effective in resolving both psychological and spiritual problems. Formal groups organized around another objective, such as Sunday school classes, ordinarily do not provide the right atmosphere for intimate sharing. Consequently, special groups composed of individuals who feel the need for intimate sharing must be formed.

References

Adorno, T. W., Frenkel-Brunswick, E., Levinson, D., & Sanford, R. N. *The authoritarian personality*. New York: Harper & Row, 1950.

Budner, S. Intolerance of ambiguity as a personality variable. *Journal of Personality*, 1962, *30*(1), 29–50.

Budner, S. Intolerance for ambiguity and the need for closure. *Psychological Reports*, 1978, *43*(2), 638.

Frenkel-Brunswick, E. Intolerance of ambiguity as an emotional and perceptual personality variable. *Journal of Personality*, 1949, *18*, 108–143.

Harrington, D. M., Block, J. H., & Block, J. Intolerance of ambiguity in preschool children: Psychometric considerations, behavioral manifestations and parental correlates. *Developmental Psychology*, 1978, *14*(3), 242–256.

Leslie, R. C. *Sharing groups in the church*. Nashville: Abingdon, 1971.

21

Consciousness
Elizabeth L. Hillstrom

In contemporary use consciousness usually means conscious experience, a phenomenon so general and so obviously a part of many aspects of psychology that it would seem impossible to describe in one short chapter. Actually the meaning of the term has shifted with both time and the interests of the people investigating it. Currently consciousness is a topic of great interest to psychologists in at least two different branches of the discipline.

Those who wanted to make psychology into a science in the latter half of the last century believed that they should study conscious experience. In subsequent years attempts to study sensation and even memory by applying the new techniques of the physical sciences were fairly successful, but attempts to study conscious experience were not. In fact, structuralism, an attempt to isolate the "elements" of conscious experience and to deduce the rules by which these elements might combine (an idea borrowed from atomic theory), was such a sterile approach that psychologists began to wonder if the scientific study of such phenomena was even possible. About this time Watson (1913) argued very convincingly that conscious experience could not be studied with experimental methods and proposed instead that psychologists confine their investigations to behavior. His arguments helped launch behaviorism, an approach which dominated psychology in this country up to the late 1960s. Behaviorism's influence was so strong and pervasive that for many years consciousness was simply ignored. Now, however, it is being investigated once more.

One group of researchers interested in conscious experience are the new cognitive psychologists who are studying such things as decision making, problem solving, and mental imagery (Block, 1980). A second group is interested in the nature of the mind and how it is related to the brain, in altered states of consciousness, and even in the spiritual nature of man. This second area of consciousness research falls into two categories—mind-brain relationships and the "consciousness movement."

Mind-Brain Relationships

Studies done on the mind-brain issue are currently of great interest to many people besides those aligned with the consciousness movement, especially those who have a vested interest in a materialistic view of human beings. For many years most psychologists have been materialists, assuming that man is nothing more than a physical being, a highly advanced animal who is programmed by past learning, internal physical events, or external environmental events. They either deny that a person has a soul or spirit or claim that these things are merely words we have invented to describe some of the phenomena we all observe. For them all experience can ultimately be explained by physical or chemical events occurring in the brain. Mind, then, would refer to subjective feelings we experience as a result of certain brain states. Mind does not produce the brain states but instead is produced by them. The brain states, in turn, depend on programming from genetic influences and past experiences, or on one's present physiological state or circumstances.

Recently several scientists have described evidence and produced arguments that are difficult to reconcile with a purely materialistic explanation (see Custance, 1980). One of the most noted of these is Eccles, who was awarded the Nobel Prize in Physiology and Medicine in 1963. Eccles has written and edited several important books on this topic. Although he would be among the first to acknowledge that certain brain injuries can drastically affect the functioning of the mind or even personality, he points out that there are even more drastic injuries which do not seem to affect either. For instance, some individuals with life-threatening tumors in their brains have had their entire nondominant cerebral hemisphere removed and have not been perceptibly changed psychologically. In fact the operation can be carried out under local anesthesia and they do not even lose consciousness as it is being done. (They do suffer loss in their visual fields and weakness in limbs on the opposite side of the body.) If mind is totally dependent on the brain, one would expect some significant change psychologically as a result of the loss of so much brain tissue. When hemispherectomies are done on the dominant hemisphere (the one that is necessary for speaking and apparently self-awareness), they are usually limited to children under 10 years of age because in young brains the entire language and awareness function can shift to the other hemisphere. In older children and adults these functions do not shift and the individual will remain severely aphasic and handicapped. The fact that the hemispheres can shift function is also hard to explain from a strictly physical point of view since the neurons which presumably provided these functions are completely destroyed and are not replaced by new ones. What, then, is left to reorganize the neurons on the other hemisphere to restore these vital functions?

Another interesting paradox observed by Libet (1982) is an apparent time lag between the brain state produced by a sensory stimulus (such as a light touch on the finger) and the conscious awareness of that stimulus. Similarly Kornhuber (1973) has shown that there is a substantial time lag between willing to move some part of the body and the achievement of a brain state capable of initiating that movement. If conscious experience is merely an aspect of a particular brain state, there should be no time discrepancy at all.

Another area of brain research that yields very interesting information about brain-mind relationships comes from patients who have undergone the "split-brain" operation. This operation, done to relieve seizures that cannot be chemically controlled, involves severing the corpus callosum, a broad band of some 200,000,000 fibers that carries visual and tactile information from one cerebral hemisphere to the other. (It is cut because it also transmits the abnormal seizure activity from one hemisphere to the other, causing the person to lose consciousness.) The operation is effective, and after recovery neither the patients nor their families are able to detect psychological or other changes. However, tests in more stringent laboratory conditions do reveal some rather startling differences.

In one type of test patients are seated in front of a screen; while they look straight ahead a word is flashed briefly on the left or right side of the screen. The information travels to either the right or left hemisphere, and since the callosum is cut it is isolated there. When a word is flashed to the left hemisphere (which is also the dominant, language hemisphere in 95% of the population), the person can say the word and use the right hand (also controlled by the left hemisphere) to reach under a screen to pick up the object named. When the word is flashed to the right hemisphere, however, the person is not aware that any word has been flashed. If persuaded to reach under a screen with the left hand to try to identify the object, they can usually do so. Oddly, even when they have the object in their left hands they cannot verbally identify what they are holding.

The results of this and many other types of tests on split-brain patients indicate that when the hemispheres receive different and discrepant visual or tactile information, they seem to act independently, as if they are really two separate minds in one head. (See Springer & Deutsch, 1981, for a comprehensive review of this area.) At first, these results seemed to confirm the materialist's assertion that mind is nothing more than a manifestation of the physical brain. After all, splitting the brain seemed to split the mind. However, later information has been difficult to reconcile with this position.

One important question is whether the mute right hemisphere is really conscious in a human sense when disconnected from the left, since it seems to have neither the ability to produce language nor self-awareness, depending, of course, on the way self-awareness is defined. Sophisticated research techniques have shown that the right hemisphere excels in some things—for example, recognizing patterns or faces, directing spatial tasks (drawing, sculpturing), or discriminating musical chords. Sperry (1982) indicates that the right hemisphere can also identify its own face, members of the family, pets, and acquaintances, and seems to show appropriate emotional response to all these things. It also seems to be cognizant of the person's daily and weekly schedules, important dates, and the need for fire or health insurance. He argues that these abilities are sufficient to establish self-awareness. Others define self-awareness as our subjective stream of consciousness not only of events, but of our reactions to them, of our thoughts and feelings from moment to moment (James, 1916). If this definition is used, the right hemisphere is not self-aware, because when information is sent to the right hemisphere alone, that part of the psyche that the patient identifies as the self is not aware that anything has happened.

If this argument is valid, it puts to rest the disturbing possibility that a single brain operation could create two persons out of one, but it does not eliminate the fact that a separate, semiautonomous aspect of the person does exist that can interact intelligently with its environment, perhaps with the same level of consciousness available to animals (Gazzaniga & LeDoux, 1978). Gazzaniga has often set up situations in which the right and left hemispheres receive different information and the patient's two hands seem to do contradictory things. When this happens, the patients are very adept at explaining the inconsistencies and do not seem disturbed by them. Gazzaniga proposes that this phenomenon in split-brain patients is not really so strange but rather is a characteristic common to all of us. Human beings can be notoriously inconsistent, intending to do one thing and then doing the opposite, but are then adept at providing rational reasons for the unexpected switch. Perhaps we are inconsistent because we also have a duality. Since we become so accustomed to inconsistency, we also become proficient at covering it up without really wondering about it.

One final observation about the split-brain studies is that they are producing a rather profound change in the way that brain scientists are viewing mind-brain relationships. For instance, Sperry (1982), one of the most noted researchers in the area, has come to the conclusion that conscious experience (mind) is very real and that, besides being different from and greater than the sum of its parts, mind also causally determines the fate of the parts. Sperry believes that as more and more brain scientists accept this perspective, the old conflict between the scientific and humanistic view of human beings will disappear and that the study of the mind and of human judgments and values will become important.

The Consciousness Movement

The individuals contributing to the consciousness movement come from very diverse disciplines and include biologists who specialize in understanding the brain, psychologists, parapsychologists, medical doctors, physicists, and even specialists in Eastern and other religions. A substantial proportion of the authors within this group perceive and present their efforts as scientific attempts to understand man's spiritual nature, yet very few of them accept or will even seriously consider Judeo-Christian beliefs. Instead they embrace Eastern religions, espousing such doctrines as reincarnation. Many have also adopted a modified theory of evolution which proposes that men are evolving mentally and even now are on the threshold of revolutionary change. These changes would include new (or newly discovered) mental powers such as telepathy, psychokinesis (the ability to move objects by mental powers alone), the ability to enter into altered states of consciousness, to heal physical disorders in others by mental means, the ability to experience other "spiritual realities" (i.e., to contact spiritual beings), or even the ability to separate at will from one's body. (See Goleman & Davidson, 1979, for a general collection of readings on this topic.)

Many of these researchers seem to believe that these mental powers may be more accessible through altered states of consciousness and thus are very eager to study them. Some of the specific areas of interest include hypnosis (Bowers, 1979), drug states (Tart, 1969), psychotic states, meditative states (Deikman, 1973), and even possession states (Ludwig, 1967). Comparisons of the characteristics of these altered states reveal surprising similarities among them, including passivity, loss of ability to control one's mental processes, hallucinations, vivid visual imagery, and extreme emotional experiences.

If these experiences were the only gratifications that altered states provided, one might wonder why anyone would repeatedly risk his health to pursue them. The real reasons for their appeal may lie in their more subtle enticements. Any of the altered states can induce people to attach great significance to their subjective experiences, ideas, or perceptions, making them believe that they have been privy to profound insights or have grasped ultimate truths. Unfortunately, however, these insights frequently bear no relationship to reality, but they can and frequently do linger on and influence thinking long after the experience. The various altered states may also provide mystical and transcendent experiences in which supernatural forces or beings may be sensed, seen, or even communicated with. These experiences are especially vivid, and their importance is exaggerated by the hyper-suggestibility and suspension of critical thinking that also accompany altered states. Such experiences have changed people's lives (Ludwig, 1969).

Researchers in the consciousness movement have also been interested in studying psychic healing and other paranormal abilities, including the scientific study of mediums. They have studied the near-death phenomenon, first described by Moody (1975), and some have even been working on scientific methods to help people leave their physical bodies. According to Brooke (1979), who worked on one such project before his conversion to Christianity, the information on how to do this is coming from what the believers call "spirit guides," who are presumably trying to help mankind on to the next stage of spiritual evolution.

From a Christian perspective these developments within the consciousness movement are unsettling because the "spirit guides" sound hauntingly similar to demons, and the "spiritual evolution" they presumably promise seems to be no more than an elaborate scientific cover-up for one more diabolical attempt to deceive and destroy. The movement, whose stated goal is to unite science and religion, is apparently attracting fairly substantial numbers of educated men and women who may perceive it as a way to satisfy their spiritual longings without meeting the costly demands of Christianity. Christians should certainly be made aware of the potential implications and dangers in this new area of study.

References

Bowers, K. Hypnosis and dissociation. In D. Goleman & R. Davidson (Eds.), *Consciousness: Brain, states of awareness and mysticism*. New York: Harper & Row, 1979.

Brooke, R. T. *The other side of death*. Wheaton, Ill.: Tyndale House, 1979.

Custance, A. C. *The mysterious matter of mind*. Grand Rapids: Zondervan, 1980.

Deikman, A. Bimodal consciousness. In R. E. Ornstein (Ed.). *The nature of human consciousness*. New York: Viking Press, 1973.

Gazzaniga, M. S., & LeDoux, J. E. *The integrated mind*. New York: Plenum, 1978.

Goleman, D., & Davidson, R. *Consciousness: Brain, states of awareness and mysticism*. New York: Harper & Row, 1979.

James, W. *The varieties of religious experience*. New York: Longmans, Green, 1916.

Kornhuber, H. H. Cerebral cortex, cerebellum and basal ganglia: An introduction to their motor functions. In F. O. Schmitt & F. G. Worden (Eds.), *The neurosciences third study program*. Cambridge: MIT Press, 1973.

Libet, B. Subjective and neuronal time factors in conscious sensory experience, studied in man, and their implications for mind brain relationships. In J. Eccles (Ed.), *Mind and brain*. Washington, D.C.: Paragon House, 1982.

Ludwig, A. M. The trance. *Comprehensive Psychiatry*, 1967, 8, 7–15.

Ludwig, A. M. Altered states of consciousness. In C. T. Tart (Ed.), *Altered states of consciousness*. New York: Wiley, 1969.

Moody, R. *Life after life*. Atlanta: Mockingbird Books, 1975.

Sperry, R. Some effects of disconnecting the cerebral hemispheres. *Science*, September 1982, 1223–1226.

Springer, S., & Deutsch, G. *Left brain, right brain*. San Francisco: W. H. Freeman, 1981.

Tart, C. T. (Ed.). *Altered states of consciousness*. New York: Wiley, 1969.

Watson, J. B. Psychology as a behaviorist views it. *Psychological Review*, 1913, 20, 158–177.

Additional Reading

Eccles, J. (Ed.). *Mind and brain*. Washington, D.C.: Paragon House, 1982.

22

Determinism and Free Will
John A. Hammes

The question of whether or not a person's choice of behavior is free, and to what extent, has plagued thinkers for centuries. Each answer has its defenders and critics. The position supporting free will or free-choice behavior has been called libertarianism (D'Angelo, 1968), or voluntarism (Hammes, 1971). Freedom here refers to the absence of intrinsic necessity in the performance of an act. That is, given alternatives from among which to choose, one can select freely, without coercion. Freedom in behavior does not mean absence of causality. The libertarian does not contend that human behavior is uncaused, but rather that there is a cause (the self) which can operate in a free manner to produce effects (choices).

Freedom is not the same as variance, as some would contend (Boring, 1957). The statistical variability of accumulative behavioral responses, referred to as the standard deviation of a distribution, does not constitute human freedom. Animals lower than man, even the earthworm, possess behavioral variability. However, the voluntarist does not attribute freedom to such behavior. Human freedom can induce variability, but the presence of variability does not necessarily infer freedom.

There are certain prerequisite conditions that must be met before a free choice is possible. The first is awareness, or a normal state of attention. A second condition is deliberation. The person must have opportunity to consider choices of action prior to decision. When awareness and deliberation are lacking, either in degree or in entirety, there is corresponding attenuation of freedom and responsibility—for example, in actions of the retardate or the psychotic, and in spontaneous emotional impulses (Hammes, 1971).

Evidence for Free Will

Various kinds of evidence have been adduced to support freedom in human choices. First, there is the capacity for voluntary attention, the act of directing the focal point of awareness to some object (Bittle, 1945). At this moment, the reader's attention is on this page. Since the present behavior is deliberate, the state of attention is called voluntary. If, however, a sudden noise were to draw this attention aside, the interruption would illustrate involuntary attention. The fundamental awareness that attention is at times under personal control, and in other instances is not, demonstrates human freedom and is the basis for differentiating the two states of attention. Indeed, the experience of intentionality itself is evidence for freedom and is a basic theme of humanistic-existential authors.

Libertarians also point to the experience of moral consciousness and conscience to support their belief in freedom (Bittle, 1945). The experience of guilt is indicative of the fundamental awareness that in the area of moral behavior one can be responsible for evil acts which need not have been done, or which could have been freely avoided. The experience of guilt is so universal that persons lacking such feelings are diagnosed as psychopathic. Libertarians also cite the experience of moral effort in support of the conviction of human freedom (Dworkin, 1970), as well as personal achievement and the pride of accomplishment (Hammes, 1971).

Another argument in defense of free will is the conviction "I could have done otherwise" (D'Angelo, 1968). For the libertarian this statement means, "If I had so freely chosen, I would have done otherwise." It would seem the original statement could be compatible with determinism, if interpreted to mean, "If the determining conditions were different, I could have chosen otherwise" (Lamont, 1967). However, the belief in free will is based on the grounds of practical experience, whereas the determinist's objections are primarily theoretical and therefore not as weighty (Dworkin, 1970).

Another defense of freedom of choice is based on the observation of indeterminacy at the subatomic level. As expressed in the Heisenberg principle, which points out that it is impossible to make a simultaneous determination of the position and momentum of atomic particles, this indeterminancy is understood to be in the very fabric of nature rather than mere uncertainty or limitation in knowledge (Bube, 1971). However, libertarians vary on this interpretation of Heisenberg.

Determinist Objections to Free Will

Determinism has been classified by some observers into hard determinism and soft determinism. Hard determinists assert that freedom is illusory, that every event has a cause and is predictable, and that all human acts occur necessarily as effects of causes. Soft determinists attempt to introduce some element of freedom while still recognizing determinism. Humanistic-existential writers such as Rollo May and Carl Rogers are sometimes placed in the category of soft determinism. Others disagree with this division within determinism. They consider soft determinism an evasion of the issue and logically reducible to either libertarianism or hard determinism. Hard determinism has been presented in a number of different ways. Each will be examined here, followed by the libertarian's response.

A primary objection to freedom is that of *skeptic determinism*. The common basis for testimony of freedom is awareness, or the consciousness of this capability. Skeptic determinism strikes at the root of this conviction by asserting consciousness to be an invalid informational source. For example, an amputee may attribute sensation to a foot no longer present; a straight stick placed partly in water appears bent, although it is not. In both instances the skeptic contends that consciousness has lied.

However, the converse is true. Past learning accounts for the discrepancy between fact and judgment in the first example, and in the second example advantage has been taken of the structure of the human eye, which does not naturally correct for refraction of light in two media. The skeptic therefore attempts to use abnormal settings to discredit the testimony of consciousness in normal circumstances. A similar argument would be that if a blind person cannot see, no one can.

A more critical reply to the skeptic, however, concerns the validity of his own positiveness. Can he doubt the trustworthiness of consciousness while using that consciousness as a basis for his doubt? Obviously not. The skeptic, in removing the basis for the validity of any doubt, consequently discredits his own. He can only hold to a doubt which is in itself doubtful.

A second form of determinism, *cause-effect determinism,* is based on law and predictability. It is contended that freedom is a conclusion based on ignorance of the causes actually present but unknown. These causes act necessarily to produce behavior as an effect. In response, the voluntarist concedes that all behavior is caused, but disagrees that all causes act necessarily to produce effects. In the instance of free choice he contends that the person, as cause, freely initiates effects (behavior). Furthermore, the principle of causality states that effects are necessarily brought about by causes, but does not demand that all causes necessarily act to produce effects. Neither is predictability a problem for the libertarian, for a person may, and usually does, choose to act consistently, since by nature we are ordered human beings. A person freely choosing to lead a good moral life, for example, can be predicted to act in ways consistent with this resolve. Predictability, being compatible with both freedom and determinism, cannot be used as an argument against freedom.

A third expression of determinism is *mechanistic determinism.* This grows out of the monistic view that man is merely a complex machine whose mental processes are neurological only, reducible to physiochemical forces subject to the determining laws of matter. However, the evidence that mind and brain are distinct within the human person, and that the mind cannot be reduced to matter, makes possible the exercise of freedom in human behavior.

Fourth is *biogenetic determinism.* Heredity, temperament, glands, and emotions are supposedly the architects of human personality and the dictators of action. Sociobiology is a contemporary example of the emphasis on genetic structure as a determinant of character traits and presumably choice behavior as well. The libertarian responds that these facts are not self-evidently deterministic and can be considered influences rather than determinants.

A fifth variety of determinism is based on learning theory and could be termed *stimulus-response determinism.* This is illustrated by Pavlov and other classical conditioning learning theorists. Conditioned behavior is sometimes used to arrive at the sweeping generalization that all human behavior is conditioned and that consequently freedom is precluded. However, some learning patterns require concentrated effort (e.g., learning to play golf or mastering algebra). The attempt to reduce all human learning to simple conditioning is, in the opinion of the libertarian, arbitrary and unwarranted.

A closely related but broader theory is that of *reinforcement determinism*. This is illustrated by Skinner and other operant conditioning learning theorists. Whatever reinforces behavior determines its repetition. However, the fact that reinforced behavior is repeated does not necessarily infer a determined relationship. It is only logical for one to choose pleasurable experiences over unpleasant ones. Knowledge of the action taken sheds no light on whether or not the choice was free or determined.

Wider still is the theory of *sociocultural determinism,* the view that behavior is shaped by forces such as home, school, church, and community. These environmental variables purportedly indoctrinate the individual and structure his choice behavior. For example, slums are said to breed criminals. Clarence Darrow believed prisoners could not help being criminals, just as those outside of jail could not help but be there (Dworkin, 1970). Skinner contends human behavior can be engineered and controlled through cultural design. The libertarian would respond that social forces should be considered as influences rather than determinants of behavior. Criminals come from high as well as from low socioeconomic levels, and good citizens as well as delinquents emerge from slum conditions. Although socioeconomic factors most certainly limit the kind and number of available opportunities, the choice among these alternatives can nonetheless be free (Hammes, 1978).

An eighth objection to free will is *motivational determinism*. This is expressed by the statement, "The stronger motive prevails." Neo-Gestalt field theorists illustrate this position (Lewin, 1935). The fault in motivational determinism is akin to that in the Monday morning quarterback. The prevailing motive is not labeled until after the decision is made. Thus, no matter what alternative is selected, the determinist would obligingly designate it as the stronger one. To do so proves nothing. The knowledge that a decision has been made gives no information on whether or not there was freedom or lack of freedom existing prior to the decision.

Another example offered by motivational determinists is that of reactive inhibition. After a person has pressed a red-light button for a hundred trials, and has then been given the opportunity to push a light button other than red, it can be predicted that the individual will invariably select the alternative, which was thereby necessitated, according to the determinist. The reader may have recognized *reactive inhibition* as a term equivalent to *monotony.* A repetitive behavior pattern will usually induce the impulse or tendency to alternate activity, a response natural to life forms, one which has survival value and which in man may even be consciously experienced. Even in such circumstances, however, the voluntarist would consider these behavioral tendencies to be influences rather than compulsive determinants.

Unconscious motivation is used as the basis for a ninth objection to freedom, termed *unconscious determinism*. This is illustrated by Freud. Some psychoanalysts, on the evidence of unconscious defense mechanisms, deny freedom of choice. Even though on the conscious level man is convinced of freedom, it is contended that there are unconscious forces unknowingly manipulating the decision-making process.

The defect in this line of reasoning is that the unconscious, being unconscious, is unknowable. The voluntarist, by the same token, could argue that the unconscious force of the rejected alternative was actually the stronger, and the chooser exerted great self-effort in his decision to overcome that option. Since the role of motivation below the level of awareness is an unknowable variable, it is arbitrary to assign various strengths of influence to one alternative over another. Unconscious motivation, therefore, cannot be used to prove or disprove freedom of choice.

A tenth theory of determinism involves the relationship between God and man and can be called *theological determinism*. Three variants of this perspective are creationistic determinism, omniscient determinism, and predestination, based respectively on God's creative power, his knowledge, and his will.

Creationistic determinism is based on the law of causality, which states that effects are utterly dependent on their causes. If so, it follows that man (as an effect) created by God (his cause) would be completely dependent upon the Creator in all human activity, including decision behavior. According to this idea man is a divinely manipulated puppet.

Defenders of human freedom consider this view to be an unnecessary application of a law in the physical world to the world of the spiritual. In the material cosmos it is true that effects are completely dependent upon, and determined by, their causes. But is it not possible that different cause-effect relations exist on the nonmaterial, or spiritual, level? God could, if he so desired, create in his image a being with free will, utterly dependent upon him for existence, but nonetheless possessing the capacity for freedom of choice. In no way would this concept do violence to the laws governing the material universe. Freedom exists as an immaterial, or spiritual, behavior pattern, since such activity is a function of the mind, itself immaterial. It could thus be argued that God created man not just "to be" but rather "to be free."

A second expression of theological determinism is *omniscient deter-*

minism. Since God is all-knowing, he knows every human choice before it is made. Consequently, it is contended that his knowledge determines that choice. The problem here lies in man's inability to experience outside of time, since the human creature is time-bound, and can only experience events as they occur. God, being independent of time, is not so bound. However, we can understand by analogy how his knowledge need not be causative. A person having seen a football game, and then reviewing it on film, could predict during the film exactly what the players would do next. Now, if one were not bound by time, he could also have predicted the play at the time of watching the actual game. In neither instance would such knowledge be the cause of the players' reactions.

Therefore, it should be apparent that knowledge of behavior, even divine knowledge, is not necessarily the cause of that behavior. God could, of course, if he so desired, control human activities completely. The question here is not whether God possesses this power; it is rather whether his knowledge alone predetermines human choice.

A final variant of theological determinism is *predestination,* the position that God chooses those to be saved. Although both Luther and Calvin, representative of this view, believed in free will in everyday choice activity, they did not extend this ability to the matter of cooperating in personal salvation. Moreover, Luther believed in single predestination, the saving of the just, whereas Calvin held to double predestination, which included the eternal perdition of the reprobate. Predestination, however, is compatible with human freedom if interpreted to mean the promise of salvation to those who freely respond to God's redemptive grace. Since we are dealing here with matters of Christian faith, determinists and voluntarists will be divided in accordance with their understanding of divine redemption.

Alternative Approaches

In addition to libertarianism and determinism, there are two other options in the argument over free will. There are those who believe the controversy to be an unresolvable paradox with which one must learn to live, and there are others who consider the controversy a pseudoproblem, reducible to semantic confusion. Some have applied Bohr's principle of complementarity, borrowed from physics, to the freedom-determinism controversy. According to this view both perspectives, being complementary, are true. Such attempts have been described as reconciliationism (Berofsky, 1966). However, voluntarists perceive the problem as involving contradictions, not mere complementarities, and resolvable only in terms of one side or the other, not both.

The linguistic analyst sees the solution in terms of describing behavior in diverse languages, descriptions which present different aspects unrelated to each other (Barbour, 1966). Thus man can supposedly be both determined and free in the same behavioral act, dependent on whether he is being described in terms of spectator language (determinism) or actor language (voluntarism). However, this approach would appear to be an evasion of the issue. For example, the preference of a scientist for spectator language or of an existentialist for actor language is irrelevant to the objective, ontological nature of the act, which in itself is independent of any descriptive language.

Resembling linguistic analysis is the multilevel systems approach (Bube, 1971), which contends that description on one level may be deterministic and yet on another level be indeterministic. All such approaches deny the determinism-free will problems. However, for reasons already considered in this chapter, many observers conclude that a real controversy exists, one that cannot be dismissed so easily and one that requires resolution.

References

Barbour, I. G. *Issues in science and religion.* Englewood Cliffs, N.J.: Prentice-Hall, 1966.

Berofsky, B. (Ed.), *Free will and determinism.* New York: Harper & Row, 1966.

Bittle, C. *The whole man: Psychology.* Milwaukee: Bruce Publishing, 1945.

Boring, E. G. When is behavior pre-determined? *Scientific Monthly,* 1957, *84,* 189–196.

Bube, R. H. *The human quest.* Waco, Tex.: Word Books, 1971.

D'Angelo, E. *The problem of freedom and determinism.* Columbia: University of Missouri Press, 1968.

Dworkin, G. *Determinism, free will, and moral responsibility.* Englewood, Cliffs, N.J.: Prentice-Hall, 1970.

Hammes, J. A. *Humanistic psychology.* New York: Grune & Stratton, 1971.

Hammes, J. A. *Human destiny: Exploring today's value systems.* Huntington, Ind.: Our Sunday Visitor Press, 1978.

Lamont, C. *Freedom of choice affirmed.* New York: Horizon Press, 1967.

Lewin, K. *A dynamic theory of personality.* New York: McGraw-Hill, 1935.

23

Dogmatism
Richard D. Kahoe

The concept of dogmatism in psychology is most closely associated with the work of Milton Rokeach and is discussed most fully in his book *The Open and Closed Mind* (1960). The Dogmatism Scale developed by him promoted and popularized research on the subject. Hundreds of published studies relate dogmatic tendencies to attitude, personality, and behavior variables, including religion.

Political extremes of World War II inspired theories and research about authoritarian personalities, most notably *The Authoritarian Personality* (Adorno, Frenkel-Brunswik, Levinson, & Sanford, 1950). Whereas these studies emphasized fascist, conservative authoritarianisms of the "right," Rokeach observed that liberals or "leftists" can be equally authoritarian or dogmatic.

Any communication includes both relevant and irrelevant information. The relevant facts concern the immediate problem to which one must react. Irrelevant facts indicate the source of the message, authority figures, rewards and punishments for alternative actions, and relationships of these to our belief systems, defenses, and motivations. Open-minded people, Rokeach said, discriminate and respond primarily to the relevant information. Dogmatic or closed-minded persons fail to discriminate the relevant facts and tend to respond to irrelevant factors, such as the authority and personal needs. The dogmatic tend to see the world as threatening and hold a narrow, future-oriented (contrasted with broad) time perspective. They are also prone to hold their beliefs in isolation, without logical integration, and tend strongly to reject and to be ill-informed about belief systems other than their own. The Dogmatism Scale was based on such definitions of dogmatism.

Rokeach's theory and research related the development of closed-mindedness to an inability to express ambivalent feelings about one's parents and, by a defensive constriction, a dearth of influence by adults outside the family. Subsequent research on the origins of personal dogmatism has related open-mindedness to higher social class, larger family size, and later birth order.

Situational threat as a factor in dogmatism was demonstrated by an investigation of conversions to authoritarian or dogmatic denominations. In two studies (nationwide for 1920–1939 and Seattle, Washington, for 1961–1970) times of economic prosperity were associated with relatively more conversions to nonauthoritarian groups and economic depression with more conversions to authoritarian faiths (Sales, 1972). Rokeach (1960) said that institutions, like individuals, respond to threat with increased dogmatism. Religions are not inherently dogmatic, but dogma may be invoked to defend the institution against heresy and ensure its continuation. Rokeach demonstrated this in a study of 12 Roman Catholic ecumenical councils from A.D. 325 to 1563. The degree of threat or heresy preceding each council was strongly related to dogmatism of the resulting canons, both in degree of authority invoked and in the punishment ordained for violators.

Subsequent research supports dogmatism as generalized authoritarianism—political and religious, left and right. Dogmatism is associated with racial prejudice, sex-role stereotypes, and rejection of unconventional music. Persons with dogmatic personalities tend to show anxiety, low self-esteem, the need to receive support from others, general maladjustment and instability, defensiveness, impatience, timidity, and conformity (Vacchiano, Strauss, & Schiffman, 1968).

Catholics were more dogmatic than Protestants in Rokeach's (1960) Midwest studies, but some Protestants are more dogmatic, particularly in the South. Churchgoers tend to be more dogmatic than the nonreligious, but radical atheists are also dogmatic. Dogmatism tends to accompany an extrinsic or self-serving religion, but usually it is not related to an intrinsic or committed religious orientation. If, as Allport said, mature, intrinsic faith develops out of self-serving religion, dogmatism may be a normal phase in the development of religious faith. The theories of Kohlberg, Fowler, and Loevinger (in development of moral judgment, faith, and ego, respectively) all include rigidly held beliefs and reliance on authority at early developmental stages. Similarly, in the growth of a personal religious faith, openness to relevant new information tends to replace defensive reliance on authority as the faith becomes more committed, mature, and secure.

References

Adorno, T. W., Frenkel-Brunswik, E., Levinson, D. J., & Sanford, R. N. *The authoritarian personality.* New York: Harper & Row, 1950.

Rokeach, M. *The open and closed mind.* New York: Basic Books, 1960.

Sales, S. M. Economic threat as a determinant of conversion rates in authoritarian and nonauthoritarian churches. *Journal of Personality and Social Psychology,* 1972, *23,* 420–428.

Vacchiano, R. B., Strauss, P. S., & Schiffman, D. C. Personality correlates of dogmatism. *Journal of Consulting and Clinical Psychology,* 1968, *32,* 83–85.

24

Doubt
James R. Beck

Doubt is a state of mind characterized by an absence of either assent or dissent to a certain proposition. It is a suspension of commitment to belief or disbelief, either because the evidence pro and con is evenly balanced (positive doubt) or because evidence is lacking for either side (negative doubt, exemplified by the apostle Thomas). Doubt is thus an integral part of each person's belief system, since it is impossible for anyone to firmly believe or fully disbelieve all propositions of which he or she is aware. Yet in spite of the natural occurrence of doubt in human cognition, many people view doubt as a negative mindset to be avoided if at all possible.

Doubt is a topic of interest to scholars from three academic disciplines. Philosophers study doubt because of its epistemological implications in relation to knowledge, truth, and awareness of existence. Theologians are concerned with doubt because it often occurs as a prelude to belief or as a precursor of disbelief. Psychologists investigate doubt because of the emotions which often accompany it (anxiety, depression, or fear) and because in certain pathologies doubt can become obsessional and debilitating.

Doubt, Unbelief, and Ambivalence

Doubt should be differentiated from unbelief. Unbelief is a positive conviction of falsity regarding an issue and hence is a form of belief. Doubt does not imply a belief in a contrary position; it is simply being unconvinced. If, however, doubt becomes pervasive and dominates the thinking of a person regarding all issues, it is more appropriately called skepticism (or definitive doubt). The skeptic despairs of ever knowing truth with certainty.

Doubt can also be distinguished from ambivalence. Ambivalence is a state of mind characterized by the concurrent presence of two or more differing feelings toward the same object. Ambivalence, in massive quantities, is classically seen as a primary indicator of schizophrenia, whereas massive doubt is more often a part of obsessional disorders. Indecisiveness and vacillation, although related to doubt, refer more to a lack of commitment to a proposition or to a frequent change of opinion.

Normal doubt can be differentiated from abnormal doubt chiefly by the degree to which the doubt impairs daily living. Doubt is normal when it does not dominate a person's thinking, when it is overshadowed by stable beliefs, and when the goal of the doubt is resolution into belief or disbelief. Doubt is also normal when employed, as Descartes advocated, for the purpose of seeking truth. Normal doubt is a type of mental clarification and can help a person better organize his or her beliefs. Developmental theorists have noted several phases of life when doubts are characteristically found: in adolescence, when the teen-ager moves from childhood credulity toward a personalized belief system, and in the middle years, when issues of competence and direction predominate (Grant, 1974). Abnormal doubt focuses on issues having little consequence or issues without grave implications of error.

Religious Doubt

Religious doubt has been a concern of believers from biblical days to the present. In the Garden of Eden the serpent used doubt as a tool to move Eve from a position of belief to one of disobedience. Abraham, Job, and David all had times of doubt which were painful yet growth-producing. The best-known example of doubt in the Bible is Thomas, who was absent when Jesus made a postresurrection appearance to the apostles. Jesus showed the 10 his hands and his side (John 20), evidence that dispelled their doubt as to his identity. When told of Jesus' appearance, Thomas replied that he would not believe until he too had seen the evidence. Eight days later Jesus reappeared, showed Thomas his wounds, and made a gracious plea for faith.

By way of contrast, Jesus consistently condemned unbelief wherever he found it. Presumably, Jesus tolerated doubt because it was a transitory, nonpermanent state of mind, whereas he condemned unbelief because it was a fixed decision often accompanied by hardness of heart. In general, the evidence seems to indicate that Jesus showed a tolerant attitude toward doubt and a negative view toward unbelief. Guinness (1976) cautions, however, that Scripture sometimes uses the word *unbelief* to refer to doubt (Mark 9:24). Hence exegetical care is needed when interpreting the Bible's teachings regarding doubt.

Doubt is a problem in theological systems committed to inscripturated truth. For example, evangelical Christians are generally not tolerant of doubt if it is prolonged, unyielding, and centered on cardinal truths. Doubt is not so much a problem in liberal theologies since truth is more relative and less certain. Thus, the conservative Christian community sees doubt as risky and dangerous, whereas the liberal Christian community sees doubt as a sign of healthy intellectual inquiry. Doubt is resolved into belief or disbelief in any of four ways: through conversion, through liberalization, through renewal, or through emotional growth (Helfaer, 1972).

Normal doubt tends to appear when a person's belief system "does not protect the individual in his life experiences and from its more painful states" (Helfaer, p. 216). Even so, it is possible for someone to construct rigid defenses designed to ensure belief and prevent doubt at all costs. Cults are noted for such an approach, which discourages any reexamination of beliefs (Cohen, 1972).

Doubt and Psychopathology

In psychopathology doubt often occurs as a prominent symptom in the obsessive-compulsive disorders. Earlier in the twentieth century a special diagnostic category was created called *folie du doute*, or doubting mania. The disorder was described as an extreme self-consciousness and a preoccupation with hesitation and doubt. The condition was frequently considered progressive and incurable. Eventually the disorder was seen as but one variety of an obsessive-compulsive disorder, since the doubting mania was accompanied by overconscientiousness, fears of contamination, and other obsessive-compulsive characteristics.

The obsessive doubter is one whose symptoms have taken a cognitive rather than a predominantly behavioral form. In other words, the doubter is usually more obsessive than compulsive, although the dynamics behind either form is similar. The obsessive doubter usually centers his or her thinking on some imponderable issue which is just beyond the pale of provability. For example, the doubter may fret over issues of existence (Do I really exist?) or over issues of reality (Did I actually put a stamp on the letter I just mailed?). As the doubter becomes more and more proficient in his or her ruminations, an elaborate network of essentially futile mental operations is created. This network of doubts serves several secondary purposes usually described as secondary gains. For example, decisions can be delayed, responsibilities can be laid aside, and action can be postponed. Obsessive doubters with high intellectual capacity can create such doubts that their friends are likewise captivated by the issues. Other issues over which doubters can obsess include paternity, memory, and length of life.

If the obsessive doubter is religious, the doubts will likely involve issues of God's existence, God's involvement in human affairs, salvation, security, and one's eternal state. Doubters who are serious students of Scripture will find an ample supply of issues that qualify for genuine obsessing—that is, issues that are essentially unanswerable or imponderable. For example, the obsessive doubter who reads Jesus' statement, "If anyone is ashamed of me and my words, the Son of Man will be ashamed of him" (Luke 9:26), will worry about a specific time of embarrassment or shame in the past. Soon all confidence and security disappear, and the doubter fears eternal damnation.

There are several characteristics of the teachings of Jesus which seem to aggravate the obsessive doubter (Beck, 1981). Jesus frequently used themes of exclusivity (Matt. 10:33), absoluteness (Luke 18:22), abstractness (Mark 9:43,45), impossibility (Mark 10:25), and prohibition (Luke 13:28). Any of these themes can aggravate the obsessive's tendency to be overconscientious, rigid, and concrete, resulting in doubts.

The etiology of obsessive doubting is similar to that of the obsessive-compulsive disorder in general (Salzman, 1968). Professional help is indicated in cases of obsessive doubting. If treatment commences soon enough in the process, the prognosis is generally favorable. Therapy can help the sufferer to learn new channels for coping with anxiety and new patterns of effective decision making.

In summary, doubt can be a valuable part of one's life if its goal is resolution and if it results in deeper commitment to existing beliefs and less commitment to extraneous or harmful presuppositions (Pruyser, 1974). All belief has about it a feeling of resolved doubt. Hence as the doubter moves toward belief, his or her life is enriched by the resulting relief and satisfaction.

References

Beck, J. R. Treatment of spiritual doubt among obsessing evangelicals. *Journal of Psychology and Theology*, 1981, 9, 224–231.

Cohen, J. *Psychological probability*. London: Allen & Unwin, 1972.

Grant, V. W. *The roots of religious doubt and the search for security*. New York: Seabury, 1974.

Guinness, O. *In two minds: The dilemma of doubt and how to resolve it*. Downers Grove, Ill.: Inter-Varsity Press, 1976.

Halfaer, P. M. *The psychology of religious doubt*. Boston: Beacon Press, 1972.

Pruyser, P. W. *Between belief and unbelief*. New York: Harper & Row, 1974.

Salzman, L. *The obsessive personality*. New York: Science House, 1968.

25

Envy
James R. Beck

Envy is a bad feeling stirred up because of the presence of something good in another person but lacking in oneself. This emotion has received considerable attention from the authors of Scripture, theologians, and psychologists. A surprising degree of unanimity characterizes both the secular and sacred views of envy; namely, envy is universal in its occurrence, is destructive in its impact on the human personality, and can become a dominant, invasive emotion if left unchecked. While not a part of the well-known pantheon of vices such as greed, wrath, or jealousy, envy is a powerful emotion that deserves more attention than it usually receives.

Envy has several components. First, at least two persons are involved: the envier and the persons being envied. The presence of envy can be completely unknown by those around the envier, since no verbal communication regarding the envy must occur in order for it to be present. Second, the envier must be aware of some feature or facet of another's life which he regards as good and which he feels is missing in his own life. In other words, envy can only occur when a person perceives himself or herself in a position inferior to another.

Hence the issue of self-esteem is related to the problem of envy. Third, the envier experiences a sadness that the missing feature is not present in his or her own life. When envy is a major feature of one's own personality, life becomes a constant, dreary calculation of how others are better, and the self is saddened because of it.

Emulation is the positive counterpart of envy (Davidson, 1908). Emulation similarly involves at least two people and a sense of inferiority or lack on the part of one of the two. But the component of sadness is replaced by a desire to obtain the missing feature of life by achievement or growth. Emulation sees the other person as a friend; envy sees the other as a rival. Envy is selfish; emulation is constructive and geared toward change. Envy often wishes harm to the other or rejoices if bad fortune befalls the envied person; emulation has a positive force to it.

Authors disagree on the precise difference between envy and jealousy. Although they are related emotions, jealousy often involves three persons, is based in fear, and includes the strong desire to possess exclusively the item or person of desire. Jealousy is wanting to hold on to what one already has, and envy is a sadness regarding what one does not have (Walker, 1939).

In the Old Testament envy is described as a powerful enemy (Prov. 27:4) and a destructive force (Job 5:2; Prov. 14:30). The insidious emotion of envy was powerful in the life of Saul (1 Sam. 18:9), Rachel (Gen. 30:1), and the brothers of Joseph (Gen. 37:11). (Many versions substitute "jealousy" for the proper "envy" in these passages.) In the New Testament the verb form for envy occurs one time, in Galatians 5:26, where the exhortation to avoid envy is strongly given. Envy appears in lists of the acts of a sinful nature (Rom. 1:29; Gal. 5:21; 1 Tim. 6:4; Titus 3:3; 1 Peter 2:1). Christian ministry can be prompted by envy (Phil. 1:15), and envy was a driving emotion behind the actions of those who called for the death of Jesus (Mark 15:10).

Catholic theologians have regarded envy as a capital (deadly or cardinal) sin because it leads a person to other sins (Meagher, O'Brien, & Aherne, 1979). Because it was regarded as a cardinal sin it was treated extensively by Dante and Chaucer. Envy is described as a sin because it is opposed to benevolence, an essential ingredient in charity (Herbst, 1967).

In psychology the theoreticians who have had the greatest interest in the emotion of envy are those of psychoanalytic persuasion. Envy was early recognized as a harmful and detrimental emotion by psychoanalysts. Freud gave extensive treatment to the concept of envy in his theory of penis envy as a factor in the development of the female personality, a concept which many recent authors dispute extensively. Freud also saw envy as a powerful factor in the sociopsychological develop-ment of a sense of community. More recent analysts such as Klein (1957) postulate a very early developmental origin for the emotion. Klein feels that an infant receives a supply of mother's milk with either a sense of gratitude (necessary for the later task of love) or with a sense of envy (the base for later pathology).

Van Kaam (1972) has aptly integrated the destructiveness of envy in a moral sense (as described in Scripture) with the psychologically harmful impact of envy as documented by the analysts.

References

Davidson, W. L. Envy and emulation. In J. Hastings (Ed.), *Encyclopedia of religion and ethics*. New York: Scribners, 1908.

Herbst, W. Envy. In Editorial Staff at Catholic University of America (Eds.), *New Catholic encyclopedia*. New York: McGraw-Hill, 1967.

Klein, M. *Envy and gratitude: A study of unconscious sources*. New York: Basic Books, 1957.

Meagher, P. K., O'Brien, T. C., & Aherne C. M. (Eds.). *Encyclopedic dictionary of religion*. Philadelphia: Sisters of St. Joseph of Philadelphia, 1979.

Van Kaam, A. *Envy and originality*. Garden City, N.Y.: Doubleday, 1972.

Walker, W. L. Envy. In J. Orr (Ed.), *The international standard Bible encyclo-paedia*. (Rev. ed.). Grand Rapids: Eerdmans, 1939.

26

Jealousy
James R. Beck

Variously described as a sin, an emotion, an anxiety state, or a trait, depending on the perspective of the definer, jealousy is almost as old as the human race (Cain and Abel). Perhaps it is because it is such a pervasive ingredient in the human experience that it is so difficult to define. Scripture describes jealousy as cruel (Song of Sol. 8:6), angry (Prov. 6:34), and frustrating (Prov. 27:4), but does not directly label jealousy as a sin. In fact, most biblical references to jealousy center around God as a jealous God. God's name is jealous (Exod. 34:14); idolatry is banned on the basis of God's jealousy (Exod. 20:5); God views the church with godly jealousy (2 Cor. 11:2); we can provoke God to jealousy through idolatrous behavior (1 Cor. 10:22). These figures of speech point to the intensity of God's affection, fervency, and sincere love for his own (Harris, Archer, & Waltke, 1980).

Jealousy always involves three persons: self, a loved one, and a rival. Feelings of fear arise in the self when there is a threatened (real or imagined) loss of the affection of the loved one. A third person is always involved. "Jealousy is never wholly rational" (Cameron, 1963,

157

p. 490). Fear can be accompanied by hostility toward the rival, and both are often intense emotions because the threatened loss strikes at one's self-esteem and narcissism. Opinions vary as to whether there is a cohesive continuum connecting "normal" jealousy with the extreme instance of morbid or delusional jealousy. Some theories posit similar dynamics for both, while others see them as different.

Jealousy is usually encountered in one or more of five different settings. The first setting occurs in the context of sibling rivalry. An only child of preschool age will often exhibit signs of jealousy when a sibling is brought home for the first time to join the family. The young child is suddenly dethroned from exclusive access to parental affection to a position where all the good emotional supplies in the family must be shared, and with a newcomer at that. Regressive behavior (soiling, thumb sucking, baby talk) may occur, or the displaced child may exhibit aggressive behavior toward the new infant (Anthony, 1970). Sibling rivalry can persist throughout childhood and even into the adult years (cf. Jacob and Esau). The second setting for jealousy is in the peer relationships which children establish in schools and neighborhoods as their social skills develop. The success or failure children experience as these friendships develop can have a powerful impact on their adult social behavior.

Love and romance provide the third major setting for jealousy. Insecure persons who are enjoying the affections of a loved one can become obsessed with losing that affection to another. Jealousy in this context can become insidious, since it preys on the unknowable aspect of a relationship and can grow into monstrous proportions. Jealousy will eventually destroy a relationship, sometimes even creating what it mistakenly suspected initially. In the Old Testament a special provision was made for the jealous husband: the offering of jealousy and the waters of jealousy (Num. 5:11–31). If a husband suspected his wife of adultery and she denied it, they were to go to a priest and present an offering. The wife would drink water mixed with soil, which would produce health in her if she were innocent and would cause her death if guilty.

The fourth occurrence of jealousy is rare but indicative of the destructive quality of jealousy: the morbidly jealous murderer. Mowat (1966) found that morbid jealousy accounted for 12 percent of insane male murderers incarcerated at Broadmoor in England. The crime was most frequently committed by bludgeoning or strangulation. Most morbidly jealous murderers are male; most victims are wives or mistresses. On the average these murderers had been married 10 years and had been delusional for half that time.

Finally, jealousy is a frequent symptom among the paranoid. Jealousy operates under the defense mechanisms of denial and projection and thrives in personalities with narcissistic wounds and fragile self-esteem structures. Suspicion and mistrust abound in the jealous person (Meissner, 1978), and false judgments, illogical deductions, and misinterpreted trivia feed it. While not the most important symptom of the paranoid person, jealousy is a significant one and one that greatly impairs the quality of life.

References

Anthony, E. J. The behavior disorders of children. In P. H. Mussen (Ed.), *Carmichael's manual of child psychology.* New York: Wiley, 1970.

Cameron, N. *Personality development and psychopathology.* Boston: Houghton Mifflin, 1963.

Harris, R. L., Archer, G. L., & Waltke, B. K. *Theological wordbook of the Old Testament.* Chicago: Moody Press, 1980.

Meissner, W. W. *The paranoid process.* New York: Aronson, 1978.

Mowat, R. R. *Morbid jealousy and murder: A psychiatric study of morbidly jealous murderers at Broadmoor.* London: Tavistock, 1966.

27

Love
Ronald H. Rottschafer

The word *love* is used broadly and has such a variety of meanings that the concept, although familiar, is difficult to define. It helps to define love by specifying the context in which it is used. When a person says to an intimate friend, "I love you," there is quite a difference from the meaning of the word in the sentence, "I love your outfit."

Love, then, has specific, contextual meanings. However, in the widest usage it generally refers to a strong attraction toward an object—a desire to reduce the distance between that object and oneself. For example, if one loves either a person or a thing, one exhibits more of a yearning for that person or object, a desire to clasp it excitedly or fondly, than if the object were merely attractive or of some interest. To love always implies personal investment in the object of love; where there is no evidence of such personal caring, one may question whether love exists for the object.

Kinds of Love

The ancient Greeks specified four kinds of love, a classification that is still widely used today. The most general form is brotherly love, *philia*, love for one's fellow humans including care, respect, and some compassion for the plight of others. The most common form is friendship. A second kind of love, *agapē*, is seen in our love for God, a reverence for and deep acknowledgement of the divine being of God, including his commandments for mankind. Third, there is erotic love (*erōs*), an affectionate, tender hungering for union with the loved one, a passionate yearning for full relationship which, although it may include genital stirrings, does not necessarily have to do so. Both the Latins and the Greeks had different words for love and sex. Eros was made a god, not sex (May, 1969). The fourth kind of love is *libido*, sexual love, physical and emotional need that ends in the physical release of tensions in the act of sexual intercourse. Erotic love grows on and on; libidinal love builds up and is released.

In modern usage the word *love* most commonly connotes deep feelings between a man and a woman. There is a differentiation between the state of love and the actual feelings of love. The state of love implies a sense of committed caring and responsibility whereby there is concern and action taken for the well-being of the loved one. This state does not necessarily have to include actual feelings within a person toward the love object. When one allows himself or herself to *feel* love, however, there is an inner awareness of affect, of involvement from the heart rather than from habit or obligation. A state of love without corresponding feelings within leaves the persons involved somewhat distant and colorless. Many suspect that such love is not genuine. Whether that is true or not, when one does not feel something within, this many reflect the person's inability to do so. Some persons are not emotionally mature enough to feel the inner stirrings of love.

How We Learn to Love

The study of early mother-child interactions has made clear that infants need a symbiotic acceptance by the mother that conveys adequate nurturance both physically and emotionally. The infant, and later the child, grows best in a climate of unconditional love where the mother's patient responsiveness clearly demonstrates that she is here to take care of the baby, not vice versa. Love grows best when there is no fear of driving the mother away or consuming her with one's neediness.

The purpose of reliable, trustworthy parental love is to provide security and hence maximize the child's growth. It also teaches the baby how to love as he or she imitates the parents. The parents' ultimate purpose is to have the child internalize the love messages so he believes he is lovable. This belief becomes the inner confidence and self-esteem that not only promotes exploration, learning, and growth, but also becomes the grounds for loving others in turn.

As the person grows through the various stages and cycles of life, he or she experiences different needs, and hence differing forms of love are sought (Orlinsky, 1972). Thus, the infant seeks nurturance, the child responsiveness, the preadolescent a close friend, the teen a lover, and the adult a spouse. Personal love relationships foster psychological growth. There is a cyclical rhythm to these relationships all through the life cycle; closeness provides the inner fuel to separate the individuate, and hence climb to a new level where one again develops a new communion before pushing on again. In communion there is cooperation and mutual sharing to satisfy each other's needs. In individuation the love of self is stressed by assertiveness and contest. Love must include mutuality and individuality, other *and* self. In Judeo-Christian thinking this same theme characterizes the relationship between God and persons.

One of the most difficult aspects of love relationships is to maintain a rich sense of self within the context of loving the other person. Many personal-emotional problems seen in psychotherapy relate to a fear of love based on the loss of self in the relationship (Branden, 1980).

Degrees of Love

There are different degrees to which one shows love, that is, various depths of loving interpersonally. Perhaps the most shallow form of love is fearful clinging. Here the person's immaturity includes an overwhelming dependency that bonds lover to loved one out of fear of loss. Up the scale one step from clinging is love by obligation, where one feels stuck with the so-called loved one and thus cares out of duty. This is seen especially in marriages where the mates feel little personal-emotional commitment but stay together for the children's sake. Both these forms of love are noteworthy for their lack of genuine mutuality and the creative joy that love should bring.

Progressing upward in terms of levels of loving, we find unrequited love, the kind of one-way loving where despite the inequality of feelings one person loves another who does not return the love. Often there is frustration for the person not receiving love, but he or she may still choose to demonstrate a genuine loving care for the love object. This may be seen in parental care for seriously retarded children or in a marriage where one mate does all the loving and is relatively satisfied.

Further upward toward full mutual love are relationships that are reasonably stable, partially gratifying, but less than one or both partners would like to have. Whether through carelessness or lack of sophistication the partners are friendly, helpful, and generally affectionate but do not dare risk the deeper revelations of self and the explorations of the full range of emotions. Perhaps most marriages settle for, or degenerate into, this kind of reasonable if not entirely satisfying kind of love.

The quality of love in relationships between persons need not necessarily be impugned because there are problems or troubles. All human relationships have difficulties, hurts, disappointments, and problems. These can, in fact, bind persons closer together as they seek to solve those issues. The worst one can expect, of course, is that the problems will erode the rapport between partners.

Mature Love

In a full sense of mutual human love we should expect several elements to exist. First of all is the willingnesss of each partner to be involved in the relationship as deeply as possible in four distinct ways: physically, intellectually, emotionally, and spiritually.

Secondly, full love involves both a giving and a receiving of love by each partner. That means that each person is responsible for giving to as well as getting from the other. Serious problems in the relationship can result when either partner is not giving or getting enough out of the relationship. Love is not giving, as popularly thought; it includes both giving and getting (Rottschafer, 1980). There has to be a daily monitoring of the balance between these two plus the willingness to correct the inequalities. The ratio of how much one gives to how much one gets (whether by taking or by receiving) may vary from day to day, but over time the health of the relationship depends on a balance between these two.

Thirdly, mature love includes as full an experiencing of the broad range of human emotions as is possible. Therefore, in full love the partners open themselves to both joy and sorrow, agony and ecstasy, always keeping in mind the needs of both self and other as the experiences and feelings of life are shared. Love is an art that needs to be learned and practiced throughout one's entire lifetime (Fromm, 1956).

Lastly, full love must include a willingness to commit to one's loved object, whether country, home, family, child, mate, or friend. Commitment involves promise, deliberate intention to take the bad with the good, and a willingness to share one's life with the loved one. Commitment brings mutual trust for quality care in the now, plus predictable, responsible, mutual involvement in the future. Many current social, emotional, and physical ills can be seen as directly related to an absence of these qualities of love.

References

Branden, N. *The psychology of romantic love*. Los Angeles: J. P. Tacher, 1980.

Fromm, E. *The art of loving*. New York: Harper & Row, 1956.

May, R. *Love and will*. New York: Norton, 1969.

Orlinsky, D. E. Love relationships in the life cycle: A developmental interpersonal perspective. In H. Otto (Ed.), *Love today*. New York: Association Press, 1972.

Rottschafer, R. H. Giving and getting: A clinical and spiritual evaluation. *The Bulletin of the Christian Association for Psychological Studies*, 1980, 6(2), 23–28.

28

Maturity
John D. Carter

Until recently psychologists who described human personality focused a great percentage of their efforts on identifying the pathological aspect of personality. The diagnosis and classification of various forms of mental illness as well as the development of numerous psychotherapies constitute a large portion of psychology. Within the last 25 years there has been a growing attempt to describe the positive potential of human nature. This positive potential does not refer to the normal personality or the personality of the average person. Rather than focusing on the normal, psychologists have attempted to define the highest characteristics of human functioning.

Most psychologists use the term *maturity* to describe the positive potential of human beings. Occasionally the terms *self-actualized, transcendent, healthy* or *authentic personality* are used by some psychologists. Since these concepts are relatively equivalent, the more frequently used concept of maturity or mature personality will be used throughout this chapter to describe the healthy personality.

Rogers (1961) lists two characteristics of the "self that truly is"; Maslow (1954) names 14 characteristics of self-actualizers; Allport

(1961) cites 6 aspects of the mature person; and Jahoda (1958) summarizes 6 aspects of positive mental health. In spite of the difference in terminology and length of their descriptive lists, these and other psychologists agree substantially on the nature of maturity. The differences are essentially over the degree of detail each author wished to address. Therefore, maturity will here be described in terms of 5 basic dimensions: 1) having a realistic view of oneself and others; 2) accepting oneself and others; 3) living in the present but having long-range goals; 4) having values; and 5) developing one's abilities and interests and coping with the task of living. While the list could be extended or elaborated upon in more detail, these dimensions cover the basic aspects of maturity.

Psychologists are not the only ones to speak of maturity. The New Testament repeatedly uses the concept to describe the character of Christian experience. The biblical word for mature is *teleios*, which is translated "perfect" in the King James Version and "mature" in most recent versions. Its basic meaning is mature, complete, or fully developed, and it refers to the potential of the person or thing to grow, develop, or become complete.

Psychological Perspective

Realistic view of self and others

This dimension involves an accurate, objective evaluation of oneself and others. Maslow (1954) lists this dimension first in describing self-actualizing people. Allport (1961) calls it self-objectification—the ability to know and understand oneself, to recognize how one's present behavior and reactions were influenced by similar experiences in the past. This dimension also represents the whole development of the ego in Freudian thinking (Freud, 1927).

A realistic view of the self often may be obtained by asking oneself such questions as, "What kind of things can I do best?" "What are my strengths and weaknesses?" At the same time it is necessary to ask, "Would others agree, and have I had some success in my area of strength?" It is important to realize that people often have more than one real talent and a host of lesser abilities. In addition, one's talents and abilities are often related to one's interests (Allport, 1961). Often a person finds that he is good at doing the things he likes to do, or can learn to do them more quickly than someone who does not share those interests. The variety of interests an individual has is related to the variety of his abilities. Consequently, in gaining a realistic view of the self, an examination of one's interests may be very helpful in discovering one's abilities and potential.

The immature person often makes one of two errors in gaining a realistic view of himself. The first is to assume he is very capable or talented in one or more areas when he is not. Coupled with this error is the assumption that others have little or no real ability, having achieved their office, job, or position of responsibility by coincidence. This first error is often observed in children and particularly in adolescents who seem convinced that they can do things much better than just about anyone. This is also the error of the "armchair" or "Monday morning quarterback," who is certain he could have done a much better job than the real player. The second error is the reverse of the first. This person says he is untalented and really can't do anything very well. In fact, he says most anyone can do almost anything better than he can.

A person with realistic self-perception avoids both errors. He knows his strengths and his weaknesses and does not over- or underestimate either. He can also laugh at himself (Allport, 1961). Just as there was a correlation between one's view of himself and others in both errors of immaturity, so there is a close relationship in a realistic view of self and a realistic view of others. When a person can perceive his own strengths, abilities, and talents as well as his lack of ability in certain areas, he can then also perceive the talents of others accurately.

One may see that his friends and neighbors have similar strengths or weaknesses or quite different ones. (Since an accurate view of self and others is related, one can begin to grow by starting with either. However, since everyone spends more time with, and has more information about himself, it is often easier to begin with oneself.)

Accepting self and others

This second dimension of maturity is closely related to the first. Rogers (1961) so stresses the importance of this dimension that he divides it into its components and discusses each separately. Adler (Ansbacher & Ansbacher, 1956) repeatedly stressed the acceptance of others, calling it social interests and social feeling—a feeling of brotherliness toward one's fellows. To Sullivan (1953) relating to others in a healthy way and mutually meeting each other's needs is the very nature of personality.

Accepting means allowing, believing, or recognizing that something is true or real in one's inner experience. It does not imply that whatever needs to be accepted is good, valuable, or right, but only that it really exists. For example, everyone has a variety of hopes, fears, desires, and aspirations. These are not all good or desirable, but they are all real.

Their reality must be accepted if one is to be mature. They must be accepted as existing now in order for change or improvement to occur. Suppose a child gets in trouble with the neighbors by walking on their grass and picking their flowers, but his parents say to the neighbors he is a good boy and wouldn't do such a thing. The longer the parents fail to accept the reality of the child's bad behavior (and thus their relationship to it), the more likely the child is to continue and the more the relationship with the neighbors will degenerate.

In addition, acceptance means that the self or other selves are approved as persons or personalities apart from however many imperfections exist. The immature individual often confuses some specific habit, attitude, or action with the total person and rejects the person, rather than accepting the total person as worthwhile and more important than the undesirable aspect.

Living in the present

The third dimension of maturity is living in the present but having long-range goals. For Adler (Ansbacher & Ansbacher, 1956) maturity involves living in the world of others and finding meaningful work. The productive orientation described by Fromm (1947), which touches on several dimensions, includes meaningful work for the person and for the common good. Rogers (1961) calls the multitude of feelings that are related to the network of interaction patterns involved in living "being complexity"—that is, one is involved in many interpersonal relationships, both in the home and occupationally, with both positive and negative feelings. A person is all of these feelings; he is a complex being in the present.

Living in the present means facing and coping with one's present circumstances and situations. This involves dealing with and acknowledging the importance of one's self, job, church, friends, family, and so on. Each and all of these situations could be described as "where I am." Each has some positive and negative qualities; it meets some needs but not others. The mature person is aware of these qualities and his needs. He is able to see what is good and bad as well as what can and cannot be changed in each situation. In each the mature person has some goals that he would like to see accomplished and is aware of the present state of progress toward these goals. The immature person tends to live with the "if only" or the "when" attitude—"if only it were as good as it used to be" or "won't it be grand when." In either case there is little or no acceptance of the present situation and the person's responsibility in it and for it, or for changing it.

In addition, the mature person is aware that the present is not all that it could be or all that he would like it to be. Consequently he develops goals toward which he directs the course of his activity and life. Maslow (1954) refers to this quality in terms of mature people being characterized by a high degree of autonomy—that is, the ability to set their own goals. White (1959) describes a related aspect of goal setting as competence, the learned ability to cope with life tasks and to establish one's own goals in the situation. These goals usually are spread over several areas of life, such as familial, vocational, economic, and personal. The goals vary as to their clarity, permanence, and desirability. As he moves toward them, the mature person assesses his progress and directs or redirects his effort as needed. He may even change his goals. He remains master of his goals, and they remain flexible. The immature person tends to be mastered by his goals, becoming rigid and rejecting others or himself for not obtaining or making satisfactory progress toward his goals.

Having values

At first this may not appear to be a very psychological concept, but most psychologists recognize implicitly, if not explicitly, the existence of values for the mature or healthy person. Frankl (1963) describes having values as having "the will to meaning" which organizes all of one's life. Similarly Allport (1961) speaks of mature people having a unifying philosophy of life, while Maslow (1954) says the mature have a strong ethical sense and are able to resist the cultural pressure to conform. May (1953) speaks of values in terms of choice and the courage to decide how one is going to live. According to the psychologist, therefore, values must be self-chosen. They are not values the individual accepts because he is coerced by a society or a religion. Rather they are chosen by the mature person and integrated in the person's self-concept and behavior. They are thus not external but internalized values. Internalization and integration of values in the person implies harmony within the personality and purposefulness of his plans and actions. The immature person operates without values (e.g., a psychopath or a child) or with a rigid, threatening set of moral values (e.g., an obsessive-compulsive individual or a preadolescent) (White, 1964). Some immature persons alternate in various ways between these polarities of no values whatsoever on the one hand and rigid values on the other. The mature person is free of coercion because his values are self-chosen, and he acts accordingly. His values may be those of society or religion, but they have become his own by choice and internalization. Having values is clearly related to the long-range goals described above.

Developing one's abilities

Developing one's abilities and interests and coping with the problems of living is the final characteristic of maturity. The first characteristic focused more on self-perception, while this last one focuses on developing one's potential and skills and then utilizing them to create, make, and do things, both from necessity and for fun. This characteristic has a certain global and integrative quality which Freud would call reality orientation. In general, Rogers and Maslow call it self-actualization. More specifically Maslow (1954) refers to mature people as problem-centered, while Schactel (1959) refers to this ability to be involved in life as allocentricity, the ability to concentrate intensely on problems outside of oneself. Mature people are interested in their job, home, family, community, church, themselves, and so on. Of course their degree of interest may vary from area to area, but they have interest. They are not only capable of purposeful, creative action but they like to do things. They have a high degree of ability to concentrate on the task at hand but also to leave it when necessary. The immature person seems to have more dislikes than likes and has not developed his creative abilities nor the interest or ability to cope with life's daily tasks.

Coleman (1960) summarizes this final aspect of maturity as a task-oriented approach to life versus a defensive orientation. The immature person is trying to protect or defend himself from life, the world, others, and himself as well, while the mature person is involved in the tasks of life. He is able to modify his approach and try an alternate approach, and to accept a substitute goal and make compromises when necessary.

The Biblical Perspective

The biblical parallel to the psychological perspective becomes evident. The Bible asks man to have a realistic or objective view of himself and others. The basic requirement is to perceive the self, others, and the world from the divine perspective. God views each and every person as fallen and in need of a savior (Rom. 3:23). Once a person recognizes his need for a savior and responds, he becomes a new creature, with a new relationship to God, other men, and the world (2 Cor. 5:17). Another aspect of a realistic biblical view of self and others is the recognition of natural traits and abilities as well as one's spiritual gifts (1 Cor. 12:14–25) and his place in the spiritual body (1 Cor. 12:14; Eph. 4:4). A realistic perception of the need of others, both believers (Gal. 6:2) and unbelievers (Matt. 25:34–40), is the biblical expectation as well as a divine view of the social order (Rom. 13:1–3).

A second aspect of biblical maturity involves accepting oneself and others. Perhaps the clearest statement of this principle is given by Jesus: "Love your neighbor as yourself" (Matt. 22:39). It is important to note that the love of neighbor depends in quality and amount on love of self in the sense of acceptance, as described above. Acceptance means allowing the biblical view of sinfulness and fallenness to be true or real in my inner experience both before and after I become a Christian. Sinfulness and fallenness are not eliminated by being saved. Righteousness always belongs to Christ and is legally attributed to the person by God. It does not become a personal quality so the person can brag (Phil. 3:9) either before God or others. A corresponding view of others is also characteristic of the spiritually mature.

In accepting self and others one must recognize that both self and others are sinful and fallen. Each person is created in God's image (Gen. 1:27) and is also fallen (Rom. 5:12); each is redeemed or in need of redemption. God loves everyone whom he created, which means that everyone is worthwhile as a person. Hence, everyone should be accepted as a person. Acceptance as a person does not imply approval of all the person's behavior or motives. However, the Bible calls the mature believer to a very high level of love for other believers (1 John 3:16), to a deep sensitivity to their weaknesses (Heb. 12:12), and to the whole body as brothers and sisters in Christ (1 Cor. 12:25–26). The biblical words *agapē, philia,* and *koinōnia* call for a greater depth of warmth and maturity in a relationship than perhaps any psychologist emphasizes, other than Carl Rogers, who came from a Christian home (Rogers, 1961).

Third, living in the present with long-term goals is basic in the Scriptures. Now is the day of salvation, for the believer as well as the unbeliever. Salvation has an eternally present aspect. While the Bible describes the future life with God, there is very heavy emphasis on present actions and attitudes. The believer is to manifest the fruit of the Spirit in his life. Christ makes an observable difference in the believer's ongoing action. It is the carnal or immature who does not show an observable change. In fact, believers are warned not to long to leave the world but to live in it now (1 Cor. 5:9–10). "Abide" and "grow up in Christ" are repeatedly used to emphasize the current ongoing focus of the Christian. However, the Christian life is also described as a race with a prize (Phil. 3:14). Most clearly Paul makes the third aspect of maturity the model of the mature Christian life: "As many as would be perfect [mature—*teleiōs*] be thus minded" (Phil. 3:15). He describes his previous life in Judaism (Phil. 3:4–6), which he then gives up for Christ (Phil. 3:8), but the process does not end at that point. In verse 10 Paul goes on describing the model: "That I may know him, the power of his resurrection, the fellowship of his suffering, being conformable to his death." This last verb is a present participle and is the strongest possible way of stressing ongoing action—the focus is on the present. However, Paul further elaborates the model of maturity by saying, "Not as though I am already perfect [mature] but . . . I press to that which is before. . . . I press toward the mark of the high [upward] calling of God" (Phil. 3:14). Thus the model of the Christian has a present focus with long-range future goals.

A fourth characteristic of Christian maturity is having values which are self-chosen. Joshua, in the process of conquering and possessing the land, appeals to the Israelites, "Choose this day whom you will serve" (Josh. 24:15). Values are a "package plan" because they involve an integrated set of motives and actions, not just something one says he thinks is right. The value packages are clearly indicated in the descriptions of the flesh and the works of the Spirit. Paul in Philippians 3:8 describes a complete value rethinking, and accompanying actions are reinterpreted and reversed. However, the value reassessment is an ongoing process: "Not as though I had already attained or were already perfect, but this one thing I do, forgetting those things which are past, I press toward the mark" (Phil. 3:13–14). Thus the process of reassessing is an ongoing process that merges with the realistic evaluation of the self and the focus on the present, but is pulled forward and clarified by the long-range goal of the high calling of God. It is the commitment of the self to a set of values that reorganizes the person and gives him an identity. For the Christian this is union with Christ, which is so characteristically described by Paul with the phrase "in Christ."

The final characteristic of the mature Christian is developing one's abilities and interest in everyday living. The development and use of one's talents and gifts (Eph. 4:7) is a necessary part of Christian maturity, since they are given to the church for the work of the ministry (Eph. 4:12). Timothy is encouraged to rekindle the gift of God within him (2 Tim. 1:6). The encouragement of growth toward Christian maturity seems to be the purpose of the gifts and the goal of the ministry (Eph. 4:15–16). Interest in everyday living involves working to support oneself (1 Tim. 5:8). The daily tasks are not to be neglected or done grudgingly (Eph. 6:6; Col. 3:22). Thus, the developing of one's abilities, talents, and gifts begins to merge with Christian values and a biblically appropriate perception of oneself and others. This merger produces congruence in the mature Christian of all that he says and does (James 2:26; 1 John 3:18).

Perhaps this is best illustrated in the First Epistle of John where the apostle describes three criteria of mature Christian faith: believing the truth (Jesus is the Christ), loving the brotherhood, and practicing righteousness. These three criteria are repeated three times in the epistle. They tend to focus on three different aspects of the human person. Believing the truth has a strong cognitive component, while practicing righteousness has a strong behavioral focus and loving the brothers involves the emotional-motivational aspects.

These joint criteria thus emphasize the unified or integrated aspect of Christian maturity in the personality. The mature Christian's behavior, beliefs, and emotions are thus organized in a consistent, congruent, and unified pattern. He is interested in his daily life because this is where God has placed him (1 Cor. 7:20; Phil. 4:11; Heb. 13:5) and he acts as unto the Lord (Eph. 6:8). Every task or sphere of activities is infused with spiritual meaning and interest. He recognizes that every good thing in life is from God (James 1:17) and that there is much that is worthy of his attention and enjoyment in this life (Phil. 4:8). Furthermore, the mature believer is aware that the mandate to subdue the earth (Gen. 1:28) has never been revoked. On the other hand, the immature Christian is torn by conflict because he is pulled in two directions (James 1:8; 4:8) and because he is unclear about his identity; that is, he has not reckoned himself dead to sin and alive to God (Rom. 6:11). He has not embraced his identity as a new man or self but rather tries to operate as the old man which he is not.

By way of summary, five aspects or dimensions of maturity have been outlined. The parallel between the psychological and biblical implications has been developed and illustrated. However, when all five aspects of maturity are taken together, two new higher dimensions emerge: actualization and congruence. In discussing the five aspects a certain degree of overlap was evident. The overlap occurs because a mature person in either a psychological or biblical sense is integrated, has a purposeful or goal-directed quality about his life, and is open to himself and others; the immature person is disorganized, having either conflicting goals or no goal, and is unaware and unaccepting of various aspects of himself and others.

Christian Maturity and Actualization

As each of the aspects of maturity has a psychic and biblical parallel, so the processes of self-actualization and congruence have parallels.

Psychologically, actualization means developing one's body, mind, and emotions into a fully functioning person. Biblically it is the same; the process is parallel but the content is different. The non-Christian may actualize his full potential as a person made in God's image but fallen. The fall limits the potential and direction of self-actualization. It does not prevent the person from becoming a good, healthy, kind, and developed person, since the image is more fundamental than the fall. The fall marred the image of God in man (Berkhof, 1941). Some Christians seem almost to reverse the pattern, emphasizing the fall so much that it appears that fallen man is only tainted by the image. Counts (1973) calls this latter view "worm theology."

Many non-Christians show varying degrees of behavior and attitudes similar to the fruit of the Spirit. An individual may develop his humanity (the God-given divine image) by utilizing the principles of psychology and mental health, with or without the aid of a therapist, to become a more mature, healthy, self-actualized person. However, the most fully functioning non-Christian will not be characterized by a relationship to Christ or the body of believers, nor will he be motivated by *agapē* love, and his self-perception and perception of the cosmos will not be Christ-like in character.

The Christian, on the other hand, actualizes his potential as created, fallen, and redeemed. In the Christian the image is being renewed (Eph. 4:24; Col. 3:10). Christ becomes the model or ideal for the Christian and the Scriptures his guidelines. Since the Christian is related to the God of the universe, he becomes more in harmony (if he is growing and maturing) with the divine purpose and pattern in both himself and the world. This is the meaning of the renewing of the image; but note that it is a process—the removal of the effects of the fall on the image. Christian self-actualization moves toward perfection after Christ (Phil. 3:10–14). The non-Christian can become complete as a created and fallen person, while the Christian becomes complete (or rather, perfected) as created, fallen, and renewed.

The image here is the Greek long-distance runner moving through the race to the finish line. The runner forgets what is behind and does not consider himself to have arrived but presses forward toward the goal. This is similar to the growth process of self-actualization. The past becomes irrelevant because the person is moving forward, realizing that his goals are not yet achieved. Thus there is an awareness of one's progress without a sense of either failure or arrival. The focus of Christian maturity is the present, but with the knowledge that one is currently moving toward the goal. This goal is self-chosen. The mature believer wills or chooses to follow Christ, and Christ becomes his choice. Thus the biblical concept of salvation in its various facets parallels the psychological process of self-actualization described by Rogers (1959), Gendlin (1964), and Jung (1970).

Christian Maturity and Congruence

The dimension of congruence, consistency, or balance is also a biblical principle, and it is related to salvation and Christian maturity. While the Bible does not use the language of personality theory, it does describe human congruent functioning in its own terms. The congruence emphasized in Scripture usually involves a consistency between cognitive, affective, and/or motivated behavior. For example, "Faith without works is dead" (James 2:26); "Let us love not in word or tongue but in deed and in truth" (1 John 3:18); "If you love me keep my commandments" (John 13:34); "Out of the abundance of the heart the mouth speaks" (Matt. 12:34). In each of these examples consistency between inner aspects of the person and outer behavioral aspects is either described or encouraged as part of Christian living.

Furthermore, congruence in the Christian life is described by such concepts as fruit of the Spirit (Gal. 5:22–23) and the new man (Eph. 4:24; Col. 3:10). In each case a consistent pattern of behavior, attitudes, traits, and/or motives is described. Each is also contrasted with an antithetical pattern of the works of the flesh or the old man. In addition there is strong biblical exhortation and encouragement to try to live congruently. Regular incongruent living is biblically described as carnal (1 Cor. 3:3), or double-minded (James 1:8; 4:8). Finally, congruence in the Christian life is one of the major themes of 1 John. While more evidence could be cited, enough has been given to indicate that Scripture represents the mature Christian as living a congruent or consistent life in which his thoughts and beliefs, motives and feelings, and attitudes and behavior are consistent with each other and with Scripture.

Summary

To summarize, Scripture grounds Christian maturity in two process dimensions: actualization and congruence. Actualization has two aspects: 1) the process of salvation, which is described in terms of being saved, sanctified, glorified, and made like Christ; and 2) Scripture also uses the word *teleios* (perfect, mature, complete) to describe maturity. The process of salvation focuses on something that God causes to happen to the believer, while *teleios* seems to focus on the believer's choice or will (Phil. 3:14–15). Hence, the mature Christian becomes what he is—a son being renewed after the image—and becomes what he chooses, pressing toward the mark of the high calling of God.

The second process of Christian maturity is congruence, integrity, or consistency. The mature believer is characterized by the fruit of the Spirit. His actions and words flow consistently out of an inner thought and emotional life which has been committed to Christ. Since the mature believer lets the mind of Christ dwell in him, his actions follow congruently (Phil. 2:5–8)—that is, they are both Christ-like and self-congruent.

References

Allport, G. W. *The pattern and growth of personality.* New York: Holt, Rinehart, & Winston, 1961.

Ansbacher, H. L., & Ansbacher, R. R. (Eds.). *The individual psychology of Alfred Adler.* New York: Basic Books, 1956.

Berkhof, L. *Systematic theology* (2nd rev.). Grand Rapids: Eerdmans, 1941.

Coleman, J. C. *Personality dynamics and effective behavior.* Chicago: Scott, Foresman, 1960.

Counts, W. M. The nature of man and the Christian's self-esteem. *Journal of Psychology and Theology,* 1973, *1*, 38–44.

Frankl, V. *Man's search for meaning.* Boston: Beacon Press, 1963.

Freud, S. *The ego and the id.* London: Hogarth, 1927.

Fromm, E. *Man for himself.* New York: Holt, Rinehart, & Winston, 1947.

Gendlin, E. T. A theory of personality change. In P. Worchel & D. Byrne (Eds.), *Personality change.* New York: Wiley, 1964.

Jahoda, M. *Current concepts of positive mental health.* New York: Basic Books, 1958.

Jung, C. G. The structure and dynamics of the psyche. *The collected works* (2nd ed.). (Vol. 8). Princeton, N.J.: Princeton University Press, 1970.

Maslow, A. H. *Motivation and personality.* New York: Harper & Row, 1954.

May, R. *Man's search for himself.* New York: Norton, 1953.

Rogers, C. R. A theory of therapy, personality and interpersonal relationship, as developed in the client-centered framework. In S. Koch (Ed.), *Psychology: The study of science* (Vol. 3). New York: McGraw-Hill, 1959.

Rogers, C. R. *On becoming a person.* Boston: Houghton Mifflin, 1961.

Schactel, E. G. *Metamorphosis.* New York: Basic Books, 1959.

Sullivan, H. S. *The interpersonal theory of psychiatry.* New York: Norton, 1953.

White, R. W. Motivation reconsidered: The concept of competence. *Psychological Reports,* 1959, *66*, 297–333.

White, R. W. *The personality* (3rd ed.). New York: Ronald Press, 1964.

29

Mind-Brain Relationship
Stanton L. Jones

Throughout history human beings have noted a fundamental dichotomy in their experience. On the one hand, there are those aspects of reality characterized by what Hasker (1983) calls physical properties. These are properties that can characterize ordinary physical objects; for example, mass, length, color, electrical charge, and chemical composition can characterize such objects as a baseball, a finger, or a brain. On the other hand, there are aspects of reality characterized by "mental properties . . . which can only characterize an entity which is possessed of some kind of consciousness or awareness" (Hasker, 1983, p. 60). Vibrant hope, ecstatic joy, excruciating pain, or a firm intention to act are examples of this latter category.

If these two aspects of reality were totally separate, there would be no impetus for inquiry into the relationship of mind and brain. But the interrelationships of the two have been noted as often as the two have been distinguished. On the one hand, physical events can result in mental events, as when compression of the tissue of the thumb with a forceful blow from a hammer results in the predictable and unpleasant mental experience of pain. On the other hand, mental events can result in physical events, as when the mental image in a dream of an ax murderer attacking one's family produces accelerated heart rate and respiration, increased sweating, and other physical reactions.

The contemporary physical and behavioral sciences have further documented this interrelatedness. Neurosurgeons can elicit such mental experiences as vivid memories by electrical stimulation of certain brain tissues. Interference with the functioning of one part of the brain through injury or drugs drastically changes mental functioning. Imagery, hypnosis, and related "mental" practices are used to reduce or moderate physical processes such as skin temperature, blood pressure, or pain produced by documented physical disturbances. Yet contemporary research in brain functioning has not eliminated the question of mind-brain relationship.

The mind-brain (or more traditionally the mind-body) problem can be stated in two major questions: "Does the common distinction between mental and physical events support a further distinction between mind and body?" and "What is the nature of the relationship between mental and physical events in human existence?" Answers to these questions are important both for the understanding of our own natures and for other practical reasons as well. How one answers the mind-brain questions relates to one's position on such issues as determinism, sanctification, and bioethical matters (e.g., when a person should be pronounced clinically dead).

Major Relationship Theories

The major theories can be divided into two groups: monistic and dualistic. (For further information on these theories see Hasker [1983], Shaffer [1967], and specific cited works.)

Monistic theories

The monistic theories answer the mind-brain question by denying there is any legitimate distinction between mind and body and arguing that one type of event totally explains the other. One group would argue that only the physical is real, while another would argue that only the mental is real.

Materialistic views include many variants. Physicalism (or logical behaviorism) is the view arguing that only matter exists and that statements about mental events must be translated into statements about actual or potential behavior. Statements that cannot be so translated are not meaningful. "He is feeling angry" would be translated into a statement like "He is clenching his fists, yelling loudly, stomping his feet, and is likely to throw that chair" to be meaningful. In extreme versions of physicalism the existence of beliefs, thoughts, and other mental events is simply denied. In general, philosophers have rejected physicalistic theories as unacceptable because there are so many human experiences, such as pain or dreaming, for which no convincing behavioristic account can be given and the existence of which simply cannot be denied.

A more sophisticated materialistic view is the central-state identity theory. According to identity theory, mental events are real. Each mental event or state is, however, "identical with the property of being in a certain neurophysiological state" (Fodor, 1981, p. 116). For example, my belief that God exists is identical with my being in a certain brain state. My belief that God is a triune God is identical with a different brain state. This view has the advantage of allowing for the reality of mental events even when they give rise to no behavioral effects. Its simplicity in proposing only one type of substance (i.e., material substance) eliminates the problems of dualism, which will be discussed later. It allows for the potential explanation of mental events according to the same deterministic causal laws applied to all physical events; this is viewed as a strength by many scientists and a weakness by others who are concerned with avoiding deterministic explanations of human choice.

Two additional problems for identity theory are the implicit notions that every mental event is identical with a *certain* neurophysiological state and that *all* mental events must be neurophysiological states. The theory of functionalism has been proposed recently to remedy these problems (Fodor). Functionalists assert that different neurophysiological brain states and even other types of states, such as specific computer operations, can result in the same behavioral outcome and thus should be viewed as functionally equivalent mental states. Thus, like the identity theorist adherent the functionalist believes that each human mental event is a brain state. Unlike the identity theorist the functionalist emphasizes not the brain state (in computer terms, the hardware) but the functional or causal nature of the operations performed (the software). Mental states in humans are neurophysiological in nature, but two persons experiencing the memory of a specific picture may not be experiencing the identical brain state. What matters is that the result—in this case the memory—is the same. A further implication is the functionalist's willingness to attribute mentality to nonhuman animals, to machines designed to exhibit artificial intelligence, and even potentially to "a disembodied spirit" (Fodor, p. 118). The functionalist's theory is new and not widely critiqued. It seems a useful improvement on identity theory but shares with that theory the problem of how one gets from a purely mechanical event to a self-conscious awareness of a mental event. The functionalist's recognition that a computer can solve an algebraic equation as well as a human is not equivalent to proving that the computer experiences a conscious awareness of the act as a human does.

The final monistic theory is the opposite of the materialistic theories: the idealism of George Berkeley, who proposed that the concept of absolute (i.e., independent) matter or substance was nonsensical. Berkeley proposed instead that "to be is to be perceived" (cited in Hasker, 1983, p. 63); that is, the only meaningful way to discuss existence is in terms of perception or ideas. He did not, as is sometimes said, assert that the world is not real or that objects cease to exist when we close our eyes. He suggested that there are many perceiving human minds, and that an all-perceiving God undergirds the constancy of creation by the pervasiveness of his perceptions. He also asserted that the fact that things exist only as perceptions does not make them any less real. Thus, Berkeley solved the mind-brain problem by reducing matter to a special subset of ideas. All that exists is mental. Berkeley's theory has never been widely accepted as a theory of metaphysics. It has had more effect on epistemology in influencing the rise of empiricism (what we know comes from what we perceive alone) over rationalism. The idea of the absolute existence of matter seems firmly grounded in human experience.

Dualistic theories

Dualistic theories suggest that physical and mental entities are not just different ways of describing the same reality, but that mental and physical are fundamentally different in being distinct substances, events, properties, states, or relations (Shaffer, 1967, p. 341).

The classic dualistic theory is the dualistic interactionism of Descartes. Similar views go back at least as far as Plato. The different proposals vary in their details, but generally assert that mind and body are differentiable entities and that the two different types of entities causally interact in a meaningful way. Thus, when I think "I'd like to scratch my ear," this immaterial mental event is in some way picked up by the physical brain (which acts something like a radio receiver), is processed, and results in the predicted action. A scratch on the knee, on the other hand, is transmitted via the nervous system to the brain, where it is processed. The resulting brain states are picked up by the mind, and at that point (and not before) they become conscious impressions such as pain or discomfort. Mind and brain are viewed as interacting, yet neither is fundamentally dependent upon the other.

A fundamental difficulty for the dualistic interactionist is the need to specify the manner in which mind and brain are supposed to interact. Descartes proposed that the pineal gland deep within the brain was the locus for interaction, but this notion has been firmly refuted. Two prominent scholars recently stunned the scientific community with a reaffirmation of dualistic interactionism. Philosopher of science Karl Popper and distinguished neuroscientist John Eccles, in *The Self and the Brain* (1977), argued forcibly for the reality of supernatural entities not dependent upon physical bodies, and suggested that the mind affects the brain not at a specific point, as proposed by Descartes, but rather at a myriad of synaptic points throughout the central nervous system. They suggest that quantum indeterminancy opens an avenue for the alteration of the purely physical synaptic processes by mental influences, thus not violating the law of the conservation of energy.

The other fundamental difficulty for a dualistic theory is the commonly observed close correspondence between specific brain functions and specific mental events. If mind is supposed to be totally removed (though interactive) from brain functions, then why does a severe lesion in a certain area of the brain's frontal lobe have such regularly observed mental results (e.g., disruption of sequential planning abilities)? If the ability to plan intentionally is a capacity of the separate mind, why does a focal brain injury disrupt that capacity? The answer that has been historically given on this issue is that specific mental faculties are received and acted upon at certain points in the brain, and that impairment of brain tissues prevents that mental capacity from being clearly articulated in neurophysiological or behavioral events.

To many this answer is unsatisfactory. One problem is that it seems unlikely that a specific mental capacity continues in existence after disruption of the related brain tissues. A version of dualism proposed to mend this problem is epiphenomenalism. This view suggests that mental events are indeed real, but that they have no causal force. Epiphenomenalists suggest that only half of the interactionist's theory is correct, that physical events give rise to mental events. Our sense of the opposite sequence, that mental events cause physical events, is merely an illusion. We might suppose that a man could think of his wife and then stop work to call her. The epiphenomenalist would argue that brain processes, under the influence of such environmental stimuli as a picture of the wife on the desk or the wedding ring on the finger, caused both the mental event of a conscious thought about the wife and the behavioral event of calling her.

The final theory of mind-brain, and the most recent, is called emergentism (see Hasker, 1983; Sperry, 1980). Emergentism suggests that the physical and the mental are truly distinct, but that the mental is fundamentally dependent upon (or produced by) the physical, that is, the brain. As analogies Haskar points to a magnet and its magnetic field and the earth and its gravitational field. In both these cases the fields are real and distinct phenomena which nevertheless cannot exist apart from the physical entity from which they arise. The emergentist further believes that mental events can cause physical events. Sperry (1980) suggests that the mental properties supersede the neurophysiological events on which they are based. He illustrates this by noting that molecules of rubber can be organized into a wheel. By virtue of this higher level structure the atoms can be made to move in ways not at all predictable from the constituent parts, as when the wheel rolls downhill, forcing its molecules to move accordingly. Sperry argues that mental events act similarly in being "self determinant" (p. 200), capable of exerting independent causal forces on physical brain events. In summary, then, the emergentist suggests that mind emerges from the brain's functioning to become a distinct, separate, and causally efficacious agency. Brain scientist McKay (1978) has a similar view of mind and brain but stops short of Sperry's position that mental processes can change physical events. He suggests rather that different types of analysis are necessary at the physical and mental levels, and that determinism at the physical level is not incompatible with responsibility at the mental level.

Christian Parameters for Evaluation

Contrary to popular opinion, the Bible does not clearly endorse one option over another. The basic parameters for a Christian solution to the mind-brain problem can be summarized as follows. First, the idea of both physical and mental essences is not anathema to biblical perspectives on this issue. Christians accept the existence of a supernatural realm that includes God and other active beings, as well as the reality of a created world of physical existence of which we are a part (Gen. 2:7). Neither domain can be summarily discarded. Second, these two domains do interact; God is active in this world. Thus, while we may not be able to specify the mode of interaction between different essences, we are nonetheless assured that such interactions do occur. Third, our natural existence is an embodied existence, as testified to by the doctrines of creation (Gen. 1:26–31), resurrection (1 Cor. 15), and incarnation (John 1). Fourth, Christian theology has fairly consistently recognized an intermediate state between death and resurrection, which suggests that in some form human life must not be irrevocably dependent upon bodily existence. Fifth, Christians are universally committed to the human capacity for responsible action, a position that must lead us away from any mind-brain theory which entails mechanistic determination of human choice. This implies that human mental experiences cannot be regarded either as trivial events or as determined results of causal processes. Finally, a Christian view will be one that emphasizes "functional integration" (Cooper, 1982, p. 17) or human unity (McDonald, 1981). A careful exposition of biblical doctrines of creation, salvation, and sanctification reveals that human beings are unified beings and that God does not deal with isolated aspects of us, as is suggested when it is proposed that sanctification occurs by suppressing the body to set the soul free.

Scientific Parameters for Evaluation

Empirical research in the neurosciences forces us to see the physical and mental as intimately interrelated. Basic research with animals and clinical (surgical, psychological, pharmacological) research with humans has documented with increasing clarity how dependent the most complex of mental functions are upon physical brain functions. A well-informed view of mind and brain will take this contemporary research into account.

The neuroscientists themselves are split on these issues. Eccles and others remain staunch dualistic interactionists. McKay and Sperry are emergentists. Fodor (a philosopher) and others have offered the functionalist viewpoint, which many neuroscientists find compelling, especially those active in research in artificial intelligence. If there is a significant trend today, it would appear to be away from views that ignore mental events or explain them away as trivial (i.e., physicalism and logical behaviorism). The behavioral sciences are emphasizing the importance of mental events as real entities. Whether they are real entities that are brain states (identity theory), functional states, real yet spurious states (epiphenomenalism), dependent yet efficacious entities (emergentism), or wholly separate but interacting entities (interactionism) is still widely debated.

Conclusion

Using the parameters developed earlier, Christians would probably be on stable, acceptable ground both philosophically and scientifically in endorsing emergentism, dualistic interactionism, or a nonde-
terministic functionalism as an attempt to answer the mind-brain
problem. At the broadest possible level empirical brain science and
solid Christian scholarship are leading to similar conclusions—that
is, an appreciative view of the irreducibility of mental phenomena
and a solid emphasis on the fundamental unity of human existence.

References

Cooper, J. Dualism and the biblical view of human beings (2). *The Reformed
     Journal*, 1982, *32*(10), 16–18.

Fodor, J. The mind-body problem. *Scientific American*, 1981, *244*(1), 114–123.

Hasker, W. *Metaphysics: Constructing a world view*. Downers Grove, Ill.: Inter-
     Varsity Press, 1983.

McDonald, H. D. *The Christian view of man*. Westchester, Ill.: Crossway
     Books, 1981.

McKay, D. M. Selves and brains. *Neuroscience*, 1978, *3*, 599–606.

Shaffer, P. Mind-body problem. In P. Edwards (Ed.), *Encyclopedia of philoso-
     phy*. New York: Macmillan, 1967.

Sperry, R. W. Mind-brain interaction: Mentalism, yes; dualism, no. *Neuro-
     science*, 1980, *5*, 195–206.

30

Perfectionism
C. Markham Berry

O ne of those profound paradoxes that constitute human experience is a deeply embossed image of the perfect, which rubs against constant reminders that human life is imperfect. Somehow, without ever having known in experience the completely right, true, beautiful, or pure, we are aware of all of these. A person who believes himself to be perfect is considered deluded, yet one who denies the perfect has sacrificed something that is uniquely human.

The concept of the ideal, that internalized measure of the utterly perfect, is both our noblest friend and greatest tormentor. It forms the focus of much of human motivation and inspiration, and is, in one form or another, the goal of life's quest. Our ideals are larger than life itself. But this same internal structure that inspires the best can also become the anvil upon which the conscience hammers one into depressing, paralyzing feelings of guilt and worthlessness.

Most religions offer some solution to the pain of falling short of righteousness, but at the same time insist on a completely righteous God. Christian theologians have attempted to resolve this human dilemma by associating the ideal with love (Wesley, 1821) or with the charismatic (see Flew, 1934), but usually end up in the same dilemma as the psychologist. One is crushed by the demands of an absolute measuring rod, yet ignores it at great risk.

The richest psychological insights into the origin and function of this fundamental human paradox have come from the psychoanalysts. Freud identified two components of this idealizing internal structure: a standard that "finds itself possessed of every perfection that is of value," or the ego ideal, and the "faculty that incessantly watches, criticizes and compares," or the superego (1920/1963, p. 428). Often in his writing the term *superego* is used for both, and has two roots in human experience. The earliest of these is the primary narcissistic bliss of the infant who is entirely cared for, thoroughly loved, and knows no sin. The other is more external, coming from a complex identification with parents as powerful and good. In the conflictual matrix of the oedipal triangle an overtone of anxious danger to parental and societal criticism and norms is added (Freud, 1923/1961; Sandler, 1960).

More recent analytic thinkers relate these structural elements to the object relations of early infantile development, a process of the first two years of life. Kohut (1968) has described this process as the formation of part objects, when good, satisfying, and soothing, experiences tend to form around foci of "good self" and "good mother." These then become developmental lines that are not lost as the infant proceeds through separation and individuation but persist into adult life. One of these, the "grandiose cohesive self," matures into healthy self-esteem and confidence. The other, "the idealized parental imago," is the foundation of one's admiration of others and the ability to relate to them effectively.

Psychologists offer three general approaches to managing this threatening element of personality. 1) The superego becomes less ominous when insight is acquired into its roots in parental and social norms. 2) Some of the harshness can be relieved by behavioral methods, desensitizing responses to guilt and shame. 3) The superego will threaten us less if we can remodel our ideals into measures that are closer to our actual behavior. None of these approaches has been effective enough to be wholeheartedly endorsed by everyone. There is a consensus that the healthy person faces legitimate guilt and shame and struggles to find a way to improve behavior without letting the superego discourage or paralyze (Meninger, 1973).

The Christian therapist offers another insight into this human dilemma. The ideal can be seen as an internal structure designed by God to maintain a constant awareness of him in life. It serves to remind us constantly of our failings and our need for a Savior. We can have confidence and hope in two primary propositions: 1) The developmental process of the believer, while not complete here and now, will be. We will be perfected. 2) For now, our expectation is in Christ, not ourselves. The work that therapists, pastors, and friends do to bring growth, healing, and unity within the body of Christ will be completed one day in him (Eph. 4:7, 16).

References

Flew, R. N. *The idea of perfection in Christian theology*. London: Oxford University Press, 1934.

Freud, S. Introductory lectures on psycho-analysis. In J. Strachey (Ed. and trans.), *The standard edition of the complete psychological works of Sigmund Freud* (Vols. 15 & 16). London: Hogarth, 1963. (Originally published, 1920.)

Freud, S. The ego and the id. In J. Strachey (Ed. and trans.), *The standard edition of the complete psychological works of Sigmund Freud* (Vol. 19). London: Hogarth 1961. (Originally published, 1923.)

Kohut, H. The psychoanalytic treatment of narcissistic personality disorders. *Psychoanalytic Study of the Child*, 1968, *23*, 86–113.

Menninger, K. *Whatever became of sin?* New York: Hawthorn, 1973.

Sandler, J. On the concept of the superego. *Psychoanalytic Study of the Child*, 1960, *15*, 128–162.

Wesley, J. *A plain account of Christian perfection*. New York: Harper, 1821.

Additional Readings

Kohut, H. *The analysis of the self*. New York: International Universities Press, 1971.

Warfield, B. B. *Perfectionism* (2 vols.). New York: Oxford University Press, 1931.

31

Prejudice
Randie L. Timpe

Prejudice is traditionally defined as a stereotype accompanied by affective reactions that predispose a person to react in a consistent way (usually negative) toward a given class of objects or persons. The actions of the priest and the Levite in the parable of the good Samaritan (Luke 10:29–37) constitute a classic example of ethnic or class prejudice.

The concept of prejudice did not receive much attention from psychologists until the racial atrocities of World War II came to light. Shortly afterward Adorno, Frenkel-Brunswik, Levinson, and Sanford (1950) published *The Authoritarian Personality*, giving specific correlates of the authoritarian personality of which prejudice was one. They had developed the California F (Fascist) Scale as a measure of prejudice and ethnocentrism without reference to specific racial groups. Subsequently Allport (1954) published the classic work on the subject, *The Nature of Prejudice*. Following the overwhelming impact of Allport's treatise, only a few systematic writings appeared (Rokeach, 1960; Ehrlich, 1973).

The etymological roots of *prejudice* lie in the Latin noun *praeju-*

dicium, which originally meant a precedent or judgment based on previous experience. Later it denoted a judgment formed before examination of the facts—that is, a prejudgment. Eventually it took on the emotional connotations of an unsupported judgment. While the emotional tone could be favorable or unfavorable, much greater use is made of the latter. The work of most social psychologists has supported this view.

Allport (1954) suggested that prejudgments become prejudices when two conditions are fulfilled: an *overgeneralization* toward the class produces an *irreversible* misconception. Overgeneralization of the underlying concept to the class of objects makes the judgment irreversible in that it prevents further evidence.

Attitudes serve individuals through two functions. They operate as a summary of past experience to guide individuals in upcoming situations. They also serve as filters to selectively admit sensory experience into consciousness. The filtering function is not random, but systematically biased. The bias of attitude filtering is in the direction of past experience. In prejudice the individual overgeneralizes from past experience, rigidly adhering to preconceptions, which renders those misconceptions functionally irreversible. Prejudices screen the contradictory evidence from awareness and prevent the individual from entering circumstances where the misconceptions would be exposed.

Social psychologists have traditionally conceptualized attitudes as having three components: cognitive (belief), affective (emotional), and behavioral (action). In the case of racial prejudices the cognitive component is represented in an ethnic stereotype. The affective component is marked by the individual's desire to avoid, malign, or express hostilities toward the ethnic group. The behavioral component constitutes the discriminatory or other action directed toward the ethnic group. Whether the behavioral component will occur depends on the intensity of the emotional component and several parameters of the situation (e.g., the proximity of the rival group, scarcity of resources important to both groups, degree of anonymity, intergroup cultural differences). Discrimination is also more likely with certain personality traits (e.g., authoritarianism).

The cognitive component of prejudice is a belief reflecting the individual's categorization of events. This stereotype contains a kernel of truth that permits the person to prejudge an event or person on the basis of class membership. The process of categorization and generalization is quite normal. When interacting with new persons or objects, the individual abstracts and sharpens essential features that distinguish the person or object. The abstraction is then applied to others that share the same features—that is, generalization. Categories formed in this way enable the individual to respond to the object. Thus the stereotype as "an exaggerated belief associated with a category" (Allport, 1954, p. 191) leads to stereotypic behavior toward the class. The individual is responded to as a member of the class or category rather than as a unique individual. In the case of prejudices the categories that are formed seem to be based on minimal information and tend to be dichotomous. Stereotypes in a given society tend to be associated with specific ethnic groups, are widely diffused throughout the society, and reflect a high degree of consensus in the society (Ehrlich, 1973). Stereotypes justify or rationalize behavior in relation to the category.

The direction and strength of the cognitive aspects are supported by emotional associations. Some theorists suggest that the cognitive aspects adapt to justify the emotional response. Disliking someone is verified in finding something to dislike about the person. Similar to other emotional responses, prejudices activate the autonomic arousal system. When physiological arousal is accompanied by appropriate cognitions and labeling of affective states, the individual is likely to engage in discriminatory behavior, provided the situation permits it. The emotional component of a prejudice is a heightened state of arousal usually accompanied by feelings of mistrust, suspiciousness, and rejection of the object of the prejudice.

Under certain conditions, the negative stereotypes and feelings are manifested in negative action toward the objects of the prejudice. The negative action includes the maintenance of social distance, discrimination, and various forms of hostility and aggression.

The seminal work on social distance was conducted by Bogardus (1959), whose social distance scale measures the willingness of an individual to admit a member of an identified race to a category: close kinship by marriage, personal friend, neighbor, fellow in one's occupation, citizen of one's country, or a visitor to one's country. Social distance indicates the normative distance advocated by a group toward others, while personal distance is the behavioral intention of the individual. Just as stereotypes are shared in groups, groups display consensus about social distance norms. Ethnic groups that have different physical appearances or different cultural heritages or are politically estranged are attributed more social distance than other ethnic groups that are more similar (Bogardus, 1959).

Other types of behavioral intentions are seen in ethnic jokes, ethnic slurs, racial hostilities, racial discrimination, rioting and lynching. The hostilities and aggression may be indirectly expressed when intergroup contact is minimal or when competition is relatively weak. They may be expressed more directly and violently in situations of extreme competition for resources, when individual anonymity is probable, or when sanctions against violence are ineffective.

Certain personality types appear to be more prone to develop prejudices than others. Authoritarianism is a personality-attitude complex that "consists of interrelated antidemocratic sentiments including ethnic prejudice, political conservatism, and a moralistic rejection of the unconventional" (Byrne, 1974, p. 86). In the work of Adorno, et al. (1950) nine dimensions of authoritarianism were postulated: conventionalism—rigid adherence to conventional middle-class values; authoritarian submission—uncritical obedience to leaders; authoritarian aggression—tendency to reject and punish those who violate conventional values; destruction and cynicism—generalized hostility; preoccupation with power and toughness; superstition and stereotypy—magical beliefs about one's fate and thinking in rigid dichotomies; anti-intraception—opposed to the subjective, imaginative, and artistic; projectivity—outward projection of unconscious emotional impulses; and exaggerated concern for sexual events. Experimental evidence has provided modest support for these proposed interrelated dimensions.

Authoritarian parents typically adopt autocratic family structures wherein punishment is physical and harsh and relations are generally restrictive in nature. Autocratic family structures tend to produce authoritarian offspring. By way of contrast, equilitarian parents adopt more democratic family structures marked by love-oriented discipline, permissiveness, and absence of punitiveness. The result is equilitarian personalities in children.

Greater social distance has been observed in authoritarians as well as in those of lower intelligence. Rokeach (1960) has argued that prejudice is more likely in individuals with closed minds. He further suggested that authoritarian and prejudiced personalities are drawn to the fundamentalist end of the religious spectrum, because fundamentalist religious dogmas legitimize that attitude and personality while providing definitive answers to critical questions. Intolerance of ambiguity and intolerance of deviance further characterize the prejudiced personality.

Theories of causation of prejudices are numerous and range from Marx's historical exploitation view to the sociocultural forces of urbanization (Allport, 1954). Psychological origins are suggested in the psychodynamic frustration (i.e., scapegoat) theory, in which intrapsychic conflict is projected outwardly in the form of out-group aggression. But most social psychological approaches conceive of prejudice as being maintained and strengthened when in-group cooperation and out-group competition characterize the social situation. While the transmission of prejudice from generation to generation involves the socialization of children by parents, teachers, and other agents of society as well as identification with and conformity to one's own reference group, these mechanisms are most operative when peculiar historical conditions and politicoeconomic structures sustain intergroup rivalries.

References

Adorno, T. W., Frenkel-Brunswik, E., Levinson, D. J., & Sanford, R. N. *The authoritarian personality*. New York: Harper & Row, 1950.

Allport, G. W. *The nature of prejudice*. Reading, Mass.: Addison-Wesley, 1954.

Bogardus, E. S. *Social distance*. Ann Arbor, Mich.: University Microfilms, 1959.

Byrne, D. *An introduction to personality: Research, theory, and application* (2nd ed.). Englewood Cliffs, N.J.: Prentice-Hall, 1974.

Ehrlich, H. J. *The social psychology of prejudice*. New York: Wiley, 1973.

Rokeach, M. *The open and closed mind*. New York: Basic Books, 1960.

32

Presuppositions of Psychology
Mark P. Cosgrove

P resuppositions are assumptions about reality that have a major impact on all the sciences, including psychology. Presuppositions about the nature of the universe, cause and effect, human nature, and knowledge help guide science by giving it a framework from which to operate. Scientists, for example, may presuppose that the laws of matter operate similarly everywhere in the universe. By assuming some regularity in the universe they are able to investigate the problems in their sciences with more confidence in their theories and tools of investigation. Assumptions about human nature are likewise important for the psychologist in both research and clinical settings.

What the natural and social sciences have been slow to recognize is that presuppositions about reality and human nature affect the scientist's ability to be objective in the scientific process. Psychological research supports the notion the individuals resist interpretations of data that run counter to their expectations. This is certainly a possibility for psychology, which has many assumptions that run counter to the biblical picture of human nature.

Interest in the subjectivity of science was kindled by Kuhn's (1962) classic book, *The Structure of Scientific Revolutions.* It was Kuhn's contention that change in scientific ideas takes place as revolutions in whole paradigms, or sets of presuppositions about reality, because people's underlying beliefs about reality have to change before new contrasting ideas can be accepted. It has been suggested that in a scientific revolution people do not change their ideas. The scientists who hold the established views eventually die, and thus new ideas can become accepted.

Presuppositions in psychology serve as a framework within which research can be conducted and therapies can be developed. On the other hand, assumptions also affect the psychologist's objectivity and can become rigid dogmas in the face of conflicting data. The importance of psychologists being aware of their presuppositions cannot be overemphasized, because all psychologists have assumptions that undergird and influence their work whether they are aware of them or not. In addition, some of the subject matter of psychology is less accessible to experimental research and thus is more dependent on the psychologist's assumptions.

The presuppositions of psychologists can affect their work by limiting the subject matter they are willing to investigate, the methods of investigation, and the interpretations they place upon their data. Psychological research on the effects of a person's belief structure on his objectivity is substantial. Research areas such as cognitive dissonance, prejudice, and social aspects of perception illustrate the biasing potential of assumptions. The research process itself is also strongly affected by the psychologist's beliefs, as is illustrated by the phenomenon of experimenter expectancy (Barber, 1976) and the effect of subject beliefs on experimental results (Silverman, 1977).

The biasing effects of assumptions should not lead anyone to reject the search for truth as hopeless, but rather should challenge the psychologist to recognize the presuppositions of his field as well as the benefits of Christian assumptions in the study of human nature.

Basic Assumptions

The presuppositions that provide the framework within which most psychology is practiced are summarized below. It is important to note that these assumptions may be held as convenient to the methodology of science without necessarily believing that they specify truth about the nature of the way things really are. For example, a belief in determinism may actually be a belief in methodological determinism, which does not mean that a psychologist does not accept the concept of human freedom but that human behavior does seem to follow regular laws. Therefore, it may be useful to think of behavior as being determined.

Naturalism

This is an assumption at the core of secular science. It means that the universe can be explained completely by natural processes. This is a rejection of the idea of the God of the universe who ultimately provides the sustaining power of the universe and who can impact the universe in ways that according to our understanding go beyond natural law (e.g., miracles). For the psychologist naturalism means that the natural causes in the universe have to be the sole explanation for all that human beings are and can do.

Materialism

Related to naturalism is the psychologist's belief in materialism, which says that everything that exists in the universe is composed of matter-energy. This means that human nature in its entirety (behavior, thinking, feeling) is ultimately reducible to material explanations. It usually means that brain activity is equated with personhood.

Reductionism

This assumption means that explanations about human behavior and personhood can be reduced to or equated with explanations in terms of physical-chemical processes that accompany human activity. MacKay (1974) calls this type of thinking "nothing buttery," since reductionistic psychologists try to describe human nature as "nothing but" neuronal or chemical activity of some sort.

Determinism

Following directly from the assumptions of materialism and reductionism is the assumption of determinism, which says that all human behavior is completely caused by natural processes. This means that human beings do not personally decide their own actions, regardless of their feelings of freedom.

Evolution

This assumption attempts to provide an explanation for the uniqueness and complexity of human nature in a naturalistic order. Evolutionary theory would say that all of human nature has evolved from simpler organisms. This includes the idea that the complex human mind is a product of the evolution of the brain.

Empiricism

This assumption is both a method of knowing and a theory about human nature. Empiricism means that one can know only through the senses and with whatever scientific instrumentation expands the senses. Empiricism may be more radically stated as whatever cannot be shown to register as sensory data, such as God or mind, does not exist. Obviously empiricism can be a benefit to careful, scientific observation and control, but it also sets limits on what can be observed about human nature.

Empiricism may also be defined as a theory of human nature. The person in the empirical sense is a product of sensory input. The mind, according to empiricist John Locke, is a *tabula rasa*, a blank slate on which sensory experience writes. British empiricism of the 1800s contributed much to the behavioristic model in psychology, in which behavior alone is seen as acceptable data in psychology and the person is seen as a product of environmental factors.

Relativism

This is the assumption that there are no absolute standards of right or value to guide psychological research, counseling, or behavioral engineering. In a naturalistic universe all things related to morality and value become arbitrary and related to the individual person. Consequently there is much debate in psychology about the value and purpose of human life, values to guide counseling, and the moral structures by which society can be organized.

There are several counterassumptions in psychology that rebel against the rigid nature of the assumptions summarized above. Humanistic psychology, for example, assumes the freedom and personality of human nature. Transpersonal psychology emphasizes the immaterial essence of the universe and human nature; this assumption is labeled *pantheism* or *panpsychism*.

Biblical Presuppositions

Since beliefs are important to the development of psychology, Collins (1977) and Cosgrove (1979) suggest that Christian psychologists should build their psychology upon biblical presuppositions about reality and human nature. While the existence of God may not seem very pertinent to psychology, it should be clear that all of psychology's assumptions depend heavily on the natural basis for the origin and operation of the universe. For this reason Christians need to state very clearly their belief in the supernatural God of the universe. The assumption of a creator God gives psychology a source for the human person, a confidence in knowledge, additional revelation on human nature in the Bible, and a source of ethics and value. The immaterial essence of human nature gives a basis for human freedom and purpose and meaning in life. Christian beliefs about the fall of human nature and sanctification can expand the Christian's view of psychological problems and therapy. In general Christian assumptions support a needed balance in psychology. They can serve to correct psychology's limited view of human nature arising from its extreme positions on empiricism, materialism, determinism, and reductionism. At the same time Christian beliefs do not rule out the physical nature of the person, the laws of cause and effect, and the strong influences of nature and nurture on the human personality.

References

Barber, T. X. *Pitfalls in human research*. New York: Pergamon, 1976.

Collins, G. *The rebuilding of psychology*, Wheaton, Ill.: Tyndale House, 1977.

Cosgrove, M. P. *Psychology gone awry*. Grand Rapids: Zondervan, 1979.

Kuhn, T. *The structure of scientific revolutions*. Chicago: University of Chicago Press, 1962.

Mackay, D. *The clockwork image*. Downers Grove, Ill.: Inter-Varsity Press, 1974.

Silverman, I. *The human subject in the psychological laboratory*. New York: Pergamon, 1977.

33

Psychology as Religion
Paul C. Vitz

The similarity between religion and modern psychological theories of mental pathology and psychotherapy was noticed from the time these approaches emerged early in this century. Each theory was a kind of general psychological interpretation of the meaning of personal existence, complete with an explanation of what facilitates and what blocks the development of a healthy or ideal personality. Since all of these psychologies were based on secular philosophy and values, they were explicitly or implicitly hostile to religion, especially Christianity.

Initially these psychologies functioned as alternative world-views or secular religions primarily in the lives of the psychotherapists, most of whom were drawn to modern psychology because they were already alienated from traditional Christianity or Judaism and were looking for an alternative understanding of life that could be interpreted as scientific and as compatible with the increasingly secular world. Even those who started training in psychology with a religious commitment often abandoned their faith or greatly reduced its importance. This replacement of religion by psychology was a common consequence of the immersion in a secular mental framework which assumed that religion and religious experience were psychological phenomena and that the supernatural did not truly exist. Religion was interpreted as an illusion at best, or as some kind of pathology at worst. This rejection of religion was largely a result of the acceptance of certain philosophic assumptions and values implicit in much of secular psychology. That psychology per se did not—and does not— logically or empirically require that one lose his religion is clear in the lives of such prominent psychologists as Stern (1981), Tournier (1957), Zilboorg (1962), and many others.

Psychology often came to serve the same religion-replacing function in the lives of the patients who entered therapy at a time of mental anguish actively looking for answers. It was a common occurrence for the patient to accept the theoretical framework of his therapist—to be "converted" to psychology. Such a change was facilitated by the frequency of the therapy sessions and by the reinforcing effect of any cures or benefits caused by, or attributed to, the therapist. Any negative experiences with religion that the patient might have had would also support the exchange of psychology for religion. Furthermore, in many respects the psychotherapist/patient interaction had something of the character of the religious relationship of master/disciple or confessor/penitent.

A fundamental way in which psychotherapy functions as a religion is that (at its best) it heals. The healing or cure aspect of psychotherapy is its primary justification, and one should not forget that healing, both psychological and physical, is a major concern of Christianity. It is probably no accident that the secular psychotherapies first developed in a period when healing was much neglected in the major Christian churches—especially those that ministered to the more educated and sophisticated.

Another important characteristic of psychology has been the serious involvement with religion and religious issues on the part of many psychological theorists and innovators. This was the case for the founders of psychotherapy, Freud, Jung, and Adler, (who converted to a somewhat liberal Protestantism from a Jewish background). The following psychologists either started with a serious religious concern or clearly expressed such in their professional life (or both): William James, G. Stanley Hall, Carl Rogers, Erich Fromm, Rollo May, Karl Menninger, Gardner Murphy, Michael Murphy (Esalen founder), and Elisabeth Kübler-Ross. Such examples strongly imply an affinity between the religious and the psychological mentality.

One interesting sociological feature of psychology has been its religious "denominational" character. Lasch (1976) has pointed out the presence of a "Catholic-Protestant" split in psychology. Freud and much of psychiatry stand for Catholicism—that is, for orthodoxy and excommunication, doctrine, priestly mediation between the "sacred texts" and the patient, formality and distance between therapist and patient. Adler and his followers—the humanistic/self psychologists such as Rogers—created a psychological "Reformation." This involved taking psychology out of a special vocabulary and putting it into the vernacular. It also meant reducing the distinction between therapist and client, emphasizing empathy and emotion and the client's own interpretations. All of this resulted in a kind of psychological equivalent to the priesthood of all believers.

This "protestantized" version of psychology has tended to follow many of the paths taken by historical Protestantism: a gradual simplifying and watering down of theory (doctrine); increasing optimism about human nature among "mainline" psychologists; the splitting of the rest of "Protestant" psychology into various sects and movements. For example, encounter group psychology is much like revivalism (see Oden, 1972); Fromm's psychology is close to the social gospel; self-help psychology is an expression of positive-thinking Protestantism (e.g., Norman Vincent Peale); transpersonal psychology and related types are analogous to Mind Cure and aspects of Christian Science.

One psychologist not discussed by Lasch is Jung. A denominational interpretation nevertheless suggests itself. Jung is a mixture of "Catholic" psychoanalytic-psychiatric psychology and the "Protestant," less formal, counseling psychology. Hence, Jung should appeal to those who identify with aspects of both Catholicism and Protestantism, to those who seek Catholic intellectuality plus Protestant freedom of choice—a kind of "Episcopalian" psychological mentality. According to this rationale Jung should be popular with the especially educated and those with an interest in symbolism, ritual, and aesthetics. This seems, indeed, to be the case, as Jung is well received in Episcopal seminaries. Also the Jungian religious writers Morton Kelsey and John A. Sanford are both Episcopalians.

With the growth of psychotherapy and the increasing secularization of society, psychological ideas began to spread throughout the culture at large. Colleges and universities with their many psychology courses, plus such phenomena as newspaper advice columns, contributed greatly to the disseminating of psychology. An important consequence has been that today the public discourse (e.g., in the media) concerning people who are facing life crises—that is, emotional, moral, and interpersonal problems—is almost entirely dominated by secular psychological theory. The older religious understanding of these issues is restricted to private life and, indeed, is no longer even understood by many secularized Westerners. There has been a triumph of the therapeutic over the theological (see Becker, 1975; Vitz, 1977; Lasch, 1978; Kilpatrick, 1983).

Specific Religious Characteristics of Modern Psychology

Psychoanalysis: Freud

The connections of Freud's thought and life with both Judaism and Christianity are deep and complex; only the most easily observed religious characteristics of psychoanalysis will be noted here.

Freud directly acknowledged the essential similarity between psychoanalytic therapy and religious counseling by describing psychoanalysis as "pastoral work in the best sense of the words" (1927/1959, p. 256). He thus recognized in psychoanalysis what is true of all secular psychotherapy and counseling; namely, that it is similar, and indeed a rival, to the long Christian tradition of confession and counseling.

In addition there were specific cultic characteristics of early psychoanalysis. Freud often functioned like the founder of a religion: he was surrounded by disciples who formed a kind of inner sanctum; the best and most loyal of these were given rings to designate their special status; a deep allegiance to Freud's ideas, especially the "dogma" of his sexual theories, was expected of any true follower. Freud likened himself to Moses and Jung (before the schism) to Joshua. Many of Freud's students broke from his ideas and were treated rather like heretics. The psychoanalytic establishment that emerged after Freud's death has often been compared to an orthodox religious organization that "excommunicated" deviants (see Roazen, 1975).

Freud was personally involved in religious issues all his life, and he wrote frequently on them (*Totem and Taboo*, 1913; *The Future of an Illusion*, 1927; *Moses and Monotheism*, 1938). In part this interest came from both religious and ethnic Jewish influence (see Klein, 1981; Ostow, 1982), but much of it came out of his complex hostility and attraction to Christianity (Zilboorg, 1962; Meng & Freud, 1963; Vitz, 1983, 1984).

Nonetheless, Freudian psychoanalysis never developed a positive synthesis to provide a clear meaning or answer to life. Instead, Freud always remained an analyst focused on the exploration of the unconscious. His attitude and that of psychoanalysis is pessimistic, stoical, and skeptical. He refused to provide a secular form of salvation since he saw religion in any form as an illusion to be rejected. Thus, Freudian theory, which is in important respects an antireligion, was never made into a positive alternative. Freud was very critical of those such as Jung or Adler who did make psychology into a kind of positive alternative to religion.

Analytical psychology: Jung

Jung also was quite aware of the religious nature of psychotherapy, and the theological cast of much of his writing is apparent—for example, *Answer to Job* (1954), an extensive exercise in Scripture interpretation. Jung's explicit awareness of the religious issue is stated when he writes: "Patients force the psychotherapist into the role of priest, and expect and demand that he shall free them from distress. That is why we psychotherapists must occupy ourselves with problems which strictly speaking belong to the theologian" (Jung, 1933, p. 278).

Unlike Freud's, Jung's psychology provided positive, synthetic concepts that could serve as a conscious goal not only for therapy but for life as a whole. Jung responded far more to the patient's demand for a general relief from distress than did Freud. Jung's positive answer to religious needs is summarized by Jacobi, a prominent student of his: "Jungian psychotherapy is . . . a Heilsweg, in the twofold sense of the German word: a way of healing and a way of salvation. It has the power to cure. . . . In addition it knows the way and has the means to lead the individual to his 'salvation,' to the knowledge and fulfillment of his personality, which have always been the aim of spiritual striving. Jung's system of thought can be explained theoretically only up to a certain point; to understand it fully one must have experienced or better still, 'suffered' its living action in oneself. Apart from its medical aspect, Jungian psychotherapy is thus a system of education and spiritual guidance" (Jacobi 1973, p. 60). The process of Jungian movement on this path is, Jacobi continues, "both ethically and intellectually an extremely difficult task, which can be successfully performed only by the fortunate few, those elected and favored by grace" (p. 127). The last stage on the Jungian path of individuation—salvation—is called self-realization. This goal of self-realization or actualization is at heart a gnostic one in which the commandment, "Know (and express) thyself," has replaced the Judeo-Christian, "Love God and others." (In certain respects all modern psychology of whatever theoretical persuasion, because of the emphasis on knowledge, can be interpreted as part of a vast gnostic heresy.)

Much Jungian psychology is not explicitly focused on individuation and self-realization but is concerned with interpreting the patient's dream symbolism. Here Jung's analysis is focused on the collective and personal unconscious of the patient and on archetypes, the anima (or animus), shadow, and other concepts. This suggests a different way in which psychology can function as religion. Jung acknowledges the patient's basic religious concerns, and Jungian psychology is directly applied to the "archetypal" expression of the patient's religious motives—for example, in dreams about the wise old man (God archetype), dreams about rebirth, and so on. Jung's discovery of the psychology of religious symbols is important, but there is with this a danger of substituting the psychological experience of one's religious nature for the religious salvation that comes through the transcendent God who acts in history (see Hostie, 1957). Those who make this mistake have truly treated psychology as religion.

Self or humanistic psychology: Rogers, Maslow, and others

The clearest expression of psychology as religion is seen in the self psychologies. These place the self at the center of personality and make the growth or actualization of the self the primary goal both of life in general and of psychotherapy and counseling in particular. More specifically, self psychologies share all or most of the following characteristics:

1) An emphasis on the conscious self as an integrated, or at least potentially integrated, system. 2) An emphasis on the true self as entirely good, not characterized by any natural tendency to aggression or exploitation or to make self-indulgent or narcissistic choices. Such undesirable phenomena are attributed to the false self created by external factors such as family, traditional religion, society, or the economic system. 3) An emphasis on the true self as having almost unlimited capacity for change through freely made decisions. This process of choosing brings about self-actualization, the ideal way of being; self-actualization is an ongoing process of change, not a finished state. 4) An emphasis on personality prior to self-actualization as primarily the result of learned social roles. That is, the false self is the product of social learning of an essentially arbitrary kind. 5) An emphasis on breaking with the past, especially with commitments to others, with tradition, with fixed moral codes. Morality is interpreted as personal, subjective, and relative. 6) An emphasis on getting in touch with and expressing emotions and feelings. This promotes a presumed greater awareness of the true self and greater self-acceptance and trust in one's instincts. 7) An emphasis on short-term counseling of relatively normal adults in contrast to theory focused on disturbed children or such problems as schizophrenia, manic-depressive symptoms, or alcoholism.

Examples of self psychology theories are those proposed by Rogers (1951, 1961), Maslow (1968), and Fromm (1947). The writings of May (1953) and the gestalt psychology of Perls (1969) are also closely related. Such self psychology had much of its origin in Adler (1924), in Goldstein (1939), and in Jung's notion of self-realization. Most of the psychology that was immensely popular in the United States during the 1960s and 1970s was a form of self psychology. For example, transactional analysis (Berne, 1964) fits into this category. Movements such as Erhard Seminar Training (EST) combine self psychology with various other elements, usually from Eastern religions. Indeed, much of recent humanistic, self, and transpersonal psychology is indistinguishable from Eastern religion (see the *Journal of Transpersonal Psychology*).

The general framework noted above served as an interpretation of the meaning of life that undermined or replaced Christianity in many cases. Some of the more specific claims of the self psychologists will make this clear. Rogers (1961) states that the goal of psychotherapy is to help the client become self-directing, self-confident, self-expressive, creative, and autonomous to such a degree that he experiences unconditional positive self-regard. The client is increasingly to experience himself as the only locus or source of values.

Fromm devotes many pages in his books to interpreting and reinterpreting parts of both the Old and New Testaments. The titles of some of his books illustrate his religious agenda—for example, *The Dogma of Christ* (1963) and *You Shall Be as Gods* (1966). Fromm (1947) explicitly states that his psychology would be untenable if the doctrine of original sin were true. He believes that evil is in no way intrinsic to man's nature; self theory follows from this fundamental assumption, for obviously the self is to be perfectly trusted only if it is perfectly free of instrinsic evil. The Pelagian assumption of "I'm okay and you're okay" found throughout transactional analysis is a popular expression of this position (Berne, 1964; Harris, 1967).

Some of the popular American expressions of self theory have gone so far as to claim that the self is God; for example, "You are the Supreme Being. . . . Reality is a reflection of your notions. Totally. Perfectly" (Frederick, 1974, pp. 171, 177; Schultz, 1979, reaches the same conclusion). Rogers's position in which the self is the sole locus of values comes close to the same thing. The influence, often indirect, of Sartre and other existential thinkers on the American self theorists has been substantial. Sartre states that once we've rejected God, "the Father," then "life has no meaning a priori. Before you come alive life is nothing; it's up to you to give it a meaning, and value is nothing else but the meaning that you choose" (Sartre, 1947, p. 58).

Since Sartre (1957) also argues that man's goal is to become God, self psychology often can be interpreted as a commercialized American packaging of much of European existentialism.

The widespread acceptance of this self psychology (called "selfism" by Vitz, 1977) has been due in large part to works that popularized the original theories (e.g., transactional analysis). The strong public response has stemmed from various cultural and economic factors, and has had little to do with scientific knowledge. Contemporary upper-middle-class Americans—wealthy, increasingly secular, and with time on their hands—have been only too happy to find a rationale that encouraged them to develop an extremely self-centered way of living. Economic support for this kind of psychology came from the needs (and pleasures) of the consumer economy of the 1960s and 70s. Indeed, these self psychologies can be viewed as justifications and descriptions of the ideal consumer (Vitz, 1977). It was not surprising that many expressions and catchwords of self theory began showing up as advertising copy: Do it now! You're the boss! Honor thyself! Break tradition!

The relentless and single-minded search for and glorification of the self is a kind of psychological self-worship and is at direct cross-purposes with the Christian injunction to lose the self. Certainly Jesus Christ neither lived nor advocated a life that would qualify by today's standards as self-actualized. For the Christian the self is the problem, not the potential paradise. Understanding of this problem involves an awareness of sin, especially that of pride; correcting this condition requires the practices of such unself-actualized states as contrition, humility, obedience, and trust in God—attitudes either neglected or explicitly rejected by self theorists.

The problems posed by humanistic selfism are not new to Christianity. Indeed, they can be traced back to early conflicts with stoicism, Epicureanism, and other sophisticated Greco-Roman philosophical and ethical systems, especially gnosticism. Self-worship in the form of self-realization is in Jewish and Christian terms idolatry operating from the usual motive of unacknowledged egoism. Disguised self-love has long been recognized as the source of idolatry. "Idolatry is well understood in the Bible as differing from the pure worship of Israel's God in the fact of its personification and objectification of the human will in contrast with the superhuman transcendence of the true God. When an idol is worshiped, man is worshiping himself, his desires, his purposes, and his will. . . . As a consequence of this type of idolatry man was outrageously guilty of giving himself the status of God and of exalting his own will as of supreme worth" (Baab, 1949, pp. 105, 110).

One of the first psychologists to identify the way in which modern psychology with its emphasis on self-acceptance tended to undermine the idea of both sin and personal responsibility was Mowrer (1961). The problem remained neglected, however, until its analysis by Adams (1970) and Menninger (1973). Menninger notes the social and psychological benefits that follow from taking responsibility for one's actions, especially one's sinful behavior that has hurt others. The same point was made by Adams in his Christian critique of secular counseling theory and practice.

Some psychologists have justified self theory by pointing out the large number of people who suffer from low self-esteem and associated depression. However, these are often caused by biological factors—something that self theorists, because of their theoretical emphasis on social learning, usually fail to observe in patients. When biological factors are not involved, low self-esteem is itself often an inverted example of self-worship. At first this proposal might appear surprising, but the rationale is simple. Depression and low self-esteem are often the result of self-hatred or aggression against the self that occur when one fails to meet one's own high standards of value and worth. Thus, optimistic pride and pessimistic depression both result from the self taking on the prerogative of creating the standards of self-worth and then judging how well one meets those standards (see Strong, 1977). In Christian terms, however, one's worth comes from God, not from one's self. A person is not to judge himself or herself as a success or failure; such judgments belong to God, and to so judge is to set oneself in God's place. Psychologically creating your own self-worth is like printing your own money; it leads to false prosperity—inflation followed by depression. It is not uncommon for self psychology sessions to give short-term elation only to be followed by depression. Kilpatrick (1983) accurately describes this creation of self-worth as wishful thinking.

Myers (1980) has collected much evidence from social and cognitive psychology demonstrating that the self is intrinsically biased in its own favor, thus documenting the natural human tendency to pride. He cites studies that show the following: 1) People are much more likely to accept responsibility for success than for failure. If I win, I accept credit, but if I lose, then it was bad luck, someone else's fault, and so on. 2) Most people judge themselves as above average on most self-ratings. For example, 70% of the high school seniors taking the College Board rated themselves as above average leaders, only 2% as below average. In most marriages each person usually sees his or her positive contributions as greater than those of the spouse. In one survey 94% of college faculty reported themselves as better than their average colleagues. 3) People have a natural but unrealistic tendency to think their own judgment and beliefs are especially accurate. 4) Most people are very optimistic about their own future as compared to that of others. For example, most college students think things will work out much better for themselves than for the average student. 5) People tend to overestimate how morally they would act as compared with how they actually do act. For example, many more people say that they would help a stranger in need than actually do help when a real opportunity arises.

These and other studies led Myers to conclude that low self-esteem is not the great problem it is often claimed to be. Like other Christian critics Myers notes that Christianity is not essentially concerned with building high self-esteem but with admitting one's pride and then, with God's grace, forgetting or letting go of the self.

Bergin (1980) has cogently summarized the many value differences between a theistic and a humanistic or self-theory approach to psychotherapy. For example: humility and obedience are virtues (theistic) versus man is autonomous and supreme, and rejection of obedience as a virtue (humanistic). Love, affection, and self-transcendence are primary (theistic) versus personal needs and self-satisfaction are primary (humanistic). Commitment to marriage, emphasis on procreation and family life (theistic) versus open marriage, emphasis on recreational sex without long-term responsibility (humanistic). Forgiveness of others (theistic) versus self-acceptance and expression of accusatory feelings (humanistic). Bergin's comparisons clearly identify how self-oriented humanistic psychology has functioned as an alternative to religion and religious values. Other important treatments of the "religious" aspects of psychotherapy are the criticisms of Bobgan and Bobgan (1979) and the reflective analysis of McLemore (1982).

Yet another analysis of how self psychology functions as religion has been presented by Kilpatrick (1983), who focuses on the way in which the psychological categories of humanistic or self psychology function to replace religious categories. Slowly, and often quite subtly, God disappears from our thoughts and concerns, and preoccupation with the self comes to dominate. This self-preoccupation has several pathological consequences, especially destructive ones being the growth of subjectivism (see Frankl, 1967) and the loss of contact with reality. A person begins quickly to perceive others only, or primarily, in terms of his or her own self-needs. This leads to serious misperceptions of others as well as to an inability to view oneself objectively. Our desire for self-esteem gets in the way of objective self-awareness. Kilpatrick also points out how close self psychology is to such American traditions as the self-made man, and the frontier man who is constantly changing, moving on, always rejecting the notion of true commitment. Thus, self psychology, in spite of its opposition to tradition, is an example of one of America's oldest social attitudes.

In summary, the overriding religious character of much psychology is its tendency to replace God with the self. Intrinsic human pride and narcissism seem to have found one of their more effective expressions in modern psychology—a discipline that substitutes for the ancient, no longer appealing worship of the golden calf what might perhaps be called today's psychological worship of the golden self.

References

Adams, J. *Competent to counsel.* Philadelphia: Presbyterian and Reformed Publishing, 1970.

Adler, A. *The practice and theory of individual psychology.* New York: Harcourt, Brace, 1924.

Baab, O. J. *The theology of the Old Testament.* New York: Abingdon-Cokesbury, 1949.

Becker, E. *Escape from evil.* New York: Free Press, 1975.

Bergin, A. E. Psychotherapy and religious values. *Journal of Consulting and Clinical Psychology,* 1980, *48,* 95–105.

Berne, E. *Games people play.* New York: Grove, 1964.

Bobgan, M., & Bobgan, D. *The psychological way/the spiritual way.* Minneapolis: Bethany Fellowship, 1979.

Frankl, V. *Existential psychology.* New York: Washington Square Press, 1967.

Frederick, C. *EST: Playing the game the new way.* New York: Delacorte, 1974.

Freud, S. Postscript to the question of lay analysis. In J. Strachey (Ed. & trans.), *The standard edition of the complete psychological works of Sigmund Freud* (Vol. 20). London: Hogarth, 1959. (Originally published, 1927.)

Fromm, E. *Man for himself.* New York: Rinehart, 1947.

Fromm, E. *The dogma of Christ.* New York: Holt, Rinehart, & Winston, 1963.

Fromm, E. *You shall be as gods.* New York: Holt, Rinehart, & Winston, 1966.

Goldstein, K. *The organism.* New York: American Book, 1939.

Harris, T. A. *I'm ok—you're ok.* New York: Avon, 1967.

Hostie, R. *Religion and the psychology of Jung.* New York: Sheed & Ward, 1957.

Jacobi, J. *The psychology of C. G. Jung* (8th ed.). New Haven: Yale University Press, 1973.

Jung, C. G. *Modern man in search of a soul.* New York: Harcourt, Brace, 1933.

Jung, C. G. *Answer to Job.* Cleveland: World Publishing, 1954.

Kilpatrick, W. K. *Psychological seduction.* Nashville: Thomas Nelson, 1983.

Klein, D. B. *Jewish origins of the psychoanalytic movement.* New York: Praeger, 1981.

Lasch, C. Sacrificing Freud. *New York Times Magazine Section*, February 22, 1976, pp. 11, 70–72.

Lasch, C. *The culture of narcissism*. New York: Norton, 1978.

Maslow, A. H. *Toward a psychology of being* (2nd ed.). Princeton, N.J.: Van Nostrand, 1968.

May, R. *Man's search for himself*. New York: Norton, 1953.

McLemore, C. *The scandal of psychotherapy*. Wheaton, Ill.: Tyndale House, 1982.

Meng, H., & Freud, F. (Eds.). *Psychoanalysis and faith: The letters of Sigmund Freud and Oskar Pfister*. New York: Basic Books, 1963.

Menninger, K. *Whatever happened to sin?* New York: Hawthorn, 1973.

Mowrer, O. H. *The crisis in psychiatry and religion*. Princeton, N.J.: Van Nostrand, 1961.

Myers, D. G. *The inflated self*. New York: Seabury, 1980.

Oden, T. C. *The intensive group experience: The new pietism*. Philadelphia: Westminster, 1972.

Ostow, M. (Ed.). *Judaism and psychoanalysis*. New York: Ktav Publishing, 1982.

Perls, F. S. *Gestalt therapy verbatim*. Lafayette, Calif.: Real People Press, 1969.

Roazen, P. *Freud and his followers*. New York: Knopf, 1975.

Rogers, C. R. *Client-centered therapy*. Boston: Houghton Mifflin, 1951.

Rogers, C. R. *On becoming a person*. Boston: Houghton Mifflin, 1961.

Sartre, J.-P. *Existentialism*. New York: Philosophical Library, 1947.

Sartre, J.-P. *Existentialism and human emotions*. New York: Philosophical Library, 1957.

Schultz, W. *Profound simplicity*. New York: Bantam, 1979.

Stern, E. M. *The other side of the couch*. New York: Pilgrim Press, 1981.

Strong, S. (Ed.). Christian counseling. *Counseling and Values*, 1977, *21*, 75–128.

Tournier, P. *The meaning of persons*. New York: Harper & Row, 1957.

Vitz, P. C. *Psychology as religion: The cult of self worship*. Grand Rapids: Eerdmans, 1977.

Vitz, P. C. Sigmund Freud's attraction to Christianity: Biographical evidence. *Psychoanalysis and Contemporary Thought*, 1983, *6*, 73–183.

Vitz, P. C. *Sigmund Freud's Christian unconscious*. New York: Guilford, 1984.

Zilboorg, G. *Psychoanalysis and religion*. New York: Farrar, Straus, & Cudahy, 1962.

34

Reductionism
Mark P. Cosgrove

As a fundamental scientific theory, reductionism states that one can explain a phenomenon of nature at one level of inquiry by showing how its mechanisms and processes arise out of a lower or more microscopic level. For example, the reductionism of science assumes that chemical reactions can be explained by appealing to the activity and properties of molecules and atoms, and ultimately to the physical forces holding atoms together. Reductionism in psychology assumes that all behavioral and mental phenomena can be explained in terms of the physical world. Physiological explanations seem to be the preferred level of explanation in psychology.

There are two forms of reductionism found in the natural sciences and psychology. Methodological reductionism in psychology refers to the decision to confine the language of psychology to expressions that are in principle reducible to a science such as physiological psychology. This is similar to methodological behaviorism, in which mental and psychological phenomena are not denied. In the interest of developing a scientific psychology, the language of private data is avoided in favor of behavioral language that is anchored in public observation. Metaphysical reductionism, on the other hand, asserts that for psychology questions of theory are to be resolved by physiological explanations. This compares with metaphysical behaviorism, which assumes that all sentences in the mental language are really translatable into sentences of physical language.

Most psychology is built on the foundation of reductionism, with metaphysical reductionism being frequently held by psychology's leading scientists. This means that much of scientific psychology takes the position that human nature can be described and explained entirely by reference to neurophysiology or conditioned responses, and not to concepts such as mind or consciousness.

Metaphysical reductionism implies a belief in both materialism and determinism. This means that human beings have no immaterial essence but are entirely material, and that there are physical explanations for every aspect of personality and consciousness. Reductionism does not agree with the philosophical idea of emergentism, which teaches that the organization of parts into a compound structure results in the emergence of new properties that could not have been predicted even from a full knowledge of the parts and their interactions. In other words, reductionism believes that the whole of a person's behavior is nothing more than the sum of its parts.

There are abundant examples of reductionism in psychology from its founding until the present. Adopting the assumptions of materialism and empiricism from the natural sciences, psychology began as a field prone to reductive explanations. The psychophysics of Wundt, the founding father of psychology, suggested this kind of analysis. The term *psychophysics* describes the relating of mind (psyche) to physical laws. Watson's school of behaviorism, which created the central philosophical foundation for psychology as it grew, encouraged the development of a unique reductive language in terms of conditioned reflexes.

One of the strongest proponents of a metaphysical reductionism in psychology today is B. F. Skinner, who believes that what have been labeled mental phenomena are really the result of physiological responses to environmental stimuli and can be totally explained by the contingencies of reinforcement in a person's environment. It is probably true that most psychologists invariably come to think of neurophysiology as the ultimate level of explanation for all mental and personal phenomena. Carlson (1980) in a popular physiological psychology textbook states, "Physiological psychologists believe that all natural phenomena (including human behavior) are subject to the laws of physics. Thus, the laws of behavior can be reduced to descriptions of physiological processes. No consideration has to be given to concepts such as free will" (p. 2).

Nowhere in science are the issues of reductionism and levels of explanation more debated than they are in psychology. The distance between psychology and any lower level of explanation is greater than between any other set of levels of explanation in science. Reducing genetics to biochemistry seems quite acceptable. But it is a much larger step to move from the human personality, with its thoughts, imaginations, and complex emotions, to the interaction of neurons in the brain.

It is precisely this metaphysical reductionism that is opposed to the Christian view of human nature. MacKay (1974) argues that even the most detailed description of the human brain will not exhaust the mystery of the person. MacKay calls the thinking of reductionism "nothing buttery" because of its tendency to say the person is "nothing but" an assemblage of functioning neurons. When the complexities of the human brain are explained in this way, they are actually just explained away. Explaining the human personality in terms of nothing-buttery allows the reductionist to deal with the complexities of human beings primarily by prior assumption. This is assumming there is nothing more to human nature than the physical; therefore, why look beyond physical explanations? The Christian has no problems with methodological reductionism, but feels that the assumptions of metaphysical reductionism clearly pass judgment on the makeup of human nature, when science should be open to investigating all levels of the human personality.

Another problem with reductionism is its decision on the proper level of inquiry. How does the reductionist decide where to base the description of human nature? Why is the organizational level of neurons a better level of description of a human being than the biochemistry of neural firing? To choose any level short of the subatomic world of physics seems to be practicing only a partial reductionism. But to explain human nature entirely in terms of quantum physics results in the loss of the subject matter entirely. It seems more reasonable to describe human nature on the levels of our ordinary experience— including spiritual, psychological, and physical levels. Descriptions at one level should never be considered complete nor be used to invalidate descriptions at other levels.

Neither neurophysiology nor Skinner's behaviorism should be considered sciences with sufficient maturity that one can immediately cancel all holistic explanations of human nature. Many schools of psychology have, in both theory and research, questioned the reductionism of behaviorism and neurophysiology. The ideas of gestalt psychologists, rationalists such as Piaget and Chomsky, and cognitive behaviorists such as Tolman and Bandura, have rejected the reductionistic notion that detailed information about the physiological or behavioral components of a person produces a complete description of the person.

The limits of metaphysical reductionism do not rule out the advantages of a methodological reductionism to the Christian who is interested in a scientific psychology. In their work psychologists should use language as carefully and objectively as possible. Objective description of human behavior or neurophysiology may be a valuable starting point for psychology. Any psychological investigation that remains at these starting levels will be unable to deal with the complexities of the human personality. A reductionist's precise, objective investigation may be an appropriate place to start, but never an appropriate place to stop.

References

Carlson, N. R. *Physiology and behavior* (2nd ed.). Boston: Allyn & Bacon, 1980.

MacKay, D. M. *The clockwork image.* Downers Grove, Ill.: Inter-Varsity Press, 1974.

Additional Readings

Collins, G. R. *The rebuilding of psychology.* Wheaton, Ill.: Tyndale House, 1977.

Turner, M. B. *Psychology and the philosophy of science.* New York: Appleton-Century-Crofts, 1968.

35

Religion and Personality
Randie L. Timpe

The concepts of religion and personality have been closely associated in Western thought. The origin of the relationship is found in their etymologies. The Latin noun *persona* developed from the infinitive *per sonare*, which indicated the theatrical player projecting the voice through a mouth hole in the facial mask that designated a theatrical role. The English terms *person* and *personality* share *persona* as their point of origin. From that context persona indicated a mask or facade suggestive of a social role. Persona was a social facade adopted in interpersonal contexts.

However, over time persona took on a second, contrary connotation. The surface designation did not correspond with the second usage which referred to the actor (and the accompanying thoughts, feelings, desires, etc.) behind the mask (Monte, 1980). The dual use of persona is an embodiment of the tension experienced when social roles and expectations lead the individual in directions that belie personal inclination, resulting in a disjointed or fragmented individual. Inner reality is divorced from outer requirements.

Religion is a binding force, uniting fragmented personality. The origin of *religion* lies in two Latin verbs. *Religio* denoted a binding or fastening together, and came to indicate a reverence and fear of deity. The reverence and fear manifested themselves in an apprehensiveness to fulfill a covenant obligation. *Religo* denoted a restraining or holding back. While the former points to the reverential aspects of religion, the latter points to the ethical-restraint role of religion's bridling of human motives and impulses. Hence, etymologically religion is seen as a force that reconnects human disjointedness and restrains errant impulses.

Psychological Analyses of Religion

The dimensions of reverence and restraint are incorporated into psychological analyses of religion. Freud's view is developed in *Totem and Taboo, Civilization and Its Discontents, The Future of an Illusion*, and *Moses and Monotheism*. For him, religion originates in the Oedipus complex and its resolution. Respect and reverence for the father figure represent a displaced and sublimated hostility. Identification with the father figure occasions the introjection of values into the superego, the ethical-moral arm of personality.

The magnum opus of the psychological analyses of religious experience is James's *The Varieties of Religious Experience*. James's definition of religion as "the feelings, acts, and experiences of individual men in their solitude, so far as they apprehend themselves to stand in relation to whatever they may consider the divine" (James, 1902, pp. 32–33) emphasized the reverential, emotional, and sentimental dimensions of religion. Consistent with his pragmatic philosophy, he was more attuned to the fruits of religion than its roots. As well as giving life a sense of hallowedness and sacredness, the fruits of religion regulate individual action through ethical seriousness.

James's approach is reflected in the work of Allport (1937, 1950). The psychological impact of religion on the person is twofold, as the individual seeks to find his personal niche in creation and to develop a frame of reference for the meaning of life. The origin of one's religious quest lies in bodily needs, temperament and mental capacity, personal interests and values, the pursuit of rational explanations, and conformity to one's culture (Allport, 1950). Religion involves the whole individual.

Modern theories of personality may be secularized versions of older theological dogmas. Oates (1973) pointed out that recent holistic or self perspectives in personality parallel ancient Hebraic views of human nature. The Hebrews used *nepeš* to portray the unity or wholeness of the person when viewed from without. When wholeness was viewed from within, the term *lēb* was used. These were translated "soul" and "heart", respectively, in the Authorized Version.

Fromm (1955, 1973) suggested that the essence of human nature was to be found in five existential needs. According to him, personal- ity originated in the needs for orientation and devotion, for rooted- ness, for relatedness and unity, for identity, and for excitation and stimulation. Religion provides a meaningful frame of reference and an object of devotion. It ties humans to the natural world, yet enables an individual to transcend the natural order. One's identity is contin- gent upon relationships with others of like orientation. Religious ac- tivities provide regular excitation and stimulation in the form of ritu- als, holidays, feasts, and celebrations.

Similar views are to be found in Buber's I-Thou relation and Maslow's hierarchy of needs. Allport (1950) suggested personality is operative in the formation of religious sentiments. Endogenous mech- anisms of organic desire, temperament, psychogenic desires and spiri- tual values, and the pursuit of meaning are tempered by the exogenous conformity pressure of culture. Thus, religion addresses the issues of individual identity as well as fostering a sense of community.

Religiousness and Personality

The relationship between religiousness and specific temperament or personality characteristics is complex (Sadler, 1970). Many theo- retical predictions about religious individuals having different per- sonalities stem from James (1902). James suggested individuals who were healthy experienced gradual conversions (were "once born"), but sudden converts ("twice born") individuals were sick of soul. In the latter case the experience of a divided self (ideal versus real self) is accentuated in evangelicalism, since it points to an incongruity of what *is* and what *ought to be*. Experienced as guilt and anxiety, the divided self motivates redemptive activities such as renunciation of the natural world. Thus, an individual needs to be twice born to change a divided self (natural and physical versus spiritual) into a unity (Oates, 1973). For these reasons it has been asserted and re- ported that sudden converts have more manifest anxiety than grad- ual converts or the unregenerate (Rokeach, 1960). Other research fails to confirm this idea (Sanua, 1969; Johnson & Malony, 1982), but in these studies there was no attempt to distinguish between state and trait anxiety.

The foregoing analysis localizes anxiety in human fallenness. However, state or trait anxiety may also involve human fraility and finiteness. In these cases anxiety may not be resolved by conversion or repentance for sin. Anxiety may involve uncertainty or fear over economic needs, human finiteness, and the existential dread of death. Growth in grace is upheld as a solution to the various sources of anxiety (Oates, 1955; Grounds, 1976).

Others (e.g., Ferm, 1959) have suggested that conversion leads to personality changes. Conversion as a radical process eventually changes behavior. If behavior is changed, then its underlying cause (i.e., personality) must have been transformed. If conversion is radical, it must alter the inner dimensions of human nature. Research into this area (Johnson & Malony, 1982) has failed to confirm such predictions, although it may be that traditional personality assessment instruments are insensitive to the nature of these personality changes.

While James did not do so, many theorists (e.g., Allport, Fromm, Freud) conceived of religiousness at two levels: the personal and the institutional. In the former the focus is on individual personality and how religion affects one's inner life. The institutional level is concerned with the external manifestations of religion, especially as group expectancies and conformity pressures influence the behavior of the individual. The question is then asked about the relative power of each level. Internal religion and institutional, external religion may countermand each other in the operation of personality.

In recent years social learning theorists (Rotter, 1966; Phares, 1973) have examined the situation-specific expectancy of the individual and its relation to belief and behavior. Individuals who expect to control their own outcomes, to dispense their own reinforcements, and to pursue self-control are described as having an internal locus of control. Individuals who expect to be influenced by the social situation, or chance, are termed external locus of control personalities. Rotter (1966) and others have developed assessment instruments to measure this internal-external dimension.

On the basis of the internal-external research one would predict that individuals who have intensely personal religious experiences would be internal in locus of control, while individuals whose religious experiences are of a more institutional, social nature would be external in expectancy and attribution. Such differences have indeed been found between various religions as well as within religious groups. Fundamentalist Protestants could be expected to have higher scores on an internal locus of control scale than liberal Protestants. Furnham (1982) found precisely those differences in clergy responding to an internal-external scale who were asked to describe their theological position, thus supporting other research literature.

Rokeach (1960, 1970, 1973) summarized his survey work as indicating that religious personalities were more authoritarian, more dogmatic, more closed-minded, and more ethnically prejudiced than less religious and nonreligious individuals. His interest in values and their relationship to religion grew out of participation in authoritarianism research (Adorno, Frenkel-Brunswik, Levinson, & Sanford 1950). His measure of religiousness was frequency of church attendance, which is more external.

Allport (1950) distinguished between intrinsic and extrinsic religious orientation, and linked these to personality differences. The extrinsic orientation to religion is pragmatic and self-serving, utilizing religion as a means to personal ends. The intrinsic orientation embodies a basic trust of others and empathetic understanding of others. Allport contended that those of an intrinsic orientation were more open-minded and tolerant than the extrinsic. Rokeach agreed, but contended that most religious individuals had an extrinsic orientation to religion.

Allport and Ross (1967) found prejudice to be curvilinearly related to religiousness, not linearly as Rokeach suggested. They differentiated between four religious orientations: 1) intrinsic religious orientation, in which religious teachings are internalized to guide daily life; 2) extrinsic religious orientation, in which religion is used to advance personal ambition; 3) indiscriminately proreligious orientation, which uncritically endorses all religious ideas; and 4) antireligious orientation, which rejects all religious teachings. They found the intrinsically religious individual to be the least prejudiced, the extrinsically oriented more prejudiced, and the prorelious the most prejudiced. Antireligious persons were slightly more prejudiced than the intrinsically religious. These findings bear some similarity to the internal-external research.

Sanua (1969) reviewed the empirical literature on the relationship of religiousness to humanitarianism, social action, and mental health. While it could be argued that healthy religion ought to augment each of these, data do not unequivocally support the assertion. Internalized dogmas (especially ethical principles) are not always externalized in action. *What* is taught in religious education may conflict with *how* it is taught.

For Christian psychologists and personality psychologists, personality's link to religion remains a riddle (Malony, 1977). The associations are complex and paradoxical. Religion has yet to fully actualize its potential in the ethical, healthy operation of personality.

References

Adorno, T. W., Frenkel-Brunswik, E., Levinson, D. J., & Sanford, R. N. *The authoritarian personality.* New York: Harper & Row, 1950.

Allport, G. W. *Personality: A psychological interpretation.* New York: Holt, 1937.

Allport, G. W. *The individual and his religion.* New York: Macmillan, 1950.

Allport, G. W., & Ross, J. M. Personal religious orientation and prejudice. *Journal of Personality and Social Psychology,* 1967, *5,* 432–443.

Ferm, R. *The psychology of Christian conversion.* Westwood, N.J.: Revell, 1959.

Fromm, E. *The sane society.* New York: Holt, Rinehart, & Winston, 1955.

Fromm, E. *Anatomy of human destructiveness.* New York: Holt, Rinehart, & Winston, 1973.

Furnham, A. F. Locus of control and theological beliefs. *Journal of Psychology and Theology,* 1982, *10,* 130–136.

Grounds, V. C. *Emotional problems and the gospel.* Grand Rapids: Zondervan, 1976.

James, W. *The varieties of religious experience.* New York: Longmans, Green, 1902.

Johnson, C. B., & Malony, H. N. *Christian conversion: Biblical and psychological perspectives.* Grand Rapids: Zondervan, 1982.

Malony, H. N. (Ed.). *Current perspectives in the psychology of religion.* Grand Rapids: Eerdmans, 1977.

Monte, C. *Beneath the mask* (2nd ed.). New York: Holt, Rinehart, & Winston, 1980.

Oates, W. E. *Anxiety in Christian experience.* Philadelphia: Westminster, 1955.

Oates, W. E. *The psychology of religion.* Waco, Tex.: Word Books, 1973.

Phares, E. J. *Locus of control in personality.* Morristown, N.J.: General Learning Press, 1973.

Rokeach, M. *The open and closed mind.* New York: Basic Books, 1960.

Rokeach, M. Faith, hope and bigotry. *Psychology Today,* 1970, *3*(11), 33–37: 58.

Rokeach, M. *The nature of human values.* New York: Free Press, 1973.

Rotter, J. B. Generalized expectancies for internal versus external control of reinforcement. *Psychological Monographs,* 1966, 80(1), 1–28.

Sadler, W. A. *Personality and religion.* New York: Harper & Row, 1970.

Sanua, V. Religion, mental health, and personality: A review of empirical studies. *American Journal of Psychiatry,* 1969, *125,* 1203–1213.

36

Self-Esteem
Craig W. Ellison

One of the unique characteristics of human beings is their ability to describe and evaluate themselves. Self-esteem is the degree of positive or negative feelings that one has as a result of such assessment.

History of the Concept

The development and nature of the self has been of interest to modern psychology since James (1890) distinguished between self as knower (I) and self as known (Me). James further identified the material, social, and spiritual Me. For him the evaluations a person arrives at involve a comparison of aspirations, or "pretensions," with achievements.

Following James sociologists Cooley (1902) and Mead (1934) stressed the social origins and development of the self. Cooley introduced the notion of the looking-glass self, which is based on a person's perception of other people's perceptions of him. He felt, much like James, that people tend toward self-appreciation. Mead saw language as an essential part of self-description and assessment, and postulated the idea of a generalized self apart from more specific selves that function in particular situations.

From the early 1900s until the late 1940s comparatively little attention was paid to the study of the self-concept and self-esteem by academic psychology. This was largely due to the preoccupation of mainstream psychology with achieving an identity as a scientific discipline. In its effort to be objective and to model after the physical sciences, it tried to divorce itself from abstract, philosophical constructs and to focus on observable behavior.

Neopsychoanalytic theorists such as Adler, Horney, Fromm, and Sullivan, who emphasized the role of interpersonal relationships in the shaping of personality, touched on various aspects of self-conception and self-esteem. Adler's emphasis on the perception of defects as the dynamic behind striving for superiority is similar to contemporary conceptions of self-esteem. A basic component of Horney's (1950) theory was the need to value oneself and to be valued by others. Fromm (1939) saw self-love as critical to healthy interpersonal relationships. Sullivan (1953) described the self in wholly social terms and felt that the self-concept was learned through reflected appraisals of others made possible by the symbolic capacity of the human being.

With the emergence of humanistic psychology and its prominent theorists, Rogers, Maslow, and May, who have made self-processes the center of their theory and therapy, considerable theoretical and therapeutic work has focused on self-perception. This has included development of experimental investigation of issues related to the self, including self-esteem. The waning of more radical forms of behaviorism and its tentative marriage with rapidly developing cognitive psychology have also legitimated the study of self-referent constructs.

Coopersmith (1967), Rosenberg (1979), and Ziller (Ziller, Hagey, Smith, & Long, 1969) have developed the most explicit contemporary theories of self-esteem based on empirical studies. Coopersmith sees self-esteem as a personal evaluation of worth that has very strong feelings associated with it. He believes that self-esteem is determined by an interplay of a person's success, values, aspirations, and defenses. Rosenberg analyzes the self-concept in terms of attitudinal structures and sees self-esteem as a positive or negative orientation that is one of the most powerful human motives. Self-esteem is viewed as a function of reflected appraisals, social comparison processes, self-attribution, and psychological centrality. Ziller conceives of self-esteem as a buffer between the self and the social environment. His analysis is primarily in gestalt, topological concepts.

Research in Self-Esteem

The importance of self-esteem is supported by a variety of empirical studies showing that it is associated with a wide variety of personal and interpersonal characteristics (Ellison, 1976). Self-esteem has been shown to be related to persuasibility and attitude change. Low self-esteem is associated with anxiety and neurotic behaviors, social inadequacy, and psychosomatic illnesses. Those with low self-esteem are more likely to be immaturely dependent, sensitive to criticism, approval oriented, and antisocial. They are more likely to feel unlovable, afraid of arguing with others, and too weak to ovvercome their deficits. Those with higher self-esteem are more active in group discussion, more intellectually curious, more likely to become leaders, less likely to conform, more satisfied with life, and more likely to have a positive relationship with God. They are less likely to be depressed, defensive in their relationships, and distrustful.

The most commonly accepted analysis of self-esteem regards it as the result of comparison between a person's perceived self, which is made up of the evaluations of other people and one's own evaluation based on self-observation, and the ideal self, which is a mixture of how one would like to be and feels he ought to be. The ideal self reflects values transmitted by the culture and emotionally significant other people. The level of positive self-esteem is a function of the degree of discrepancy between the ideal and perceived self. The greater the discrepancy, the lower the self-esteem.

Currently there is some debate as to whether there is one general, unified self-concept or whether there are many selves (Gergen, 1971) or dimensions of self-esteem. Although some recent literature suggests the existence of multiple components of the self, no personality theory has systematically identified what those components are and related them to self-esteem. There are a few scales—such as the Tennessee Self-Concept Scale (Fitts, 1965), which describes eight categories of reported self-concept—but these seem to be either empirically or theoretically limited.

Development of Self-Esteem

It is in the context of the parent-child relationship that feedback crucial for one's self-esteem begins. Acceptance of the child is basic to the development of positive self-esteem. Acceptance is communicated in various ways. For the infant and young child it is expressed through physical gentleness, time spent holding and talking, appropriateness and time lapse in meeting needs, and spontaneous play. For the older child it involves gentleness (not permissiveness) in discipline, time spent encouraging and affirming ideas and positive behavior, and use of language to express praise and affection. The impact of parental feedback in childhood is especially important because it occurs at a time when the child is developing basic conceptual categories where none existed before, and when the parent's input carries considerable weight because the child has comparatively little other feedback about himself and perceives his parents as omniscient.

Early parental evaluation is also given at the point of greatest language inability and received, therefore, in simplified emotional terms. As a result the child initially reads evaluations in "all or none" terms. With subsequent cognitive development and exposure to additional sources of input the person is able to be more selective and limited in his reception of evaluation, but a core feeling of good/bad self seems to be retained. In addition to information control the control of rewards and punishments allows the parent to communicate goodness and badness to the child. Finally, there is evidence to suggest that self-esteem is related to identification with one's parents, especially the mother. If a mother has low self-esteem, she is likely to foster a similar self-perception in her children by providing a negative model; by pushing the children so hard to make up for her inadequacies that they feel inferior because they can't meet her standards; or by being overly sensitive to their shortcomings because these might reflect on her inadequacies.

As the child develops, additional sources of feedback enter in. For the teen-ager peer evaluation is critical. For adults the assessment of marital partners, work supervisors, and peers is important. Various studies have indicated that those with higher self-esteem have higher goals and more successfully achieve them, though affirmation of the person apart from achievement seems important also.

Many of the key values that American society uses as the standards of worth are shaped by mass media and education and subsequently internalized and applied by parents, peers, authority figures, and spouses. These values center on what people do and how they compare with others. Failure to meet these criteria usually results in low self-worth. These values include appearance, achievement, affluence, assertion, and actualization. The more that one possesses or utilizes these qualities, the higher his self-esteem deserves to be, according to our society. As a result of the comparison base one's self-esteem is relatively vulnerable. Power, prestige, and personal rights are sought as ways to guard against negative self-evaluation.

Biblical Perspective

In contrast, biblical standards of self-esteem focus on what God thinks rather than what others think (1 Sam. 16:7). The biblical basis of self-esteem is grace, not works. Human beings do not have to achieve or possess anything to be worthwhile in God's eyes, though they have to be open to his love in order to experience affirmation.

The biblical building blocks of positive self-esteem are divine creation, redemption, confession, servanthood, and community. The act of divine creation contains several indications of the positive value God placed on his creation. First, he evaluated what he had made and said it was "very good" (Gen. 1:31). In addition, he assigned the major responsibility of administering his creation to Adam and Eve (Gen. 1:28). Significant responsibilities are not normally delegated unless the one charged is highly valued. God also cared for the man and woman by providing food for them (Gen. 1:29–30). Such provision is an act of love. Further, according to Psalm 139, God has special concern for each person he creates, and he gives each a special purpose in his plan (Rom. 12:3–6).

God did not stop treating human beings as worthwhile when sin entered the world. Instead he gave his most valuable possession as a sacrifice (Rom. 5:6–8) in order to redeem each person. Other passages (e.g., 1 Peter 2:9–10) specifically assert that he chose us, even while we were antagonistic toward him.

When Adam and Eve sinned, they immediately began blaming, denying, and hiding. These ego defense mechanisms were and are automatically invoked to protect the sense of self-esteem. None of them are effective, however. Unconfessed sin brings depression, disease, and guilt (Ps. 38). Instead of leaving persons without a way for the restoration both of spiritual communion and of self-worth, God provided confession as a means of cleansing, restoration, and renewed affirmation from God and others.

The key to positive self-esteem on a daily basis is to act with God's purposes and evaluation in mind. Such an orientation of servanthood (Col. 3:17,23) frees a person from much of the anxiety and damage of social comparison and negative comments by others. Work and relationships are freed to be more caring and constructive, which in turn encourages reciprocated affirmation. The inner satisfaction of God's approval becomes a stable source of self-worth.

The biblical conception of community is as a place of affirmation where love reigns and destructive criticism is foreign (Col. 3:12–14), a place of equality where each person's contribution potential is recognized and affirmed (1 Cor. 12:14–27), and a place of counterculture where the prevailing cultural bases of unstable and competitive self-worth are replaced by biblical values (Eph. 4:11–17).

According to Scripture, positive self-esteem is not to be confused with the sin of pride. Pride involves an attitude of superiority over others and a spirit of independence from God. It is refusal to admit weakness and error, which amounts to an attempt to maintain the charade of perfection, or Godlikeness. More often than not arrogance is the sign of a person who really doesn't accept himself. The Bible warns against the improper elevation and overestimation of ourselves (Rom. 12:3; Gal. 6:3), while encouraging accuracy testing in order that we might take pride in ourselves (Gal. 6:4).

The other extreme from defensive pride is false humility. This is a belief that one is no good and has no ability to do anything, which usually has religious overtones. The belief is that to have a sense of positive self-esteem is to have pride, the sin which God abhors most (Prov. 6:16–17).

In contrast, true humility is compatible with healthy self-esteem. Appropriate self-worth involves the ability to see one's strengths and weaknesses, to admit and confess sins, but to still feel positive. True humility and positive self-esteem are based on accuracy rather than on feelings of superiority (pride) or feelings of inferiority (false humility). The greatest example of true humility and positive self-esteem is Jesus Christ (Phil. 2:3–8). Christ was clearly sinless and therefore truly humble, but also asserted who he was without apology. Scripture does not allow the conclusion that he was arrogant or that he belittled himself. Because of his worth, his servanthood and sacrifice have redemptive meaning. The Bible suggests that God's people are to have the same servant attitude as Christ, and implies that we are expected to properly love ourselves, as Christ did (Mark 12:31).

References

Cooley, C. H. *Human nature and the social order*. New York: Scribners, 1902.

Coopersmith, S. *The antecedents of self-esteem*. San Francisco: W. H. Freeman, 1967.

Ellison, C. W. (Ed.), *Self esteem: A new look*. San Francisco: Harper & Row, 1982.

Fitts, W. *Tennessee self-concept scale: Manual*. Nashville: Counselor Recordings and Tests, 1965.

Fromm, E. Selfishness and self-love. *Psychiatry*, 1939, 2, 507–523.

Gergen, K. J. *The concept of self*. New York: Holt, Rinehart, & Winston, 1971.

Horney, K. *Neurosis and human growth: The struggle toward self-realization*. New York: Norton, 1950.

James, W. *Principles of psychology* (Vol. 1). New York: Holt, 1890.

Mead, G. H. *Mind, self, and society from the standpoint of a social behaviorist.* Chicago: University of Chicago Press, 1934.

Rosenberg, M. *Conceiving the self.* New York: Basic Books, 1979.

Sullivan, H. S. *The interpersonal theory of psychiatry.* New York: Norton, 1953.

Ziller, R. C., Hagey, J., Smith, M., & Long, B. H. Self-esteem: A self-social construct. *Journal of Consulting and Clinical Psychology,* 1969, *33,* 84–95.

Additional Readings

Narramore, B. *You're someone special.* Grand Rapids: Zondervan, 1978.

Vitz, P. C. *Psychology as religion: The cult of self-worship.* Grand Rapids: Eerdmans, 1977.

Wagner, M. E. *The sensation of being somebody.* Grand Rapids: Zondervan, 1975.

Wells, L. E., & Marwell, G. *Self-esteem: Its conceptualization and measurement.* Beverly Hills, Calif.: Sage Publications, 1976.

37

Sexuality
Stanton L. Jones

The term *sexuality* has been used in a variety of ways. At the broadest possible level, the term *gender sexuality* in this chapter will refer to "the way of being in, and relating to, the world as a *male* or *female* person" (Kosnick, Carroll, Cunningham, Modras, & Schulte, 1977, p. 82). A second type of sexuality, here termed *erotic sexuality,* is that of passionate desire for the other; the longing for completion through interaction with another, which possibly but not necessarily includes emotional, intellectual, spiritual, or physical interaction with the other (Thielicke, 1964). Finally, when physical sexual action is the focus, the term *genital sexuality* will be used, even though the sexual expression may not involve the genitals at all. When experience at all of the above levels is the focus, the unqualified term *sexuality* will be used.

Theological Perspectives

History of Christian thought

The thinking of the early church in the West on the topic of sexuality was deeply influenced by Hellenistic and gnostic thought forms (Bullough & Brundage, 1982; Kosnick et al., 1977). Departing from the historic Hebraic affirmation of body life and sexuality, many of the early church fathers (including Justin Martyr, Origen, Tertullian, Jerome, and Ambrose) viewed genital sexuality as at most acceptable only within marriage for procreation, while erotic passion was to be spurned at all costs. Virginity or chastity within an established marriage was viewed as a superior mode of life. Justin Martyr and others wrote approvingly of young people having themselves castrated for the kingdom; these acts were later declared self-mutilation and condemned by the church.

Augustine's writings were the central pillar of the thinking of the church until the Reformation. He argued that the conjugal act in marriage was in itself sinless since it led to procreation, but paradoxically suggested that the pleasure attached to that act was a consequence of original sin and that erotic desire was a product of man's lower, fleshly nature. Other writers later attempted to remove the stigma from sexuality (e.g., Thomas Aquinas), but Catholic thought until very recently continued to reflect Augustine's reasoning.

The Reformers, among their other amendments of Christian doctrine, rejected the Catholic doctrine of clerical celibacy and its implicit asceticism on scriptural grounds. Luther, Calvin, and others esteemed marriage and sexual union as the gifts of God; to both, sexuality was a natural part of human existence. Luther dealt with the topic in an especially frank and earthy manner. Subsequent Protestant thought on this theme tended to slip back and forth between a latent asceticism and the healthier balance achieved by the Reformers (Feucht, Coiner, Saver, & Hansen, 1961).

Biblical themes

Sexuality in all its forms was an intended part of the created order. Genesis 1:27 is viewed by most contemporary scholars as teaching that males and females were equally created in the image of God, and this gender differentiation and the institution of erotic and genital sexuality were hailed by God and man as very good. Genesis 2:24–25 persuasively refutes any notion that conjugal relations between husband and wife are in any way contrary to God's intended order.

The Old Testament also suggests that bodily existence, marriage, and sexual intercourse were all gifts of God. A major distinction between the Hebraic people and the pagan cultures about them was their refusal to overly spiritualize sex by attributing genital sexuality to God, or to degrade the gift of sexuality in general by attributing its origins to Satan or the fall. While genital sexuality in marriage was affirmed in the Old Testament, harsh condemnation was expressed for extramarital genital sexuality. At points in the Old Testament women were given a radical equality with men; in other places the Scriptures portray a patriarchal society that does not reflect the equality of the sexes indicated to have been God's intent before the fall.

To understand the treatment of sexuality in the New Testament one must first realize that the Scriptures do not attempt to give systematic attention to the topic in the same way in which they treat the great doctrines of human depravity and divine grace. Rather, the broad themes are briefly touched on in addressing specific problems of concern. Further, all New Testament writings are colored by the eschatology of the writers, who expected an imminent return of the Son of Glory. Most of Paul's writings that have been understood as antisexual (e.g., 1 Cor. 7) are better understood as being rooted in this view of eschatology. His positive, Hebraic affirmation of the place of sexuality in human existence is more clearly presented in Ephesians 5. Other New Testament passages do seem to portray a more negative view of sexuality (e.g., Rev. 14:4) but cannot be dealt with here.

Theological themes

In understanding our sexuality it is critical to affirm that human existence is inevitably an embodied, physical existence. The fact that sexuality in all its forms is intimately intertwined with physical processes cannot be used to denigrate that aspect of our being. "Thus does the 'biblical view' of man represent him as consisting of two principles, the cosmical and the holy, which unites the individual into a free and personal oneness of being" (McDonald, 1981, p. 78). While Scripture makes this differentiation, it never denigrates the physical at the expense of the immaterial, and it constantly emphasizes the unitive, integrated nature of our existence. It should be remembered that body life can be made spiritual or carnal; the term *flesh* (*sarx*) is in Scripture primarily an ethical term, and we can have a fleshly mind as well as a fleshly body.

Unlike classical Reformed theologians such as Hodge and Berkhof, the neo-orthodox theologian Barth viewed the gift of sexuality as fundamental to the image of God which humans reflect. Barth, and many since, have suggested that human sexuality reflects the differentiation of persons within the Godhead and God's intimately relational nature. "God created man in His own image, in correspondence with His own being and essence. . . . God is in relationship, and so too is the man created by Him" (Barth, cited in Small, 1974, pp. 131–132; see also Thielicke, 1964). Thus, our sexual natures reflect the nature of the Creator of the universe.

It must be remembered that all our experience of sexual life is conditioned by the fall. Brunner (1939) has suggested that as a result of the fall a "vast rent . . . runs right through human nature" (p. 348). In the area of sexuality, according to Brunner, this rent has two results: "a shame which cannot be overcome, and a longing which cannot be satisfied" (p. 348). That is, a sense of shame reminiscent of the shame of Adam and Eve over their nakedness and a lack of fulfillment of our desire to know the other (which results in an unsatisfied longing and personal isolation) are perpetually ours as a result of the fall. Further, Brunner points out that enmity between the sexes is the result of the fall. One result of this enmity is that in the agelong struggle between the sexes, in which males have largely been dominant, the original distinguishing characteristics of the sexes (aside from the obvious anatomical differences) have been blurred. We have little information about what God originally intended in differentiating male and female, as we have spent the eons since the creation recreating ourselves in our own images.

Sexual ethics

Christian theology in dealing with human sexuality has mainly been preoccupied with the clear articulation of biblical moral standards. Recently more attention has been given to areas that have been called "borderline cases" (Thielicke, 1964, p. 199). In confronting the issues presented here, we are forced to struggle with the central principles underlying the ethics of God's revelation. To paraphrase Thielicke, in struggling with the ethics of homosexual orientation we grapple with the nature and purpose of gender differentiation; the problems of divorce, remarriage, and birth control lead us to struggle with the basic nature of marriage; and abortion and artificial insemination bring us face to face with the issue of the nature of life and parenthood.

Christian ethics is inherently deontological ethics. Sexual acts have meanings in and of themselves. Some sexual acts are clearly declared moral or immoral in the Scriptures. We might term these acts "objectively" moral or immoral. Other acts (e.g., petting, masturbation, sexual fantasy, fetishism) must be judged in regard to their morality by reference to the principles that are assumed to underlie God's clearer sexual absolutes. While several Christian writers have attempted to articulate these values, the criteria given by Kosnick et al. (1977, pp. 92–95) are eloquently developed. It is argued that sexual acts are most likely to be wholesome and moral when they are self-liberating, other-enriching, honest, faithful, socially responsible, life-serving, and joyous.

Purposes of sexuality

Two of the major purposes of sexuality are the procreative and unitive functions (Kosnick et al., 1977, p. 86). Genesis 1:28 states clearly that procreation is a fundamental purpose of genital sexuality, and the Scriptures as a whole are so clear on this point that it needs no further elaboration.

Union is the other clear purpose of sex presented in Scripture. Genesis 2:24 suggests that becoming "one flesh" is foundational to marriage and that genital sexuality is in some way fundamental to this process. The exact meaning of "one flesh" is a topic of some debate. Some Scriptural passages suggest that becoming one flesh with another is in some sense an immediate and permanent result of sexual intercourse (e.g., 1 Cor: 6:16). Such a doctrine creates numerous philosophical and practical difficulties, including the question of the marital status of the person who has had intercourse with more than one person. Theologians generally conclude that becoming one flesh is used in several ways, the most important of which denotes a process of growth between married persons in which sexual intercourse is a necessary but not sufficient precondition. The end goal of the process is to be a unitary expression of fidelity, commitment, purpose, love, and ownership of the other (see Small, 1974).

Several biblical passages suggest a third purpose of sexuality, that of physical gratification and pleasure. Paul's discussion in 1 Corinthians 7 suggests that genital sexuality in marriage gratifies a passionate desire and that this function of marriage is not sinful. Proverbs 5:19 suggests that the exhilaration of physical love serves to enhance the stability of a marriage. This function is probably subservient to the larger purpose of union.

From a theological perspective a group of broader purposes of sexuality emerge. Kosnick et al. (1977) broadened the terms *procreative* and *unitive* to *creative* and *integrative* better to describe the broadest purposes of sexuality. They argue that our potential for "shared existence" (p. 85) with persons of the opposite sex calls us to the task of creative completion of our personhood, to the realization of our unfulfilled potentials. Sexuality reminds us experientially of our relational natures and thus beckons us toward integration with others, including a nongenital integration or fellowship with others beside our spouses.

Thielicke (1964) similarly argues that eros opens up the person to the experience of greater levels of self-acceptance and growth. We might also argue that sexuality was divinely created to experientially teach us important truths about our relationship to the Godhead. As argued earlier, gender differentiation reflects God's differentiated person-hood, and sexual union in marriage reflects the complementary truth of union across differentiation within the Godhead and between God and humankind. Sexuality as a part of marriage is obviously a part of the symbolic representation in that institution of the relationship be-tween Christ and his church (Eph. 5:21–33). This symbolism was obvi-ous in the Old Testament as well, where sexual passion was a prime metaphor for the relationship of Israel to her God, both in the positive, faithful sense (Song of Songs) and the negative, adulterous sense (e.g., Ezek, 23).

Biological Perspectives

Contemporary textbooks in human sexuality (e.g., Masters, John-son, & Kolodny, 1982; McCary & McCary, 1982) provide excellent presentations of the issues briefly presented here and should be con-sulted for further detail.

Sexual anatomy

Genetic gender is fixed at the moment of conception. An embryo with a pair of XX sex-determining chromosomes is a genetic female; a genetic male possesses an XY pair of chromosomes. Some individuals are conceived with abnormal chromosomal arrangements that com-plicate the process of sexual differentiation.

Development of internal and external sexual anatomy is a function of hormonal levels in the developing fetus. The internal and external sexual anatomy of males and females is indistinguishable up until the sixth week or so after conception. Differentiation is practically com-plete around the twelfth week of development. Under the influence of androgens (male hormones) the internal and external sexual anatomy of a male begins to develop. In the absence of these hormones, or when the target tissues are unresponsive to the hormones, female anatomy develops. These processes occur regardless of the genetic sex of the fetus. That is, a genetic female under the influence of androgens will develop testes, penis, scrotum, and so on, while a genetic male not exposed to androgens develops ovaries, uterus, vagina, and so on. Such conditions are called pseudohermaphroditism. The true her-maphrodite, which is very rare, is the infant born with both true ovaries and testicular tissues and almost always with a uterus.

Sex hormones also influence the brain. The most well-documented gender differentiation is in the hypothalamus, which plays a major controlling function in the regulation of sex hormones. The hypothalamus in the female is patterned for cyclical hormone production, resulting after puberty in the ovulatory/menstrual cycle, while the male hypothalamus maintains a relatively constant level of sex hormone production. Other possible brain differences between females and males have been investigated, but none has been sufficiently established to be firmly reported. It cannot be firmly asserted that the culturally stereotypical differences in aggressiveness, emotionality, or sexual responsiveness are rooted in stable brain deficiencies.

The next major stage of sexual development occurs at puberty. Under the influence of suddenly escalating hormone levels, changes begin to occur in the genitals and in other secondary sex characteristics. For both males and females puberty results in enlargement of the external genitalia, growth of pubic and other body hair, and an overall growth spurt. Females begin to experience breast enlargement, menarche (first menstruation), ovulation, vaginal secretion (including nocturnal lubrication), and development of feminine body form due to changes in bone structure and muscle/fat ratios. Males experience voice deepening (due to growth of the larynx), growth of facial hair, increased potential for muscle growth, increased incidence of erection, and nocturnal emissions. Puberty normally occurs between ages 10 and 16 (one to two years later for boys than for girls), though earlier and later dates can occur. Neither pregnancy nor impregnation is possible before puberty.

Adulthood is a fairly stable period of sexuality from a biological perspective. Menopause is the cessation of ovulation and menstruation for women, a condition that can be accompanied by discomfort and distress. A very small percentage of males experience a similar lessening of hormone production with resulting distress called the male climacteric. Most people, male and female, experience a decrease in sexual desire with aging; but a cessation of desire or capacity for sexual response is no longer viewed as a normal aspect of aging.

The most important sex organs for the male are the penis, testicles, seminal vesicles, and prostate. The glans, or head of the penis, is richly ennervated and is highly sensitive to tactile stimulation. The testicles, seminal vesicles, and prostate all contribute to ejaculation. For some men the penile foreskin is surgically removed at birth (circumcision). Presence or absence of the foreskin does not seem to affect sexual response. The testes, along with the adrenal glands, produce the male sex hormones; the testes alone produce sperm.

The major female sexual organs are the labia majora and minora, clitoris, vagina, uterus, and ovaries. The clitoris and the outer one-third of the vagina and the labia minora are the most erotically sensitive areas of the female body. The clitoris, like the penis, has a glans, or head, which is richly ennervated and extremely sensitive to stimulation. The inner (deeper) two-thirds of the vagina seems to be less sensitive to stimulation. The ovaries produce the female sex hormones and the ova, which can be fertilized by sperm and implanted in the uterus for development and birth.

Sexual physiology

The degree to which sexual drive is a biologically rooted phenomenon is unclear. Research suggests that there is some correlation between intensity of sexual drive and testosterone levels in males (produced in the testicles and adrenal glands) and androgen levels in females (produced in the adrenal glands). This relationship of hormone levels and sex drive is a complex one, however, in that sex drive is also a function of a number of psychological factors as well. Low sexual desire is not necessarily a function of lowered hormone levels, and hypersexual desire is not necessarily a function of elevated hormone levels. Hormones do nothing to direct sexual desire; there are no firmly established sex hormone differences between heterosexuals and homosexuals. While sexual response is closely regulated by female hormone levels in most animals, it appears that there is no such relationship for human females.

Masters and Johnson's (1966) conceptualization of the phases of sexual response has been the most influential in this field. Based on empirical clinical research with volunteers, their conclusion is that males and females experience four stages of sexual response: excitement, plateau, orgasm, and resolution. The two basic changes in the body during sexual response are vasocongestion (concentration of blood in specific tissues) and muscular tension throughout the body, especially in the genital area.

The excitement stage results from effective sexual stimulation of any sort, physical or psychological. Males and females both begin to experience increased muscular tension, including the beginning of elevation of heart and respiration rates. Vasocongestion in the male results in erection of the penis. Erection is a hydraulic event resulting from engorgement of blood in the penis. Vasocongestion in females results in the beginning of swelling of the tissues in the genital area, including hardening (erection) of the clitoris and lubrication of the vagina, which results from seepage or "sweating" of the vaginal walls. Vaginal lubrication does not come from glands. Nipple erection from vasocongestion is typical in women and frequent in men. Testicular elevation begins for men in this stage.

The plateau stage continues and intensifies the same physiological reactions for both sexes. In women the labia swell and deepen their color, the vagina expands, the uterus moves within the abdomen to become more erect, the clitoris continues to engorge with blood and become more sensitive, and the breasts swell. A flush on the skin of the chest is common. In men erection becomes complete, as does elevation of the testicles. A small amount of fluid may pass from the penile opening before ejaculation; this fluid may contain live sperm. This is a major reason why interruption of coitus before ejaculation is not effective as a method of birth control. The length of the excitement and plateau stages varies widely.

Orgasm, frequently called climax or coming, is characterized for both sexes by a sharp peak of overall muscular tension, but especially rhythmic muscular contractions of the genital area (for women, the outer third of the vagina and the uterus; for men, the penis, urethra, and prostrate). Males typically experience a sensation of "ejaculatory inevitability," which signals the beginning of orgasm but precedes ejaculation. After this point is reached, orgasm has begun and ejaculation is inevitable within seconds, even though stimulation ceases. For males, ejaculation and orgasm are usually parallel but differentiable events. Orgasm without ejaculation, and the reverse, are possible and have been documented.

There is some controversy about types of female orgasm. Freud believed that there were two types of orgasm, clitoral and vaginal. The clitoral orgasm was deemed less mature and more autistic, while the vaginal orgasm (produced in coitus only) was viewed as more mature. The research of Masters and Johnson (1966) and others has demonstrated to the satisfaction of most of the scientific world that there is only one type of orgasm, one which results from clitoral stimulation. They showed that the clitoris is stimulated indirectly during intercourse by penile thrusting, and that there is no physiological difference between orgasm during masturbation and orgasm during intercourse. These conclusions have not been universally accepted. For example, Singer and Singer (1978) differentiated between clitoral, uterine, and mixed orgasms. Their position, as well as those of classical Freudians and others who disagree with the conclusions of Masters and Johnson, are not now well accepted in the scientific community.

The final stage of sexual response is that of resolution. For males and females the resolution stage is most often characterized by a rapid return to the unaroused resting state. The changes of the excitement and plateau states reverse themselves rapidly. If the person has reached the late plateau stage but has not experienced orgasm, resolution takes a much longer time to occur, and this can result in a variety of uncomfortable lingering sensations. In this phase a major difference between females and males emerges. Females are biologically capable of being multiorgasmic through the continuation of sexual stimulation. Not all women desire such experience or find it pleasant, however. Males, on the other hand, experience a refractory period following orgasm during which continued sexual stimulation does not result in a return of erection and capacity for sexual response. This refractory period is typically brief in young men (seconds or minutes) and gradually lengthens in duration with age (extending to hours or even days in later years).

A number of researchers have criticized Masters and Johnson's conceptualization of sexual response cycles because of what is perceived as their physiological reductionism and ignoring of the prerequisites of sexual arousal—that is, sexual desire.

Psychological Perspectives

Sexual development

How do genetic males (or females) become psychological males (or females)? Perhaps the two predominant models of gender differentiation are the psychodynamic model and the biosocial model. The latter enjoys the greatest acceptance today.

There are actually a number of psychodynamic models; the classical one is that of Freud. Freud believed sex (libido) to be the primary drive of human existence. He believed that around ages 4–5 young children come to have strong sexual/affectional longings for the opposite sex parent. In both sexes this is not a well-focused genital sexual desire like that experienced in adolescence, but a more diffuse desire to possess all the attention and affection of the opposite sex parent. For both sexes this affection is accompanied by fear of the same sex parent, who is seen as a stronger, more competent competitor for the other parent's affection who might hurt the child in the rivalry. This fear leads, in normal development, to identification with the same sex parent (becoming like them, assuming their characteristics) as a way of vicariously having the special affection of the other parent. Gender identity develops through identification. This process can be complicated by disturbances in father-mother relationships, absence of either or both parents, and psychological disturbances of either or both parents.

The biosocial view of gender differentiation is primarily identified with John Money, who has conducted a great deal of research with cases of sexual deviancy, gender disturbance, and physical aberrations in sexual development (summarized in Masters et al., 1982). Money emphasizes the interaction of biological and learned or psychosocial factors in development. Biological factors, as discussed earlier, determine genital appearance of the newborn child. Genital appearance at birth influences the manner in which parents and others interact with the developing child, influencing the child to accept the socially defined role behaviors of male or female. Money and his colleagues believe there is a critical period for gender identity development; gender identity is usually set by age 3 and is largely impervious to change. Thus, children whose sex is misidentified at birth (e.g., the female misidentified as a male due to genital masculinization caused by high androgen levels during development) or children raised as the other sex due to parental psychological disturbance grow up with a relatively stable sense of themselves being of the other sex than they are physically.

Money believes that developments in childhood and adolescence, both physical development and the development of erotic feelings for the opposite sex, serve to further substantiate the person's gender identity. Behavioral psychologists have added speculations about development of sexual orientation to Money's formulation. They suggest that sexual desire is relatively unfocused in the child, and that each incremental experience of sexual arousal serves to "stamp in" a sexual orientation through conditioned association. Previous development of a firm gender identity can serve to channel this process. Thus, boys with a firm sense of gender identity know that they should expect sexual arousal to girls and generally seek such arousal in the forms of fantasy or experience. Arousal thus experienced further confirms gender identity and solidifies sexual orientation.

Sexual Behavior

Sexual behavior occurs throughout the life cycle (see McCary & McCary, 1982, or Masters et al., 1982, for summaries of relevant studies). Ultrasound studies have suggested that male infants experience erection within the womb. Erection in male babies and vaginal lubrication in females have been demonstrated soon after birth. Children seem to naturally experience stimulation of the genital area as pleasurable. Genital self-stimulation (masturbation) is common in young children. Orgasm is possible throughout the life cycle, even though maximal pleasure is not derived therefrom until after puberty. Prepubertal males do not ejaculate upon experience of orgasm. A variety of types of sex play continues throughout childhood for many children.

Genital sexual activity is common in adolescence. There is much disagreement among figures reported in the empirical literature from surveys of adolescent and adult sexual behavior. A major problem with this literature is the high rate of refusal to participate by teenagers contacted for interviewing (or by the parents of adolescents contacted for their permission for their child to be interviewed). Early studies suggested a large disparity between the occurrence of male and female masturbation in adolescence, but this gap has been shrinking over the years. It can be said with some firmness that the large majority of adolescents have masturbated to orgasm at least once by age 18. The number who regularly practice masturbation is thought to be somewhat below the overall incidence.

Erotic dreams and nocturnal emissions (together commonly called wet dreams) are almost universal in boys during adolescence. Erection is common throughout the life cycle as a correlate to the rapid eye movement (REM) stage of sleep, the stage when dreaming is most likely. Wet dreams may represent a mechanism for the release of sexual tensions. It is less commonly known that the female correlate of erection, vaginal lubrication, occurs regularly in sleep during REM periods. While not as common as nocturnal emissions in males, orgasm during erotic dreams is not unusual for women; up to 50% report this occurrence by adulthood.

Figures on homosexual experience in adolescence are difficult to interpret, given the common sampling problems and the differences across studies in how homosexual experience is defined. Some studies have inquired about homosexual stimulation to orgasm, while others have used a much broader definition that might incorporate any sort of same sex sexual play, even in earliest childhood. The best summary of this data suggests that a substantial number of men, and to a lesser degree women, have fleeting homosexual experiences early in life. It appears that only about 2–3% of the male population and 1–2% of the females are exclusively homosexual in experience, with an additional 5–10% of each sex having at least one significant prolonged homosexual experience. Male homosexuals outnumber females two or three to one.

Intercourse before marriage is becoming more common and more accepted in American society. The consensus of a number of studies is that by age 16 close to 35% of males and 25% of females are nonvirgins; by age 19 about 70–80% of unmarried males and 60–70% of unmarried females are nonvirgins. These figures appear to represent a dramatic change in sexual behavior among females, who are becoming much more sexually active. These figures cannot be taken to indicate a complete swing toward promiscuity, however, as most adolescents do not report large numbers of sexual partners. Whereas in the 1950s many men reported first intercourse experience with a prostitute, most young men and women now report intercourse to occur in a caring relationship. Casual sex is perhaps only slightly more widespread today than in the past, but there is a much broader acceptance of sex with affection outside of marriage than was previously the case.

In adulthood most persons marry. The frequency of intercourse in marriage may have increased moderately over the past several decades. Frequency of coitus decreases steadily with age. In this, the sexual desires of the male seem to predominate, in that it is commonly reported that males' sexual desire peaks in late adolescence and the early 20s, declining thereafter. Females' sexual desire is reported to peak in the 30s and 40s. Adultery has become more common in the United States, with most recent studies suggesting that about 50% of males and 33% of females have had at least one extramarital experience of coitus. Those proportions are higher in younger groups. Some studies suggest that a fairly high percentage (up to one-half) of married couples experience moderate to strong dissatisfaction with their sexual relationship with their spouses.

Factors influencing sexual behavior

Research with adolescents and college students (Chilman, 1978) suggests that the following factors are associated with premarital coitus: increasing age, lower religiousness, greater permissiveness of peers, lessened influence of and communication with parents, higher self-esteem in boys but lower self-esteem in girls, lower academic achievement expectation, higher value of independence from family, permissiveness of parents, and basic sexual ideology or morality.

A number of factors that influence satisfaction with genital sexual experience have been identified in the clinical treatment literature. The factors that have been implicated in decreased sexual satisfaction include lack of information or actual misinformation about sexual response, deeply ingrained negative attitudes toward sex, anxiety due to fear of pregnancy or of intimacy, performance anxiety, fatigue or illness, and relationship disturbances. Many experts in the field who have advocated greater sexual enlightenment for our society are recognizing that the cost of sexual revolution has been greater emphasis on sexual performance relative to relational intimacy and subjective satisfaction. Some have suggested that the current trend emphasizing affection and relationship (but not necessarily marriage) before sex is a reaction against these trends. Possibly as another reaction to the cultural emphasis on sexual performance, sex therapists report an increasing number of persons seeking treatment for disorders of sexual desire. Increasingly people who find sex to be less important in life are viewed by themselves and others as abnormal.

Sexual dysfunctions must be differentiated from sexual deviations (or more commonly today, "variations"). Dysfunctions represent failures to perform adequately; deviations represent disorders in response to sexual objects. The most common sexual dysfunctions in women are disorders of arousal, orgasmic dysfunctions, vaginismus, and dyspareunia. Males experience disorders of arousal, erectile dysfunction, and premature or retarded ejaculation.

Sexuality and adjustment

What is the relationship between sexual functioning and personal adjustment? Views based on early dynamic formulations tended to link the two closely, so that sexual dysfunction was viewed as symptomatic of more deeply rooted personality disturbances; from these came the description of the sexually underresponsive woman as "frigid." Some writers pushed this view further to conclude that sexual response was the best index of adjustment.

In the early stages of the development of sex therapy as a speciality within mental health practice, the opposite ideology seemed to be pressed. Sexual functioning was viewed as a learned phenomenon without necessary linkages to other aspects of personality functioning. This conception was supported by the rapid successes in treatment of sexual dysfunction reported by Masters and Johnson and others.

The current view among many prominent sex therapists (see Leiblum & Pervin, 1980) is that neither of the above broad formulations is adequate. Rather, for some individuals sexual dysfunction represents a relatively simple problem amenable to brief intervention. For others the sexual disturbance is a problem for which more fundamental change is essential.

Integration

The interrelationships between the theological, biological, and psychological perspectives on sexuality are critical, but only a sampling can be explored here. First, it should be stated that any definition of normality is conditioned by a priori assumptions regarding the nature of optimal human response and the purposes of that response. The implicit theory of most sex researchers and clinicians is that sexual functioning is, from an evolutionary perspective, intended for procreation, and has become endowed with tremendous pleasure-producing qualities as a spur to reproductive activity. Because species survival and pleasure are viewed as the highest human goods (with some emphasizing the primacy of individual hedonistic gratification and others the importance of subsuming individual pleasure to collective good), most writers in this field exhibit a broad acceptance of sexual behaviors. These writers would argue for a "scientific" basis for determination of normalcy based on empirical study of statistical frequency, pleasure derived, and harm/benefits produced by a particular behavior. Christians must recognize the implicit values behind such a scientific analysis and suggest alternatively that other purposes of sexuality must be considered in the determination of normalcy. Thus, despite the high statistical frequency, reported pleasure derived from, and lack of empirical evidence showing harm produced by premarital sex, Christians can assert that such actions are statistically frequent but not normal, in the sense that those actions violate the meaning and purpose for which the act of coitus was created by God. As noted earlier, however, Christians must struggle with empirical and clinical evidences in areas that might be called borderline (Thielicke, 1964), since these areas are not clearly dealt with in Scripture.

Our consideration of the purposes and nature of sexuality affects our definition of optimum sexuality. Optimum sexuality cannot be defined in terms of physical performance standards only, since such standards omit reference to the broader purposes of unity and reflection of spiritual truth that are important to sexual relationship. Optimum sexuality will be that which is most in accord with the purposes of sex; thus, optimum genital sexuality in marriage is appropriately open to procreation, is pleasurable, promoting of interpersonal union, and in its wholeness and holiness mirrors the nature of God and of Christ's relationship to his church. Such formulations of optimum sexuality are critical to judging the effectiveness of sex therapy in treatment of sexual dysfunctions, which to this point has been largely judged by the criteria of frequency and speed of orgasm. Such purely functional criteria can be seen from an integrated perspective to be important (to the purpose of pleasure) but limited. True enhancement of sexual life must have in focus a broader view of the meaning and purpose of sexuality.

References

Brunner, E. *Man in revolt.* London: Lutterworth, 1939.

Bullough, V., & Brundage, J. *Sexual practices and the medieval church.* Buffalo, N.Y.: Prometheus, 1982.

Chilman, C. *Adolescent sexuality in a changing American society.* Washington, D.C.: U.S. Government Printing Office, 1978.

Feucht, O., Coiner, H., Sauer, A., & Hansen, P. (Eds.). *Sex and the church*. St. Louis: Concordia, 1961.

Kosnick, A., Carroll, W., Cunningham, A., Modras, R., & Schulte, J. *Human sexuality: New directions in American Catholic thought*. New York: Paulist Press, 1977.

Leiblum, S., & Pervin, L. (Eds.). *Principles and practice of sex therapy*. New York: Guilford, 1980.

Masters, W. H., & Johnson, V. E. *Human sexual response*. Boston: Little, Brown, 1966.

Masters, W. H., Johnson, V. E., & Kolodny, R. C. *Human sexuality*. Boston: Little, Brown, 1982.

McCary, J., & McCary, S. *McCary's human sexuality*. Belmont, Calif.: Wadsworth Publishing, 1982.

McDonald, H. D. *The Christian view of man*. Westchester, Ill.: Crossway, 1981.

Singer, J., & Singer, I. Types of female orgasm. In J. LoPiccolo & L. LoPiccolo (Eds.), *Handbook of sex therapy*. New York: Plenum, 1978.

Small, D. H. *Christian: Celebrate your sexuality*. Old Tappan, N.J.: Revell, 1974.

Thielicke, H. *The ethics of sex*. New York: Harper & Row, 1964.

38

Trust
Craig W. Ellison

T rust is an act of dependency upon another person for the fulfillment of biological, psychological, social, or spiritual needs that cannot be met independently. It is subjective confidence in the intentions
and ability of another to promote and/or guard one's well-being that
leads a person to risk possible harm or loss. Trust, then, involves both
perceptual and behavioral dimensions. Perceiving another person as
trustworthy does not constitute trust, nor does simply engaging in a
risk-taking behavior without some positive expectancy about the response. Perceiving someone as trustworthy *and* placing oneself in a
position of vulnerability due to the possibility of betrayal is trust.
Trust may involve the vulnerability of one's self-concept and emotional well-being, relationships, possessions, social and economic position, or physical being.

Trust is not usually an all-or-none phenomenon. There are degrees
of trust, which can be assessed by the level of positive expectancy
about someone's trustworthiness together with the magnitude of damage involved if betrayal occurs. A process of observation and testing
typically occurs before significant outcomes are entrusted. As confi-

dence increases, subjective assessment of the risk involved tends to decrease and greater (objective) acts of trust occur. Interpersonal attraction and reciprocated acts of disclosure appear to facilitate the development of trust.

It seems that people differ in their general tendency to trust people. Some persons are so trusting they are called gullible. Others are so suspicious that they are paranoid. Erikson (1963) suggests that this basic orientation is is due to the adequacy with which basic needs of the infant were met during the helplessness of the first year of life. Two scales widely used to assess such a generalized trust orientation are the Philosophy of Human Nature Scale (Wrightsman, 1974) and the Interpersonal Trust Scale (Rotter, 1967).

Acts of trusting vary considerably. They may involve the safekeeping of property, acceptance of a persuasive communication, seeking help for problems, selection of a physician, or sharing of confidential information. The diversity of trust acts may be categorized into three general types of trust: persuasive, functional, and personal. Persuasive trust involves a belief in the validity of a message and the integrity of a messenger so that an idea is accepted or a product is bought. Acceptance of the appeals of politicians, evangelists, and vacuum cleaner salespeople requires this kind of trust. Functional trust is confidence in the capacity and expertise of the one being trusted to competently fulfill a function, such as flying an airplane or doing surgery. Personal trust is the expectancy that another will accept voluntarily disclosed intimate information, treat it with value, and act in one's best interest. This is the trust of intimate friends. More than one kind of trust may be expressed toward another person. Trust of one type may facilitate the other types in certain situations.

The act of entrusting specific outcomes to a specific person at a given point in time involves a complex mixture of one's history of trust encounters in general and in similar situations; the level and kind of felt need; information about the other person's sincerity, capability, integrity, and intentions based on direct and indirect observation; the kind of relationship that exists; the kind and degree of trust required; and the situational context.

The phenomenon of trust has been studied by psychologists from the perspectives of laboratory experimentation in bargaining and negotiation (Deutsch, 1962), developmental theory (Erikson, 1963), encounter group therapy (Schutz, 1967), self-disclosure theory and research (Cozby, 1973), and measurement (Rotter, 1967; Wrightsman, 1974).

One of the most basic concepts in the Bible is that of faith. Faith is a perspective that affects both perception and practice. It involves a sense of confidence about the truth of biblical statements regarding the existence and nature of phenomena beyond immediate sensory experience, including God, and about the ultimate spiritual consequences of various decisions and behaviors. The Hebraic and early Christian understanding of faith merged belief and behavior in a manner that is synonymous with trust. Without actions that express belief, belief is not regarded as faith (James 2:14–26).

The Bible can be understood as a record of the qualities of God that encourage perception of him as absolutely trustworthy (1 John 4:9). The illustrations of his capabilities (Eph. 3:20), integrity (1 Peter 1:17), and love (1 John 4:9) revealed in historical accounts of his relationships with specific people are intended to enable all people to believe and entrust the direction and decisions of their lives to him. The incarnation of Christ further demonstrated the desire of God to act for the benefit of humanity through his redemptive act of self-sacrifice (Rom. 5:8).

In addition, the Scriptures repeatedly demonstrate the positive consequences of actually trusting God (Ps. 22:4–5; Rev. 21:3–7) and the negative results of failing to do so (1 Kings 21:21–25; Rev. 20:15) as a means of motivating people throughout history to act on their biblically based perceptions of his character.

References

Cozby, P. C. Self-disclosure: A literature review. *Psychological Bulletin*, 1973, 79, 73–91.

Deutsch, M. Cooperation and trust: Some notes. In M. R. Jones (Ed.), *Nebraska symposium on motivation* (Vol. 10). Lincoln: University of Nebraska Press, 1962.

Erikson, E. H. *Childhood and society* (2nd ed.). New York: Norton, 1963.

Rotter, J. B. A new scale for the measurement of interpersonal trust. *Journal of Personality*, 1967, 35, 651–665.

Schutz, W. E. *Joy*. New York: Grove Press, 1967.

Wrightsman, L. S. *Assumptions about human nature: A social-psychological approach*. Monterey, Calif.: Brooks/Cole, 1974.

Part **3**

Christian Psychology

39

Biblical Anthropology
William T. Kirwan

The study of the biblical view of man has been somewhat confusing, since a multitude of terms are used to refer to humanity. *Soul, spirit, body, heart,* and *mind* are a few of the key words which refer to man in his psychospiritual functioning. In the past much debate has centered on the so-called dichotomistic versus the trichotomistic models of man. However, more recent biblical scholarship suggests that anytime the Bible speaks of an aspect of man (soul, spirit, or mind) it is always talking about the whole person (Berkouwer, 1962). Biblically, man is never fragmented or divided into parts; he is always viewed as a totality. This separates biblical thought from Greek thought, where knowledge was seen as cognitive; to the Greeks, the accumulation of facts was something that could be abstractly discussed apart from the knower or the context of a personal commitment to that knowledge by the knower. Biblical thought knows nothing of such an idea, but sees knowledge as something to be acted upon and demanding commitment from the person. Thus in the Bible *mind* and its ability to know refers to a response that involves the whole person.

It seems clear that the key biblical term for the psychospiritual nature of man is *heart*. More than any other biblical term *heart* refers to the absolute inner center of man in that it suggests a depth view. All the other biblical terms may often be used interchangeably with heart. They may give a different light on man in totality, but they do not indicate a part of man that is separate from or not included in his heart. A brief examination of a few of these other terms will help interpret the biblical concept of heart.

Soul, Spirit, and Mind

The words *soul (nepeš; psychē)* and *spirit (rûah; pneuma)* are often used as parallel expressions and probably should be viewed as synonymous. Matthew 27:50 reads, "And when Jesus had cried out again in a loud voice, he gave up his spirit *(pneuma)*." However, in contrast, in John 10:17 Jesus says, "The reason my Father loves me is that I lay down my life *(psychē)*, only to take it up again." Here both soul and spirit refer to the laying down and giving up of Christ's life and seem to be used interchangeably.

Also it should be noted that the highest experiences of life can be ascribed to either the soul or the spirit. In John 12:27 Jesus said, "Now my soul *(psychē)* is troubled and what shall I say? Father, save me from this hour?" In contrast John 13:21 says, "After he had said this, Jesus was troubled in spirit *(pneuma)* and testified, I tell you the truth, one of you is going to betray me." To attempt to differentiate soul and spirit based on these examples would be extremely difficult. Those who make a distinction suggest that soul refers to the individual's personal life, while spirit refers to the principle of life—that is, the sense of man's being a spiritual being.

With the term *mind (nous; dianoia)* we find the same emphasis. The total man is always in view. In Deuteronomy 6:5 God says "Love the Lord your God with all your heart and with all your soul and with all your strength." There was no technical word in Hebrew for the mind, so we have the word *strength*. In repeating this commandment Jesus says in Matthew 22:37, "Love the Lord your God with all your heart and with all your soul and with all your mind *(dianoia)*." Clearly his reference to loving God with the mind implies the whole personality is to be committed to an intimate and personal relationship with God.

Heart

Heart is emphasized as the more absolute center, the core of psychospiritual life. "Above all else guard your heart, for it is the wellspring of life" (Prov. 4:23). In some of his harshest teachings Jesus rebuked the Pharisees, and in doing so picks up the theme of the heart as central to human personality: "But the things that come out of the mouth come from the heart, and these make a man unclean. For out of the heart come evil thoughts, murder, adultery, sexual immorality, theft, false testimony, slander" (Matt. 15:18–19). The heart refers to the person's inner essence. It represents the ego or the person. "Thus the heart is supremely the one center in man to which God turns, in which the religious life is rooted, which determines moral conduct" (Kittel, 1976, p. 608). Brandon notes that the heart is the source of motives, the seat of passions, the center of the thought processes, and the spring of conscience. He further notes that this incorporates what is now meant by the cognitive, affective, and volitional elements of personality (Brandon, 1967).

It is interesting to note that the uses of *heart* which refer to thinking, feeling, and acting are balanced enough so as to represent nearly equal emphases. The heart can then be said to contain cognition, affect, and volition. Delitzsch (1867/1977) states that the heart is the center of the pneumatico-psychical life, the life of thought and perceptions, the life of will and desire, and the life of feelings and affections. According to Scripture the heart is not the seat of emotion only, but also of the will and thought; all three spiritual activities converge in the heart (Delitzsch, 1867/1977, p. 307).

This biblical perspective underlines the importance of the heart and its key role in Christian life and thought. It is upon the heart that God looks (1 Sam. 16:7), with the heart that we believe unto salvation (Rom. 10:10), and from the heart that obedience springs (Rom 6:17). It is the heart which is wicked and evil (Jer 17:9), and finally the heart is the internal source for all that is external in us (Luke 6:45). As the center of the person, the internal source of one's life, it is the core and seat of emotions, the center of emotional reaction, feeling, and sensitivity. The full spectrum of emotions, from joy to depression and from love to hatred, are ascribed to the heart. Says Delitzsch, "The heart is the laboratory and place of issue of all that is good and evil in thoughts, words and deeds" (p. 148).

If God views the heart as the central influence in the Christian life, then how is the heart transformed from being "deceitful above all things" to "white as snow"? How is the condition of the heart altered? Perhaps no more important question can be asked in philosophy as well as psychology. The biblical answer is quite clear. The heart is changed only through relationship with Jesus Christ. All theology which deals with a person's change, salvation, sanctification, and glorification ultimately focuses upon the simple relationship that an individual can have with Christ. Biblically, neither the heart nor the human person is ever changed in any other way. Evidence for this cardinal truth can be seen throughout Scripture. In the Old Testament only a personal relationship with Jehovah, the covenant God, changed a person. David says, "Create in me a pure heart, O God, and renew a steadfast spirit within me" (Ps. 51:10), and again, "Search me, O God, and know my heart; test me and know my thoughts" (Ps. 139:23). The primacy of the heart is also set forth in Ezekiel. God says, "I will give them an undivided heart and put a new spirit in them; I will remove from them their heart of stone and give them a heart of flesh" (Ezek. 11:19). Paul repeats the same thinking in the New Testament (Eph. 4:16–19).

Implications for Psychology

This meaning of the biblical use of heart has several implications for the study of psychology. First is the emphasis on the hiddenness of the heart. It is presented as that which lies at the root of thinking, feeling, and acting, the core of man's psychic processes. Its depth and unknowability strongly hint at the modern concept of the unconscious. This is substantiated by David's prayer, "Search me O God and know my heart, . . . and see if there be any wicked way in me" (Ps. 139:23–24). Again, "The heart is deceitful above all things and desperately wicked; who can know it?" (Jer. 17:9). The primacy of the intellect versus the primacy of the inner man or his heart needs to inform the direction of Christian thought in psychology.

Second, the heart shows the importance of affect or feeling. Clinically the power of feelings is easily observable, but to have the Bible point to emotions and feelings as a key and important part of man is significant. Since Christians have often tended to downplay emotions or make them subordinate to other functions, the heart stands as a corrective against such views.

Third, the importance of relationships can be seen by the fact that the heart is changed only by relationship with Christ. This emphasis is found through the entire Bible, and it too has tended to be overlooked by Christian thought. The heart calls relationships to the fore in any discussion of Christian theology or psychology.

Fourth, the heart serves to inform us about the use of psychological thought today. If a person's chief areas of functioning are knowing, being, and doing, it can be seen that congnition, feeling, and behavior correspond closely to these. Therapy should therefore involve all three if it is to be biblical.

Last, the heart must be the core which corresponds to the modern concept of identity. Cognition would emphasize self-image or one's rational view of himself. Affect would emphasize self-esteem or one's feeling about his worth, value, or image. Volition would emphasize self-control or one's ability to control his impulses and feelings. The biblical emphasis on heart suggests that all three components would apply to man as an observer of himself. Thus a comprehensive psychology of identity must include self-image, self-esteem, and self-control mechanisms and structures.

References

Berkouwer, G. C. *Man: The image of God.* Grand Rapids: Eerdmans, 1962.

Brandon, S. G. F. *Jesus and the zealots.* New York: Scribners, 1967.

Delitzsch, F. J. A *system of biblical psychology* (and ed.). Grand Rapids: Baker, 1977. (Originally published, 1867.)

Kittel, G. Kardia. In G. Kittel (Ed.), *Theological dictionary of the New Testament* (Vol. 3). Grand Rapids: Eerdmans, 1976.

40

Christian Psychology
Randie L. Timpie

Although the term is not widely used at the present (for an exception see Myers, 1978), *Christian psychology* refers to a movement within psychology which seeks to integrate the evangelical understanding of biblical doctrine with scientific and applied aspects of psychology. The critical focus of the movement is to reconceptualize psychology in such a way as to be consistent with the tenets of an orthodox, Protestant cosmology and anthropology. However, the general purpose is broader than purely cognitive reconceptualization; theological and psychological insights are applied to bolster one's personal faith.

The Desacralization of Psychology

The past century of psychology has witnessed the gradual but complete secularization of concepts about human personality which had theological origins (Roback, 1952). During the first half of the twentieth century psychologists were more disposed to discuss sexual matters (unheard of in the Victorian period of 1830–1900) than religion

254

(except for the noble examples of James and Allport). In spite of recent antipathy between psychologists and theologians there is a close historical link between them. The Latin term *persona*, from which the English term *personality* developed, denoted both the mask used to indicate a particular theatrical role and the real self or actor. *Persona* suggested that the inner nature may be split from outward action. But the Latin word *religio* meant a binding or fastening, especially in the form of reverence or fear of a more powerful being. Thus the person had internal integrity because of the religious nature of personality (Oates, 1973).

The ancient Greeks used two words to portray the essence of human nature. *Psychē* originally meant the breath or spirit which distinguished the animate from the inanimate. Later it developed connotations of soul and mind, and the study of psychology ensued. *Pneuma* was a close parallel to *psychē; pneuma* referred to life, but in its relationship to the eternal. From the study of the *pneuma* came theology; religion was a human expression of *pneuma*. The secularization of *psychē* inevitably led to the development of psychology as a discipline distinct from philosophy and theology.

The language of psychology has been desacralized at other points. The Hebrews used the word *nepeš* to describe the whole person, a union of inner and outer aspects of *lēb* and body. In the Old Testament *nepeš* is commonly translated *soul*. However, when *soul* gradually developed connotations of transcendency and eternity, psychologists adopted the term *self* to refer to human wholeness. Self to the holistic psychologists is essentially the rebirth in a desacralized form of the Hebraic concept of soul. Secularization of will is recounted by Roback (1952) and Kantor (1963).

The Integration of Psychology and Christianity

Christian psychology originates from a drive to construct a more adequate psychology by reconnecting the severed relationships with theology; the drive embodies a desire to adopt the best of science and faith. The goal is to integrate faith and reason by linking theology and science. The reassertion of biblical orthodoxy as the basis of one's science is a reaction to modern psychology's endorsement of the religion of secular humanism (Collins, 1977; Vitz, 1977). Although the relationship between theology and psychology has been strained and one of mutual suspicion and denigration, this need not be the case (Ellison, 1972).

The attempt to integrate psychology and theology strives for "the unity of truth." The task of integration involves an explicit relating of truth gleaned from general or natural revelation to that derived from special or biblical revelation, of interrelating knowledge gained from the world and knowledge gained from the Word. Of critical importance are the issues regarding the nature of reality (metaphysics) and the nature of knowledge (epistemology). The conflict between science (e.g., psychology) and theology at this point stems from variations in original assumptions. The naturalistic, objective, and inductive biases of scientists are juxtaposed to the supernaturalistic, subjective, and deductive premises of the theologian. The integration movement offers a rapprochement by proposing the adoption of two premises: 1) God is the source of all truth no matter *where* it is found; 2) God is the source of all truth no matter *how* it is found (Timpe, 1980).

To the integrationist, natural revelation supports special revelation instead of being a rival methodology. That is, if God is consistent (i.e., immutable) as the Scriptures suggest (e.g., Mal. 3:6), then knowledge based in revelation should parallel and complement that derived from reason. Both will complement that founded in replication and observation. Underlying this approach is a faith statement common to scientist and theologian alike: the laws that govern the operation of the world are discoverable.

Models of integration

Those who seek to understand the relationship between psychology and theology employ one of four strategies (Carter & Narramore, 1979). Some models of integration have sacred and secular versions. Perhaps the oldest and most familiar description is the *against* model, in which psychology and theology are portrayed as mortal enemies. Each defines one exclusive approach to truth (empiricism vs. revelation), one cause for human discomfort and misfortune (environmental conditioning vs. sin), and one solution to problems (psychotherapy vs. salvation). Freud and Ellis espoused a secular version of this approach; Adams adheres to the sacred version.

The *of* model (e.g., the psychology of religion) holds that human beings are moral-spiritual creatures not reducible to a collection of naturalistic forces. Humans are fundamentally good, and whatever pain is experienced is attributed to environmental or psychological factors rather than sin. Psychological insights aid persons in spiritual development. In the secular version human personality tends to be deified, while in the sacred version of the divine is desupernaturalized. The works of James, Allport, and Hiltner exhibit this mode of thought.

In the *parallels* model psychology and theology are held to be separate disciplines with separate goals, contents, and methods of inquiry to describe separate dimensions of human nature. There is a dualism in which spiritual dimensions constitute the province of theology, while physical and social dimensions concern psychology. Psychological insights parallel those of theology, but neither purports to offer a comprehensive description of human totality. In one respect psychology and theology have chosen to limit the focus of their study, both attempt to conceptualize the given aspects of human nature.

Etymologically, the word *psychology* has origins in two Greek words, *psychē* and *logos*, so that literally psychology is human words about life and personality. Similarly, the term *theology* comes from the Greek *theos* and *logos*. Theology is human words about God. Individuals who favor the parallels model suggest that psychology and theology are theory and conceptualization, regardless of what evidence each is based on. Psychology and theology are free to change when new facts are discovered or when old facts are reinterpreted. Humans are not obliged to act as psychologists have constructed them, nor is God obligated to correspond to theological ideas.

Moreover, the parallelists have defined different goals. Psychology is often described as the science which seeks to understand, predict, and control behavior. The choice of following the scientific model has had the effect of limiting study to regular, lawful, and aggregate events. Theology has sought to reason and deduce the nature of God and his laws aided regularly by divine revelation via the Scriptures. The focus in theology is often on unique, one-time events (e.g., incarnation, miracles). Psychology may be described as a science that tells the "how" of personal motivation and social relationships, whereas theology explains the "why" of creation and redemption (Jeeves, 1976; Timpe, 1980). Psychology is horizontal, theology is vertical in perspective. Each discipline couches its insights in a separate set of linguistic conventions, with parallels between conventions being mentioned (e.g., personality theory and anthropology, psychopathology and hamartiology, developmental psychology and soteriology). Furthermore, the parallel model holds that the Bible was inspired to be not a science book but rather history (i.e., the story about God's redemptive efforts to save his people). As history it contains all truth necessary for an individual's salvation.

According to Carter and Narramore (1979), the *integrated* model is to be perferred, since it is the most comprehensive. Psychology is not treated as a system of thought about human nature but rather about the actuality of created humanness. In like fashion theology is more than a body of thought about God; it takes on the character (or caricature) of cosmology. Knowledge is not pigeonholed into discipline-defined units, but all sources of knowledge are interrelated into one body of truth. Of necessity, the integrationist must be competently knowledgeable in both fields, and then be able to transcend the traditional limits of each. Tournier seems to have been able to accomplish those ends in much of his writing.

Levels of integration

The various models of integration may be applied at several levels (Larzalere, 1980). The broadest level of analysis is cosmological, in which assumptions about one's world-view are articulated. These are in essence faith statements, since neither psychology nor theology can prove the correctness of their assertions about the nature of reality. Embedded within the world-view is the second level of special assumptions: those assumptions pertain to content (e.g., human personality) and approved methodologies. Most of the tension existing between psychology and theology occurs at these two levels.

Foundational presuppositions in large measure determine the shape of the superstructure (i.e., theory). The central and non-negotiable assumption for the Christian psychologist is that God exists and is Creator-source of all truth and power (i.e., omniscience and omnipotence). Furthermore, God has chosen to reveal to humans, individually and collectively, some of his nature through the created world, through the inspired Scriptures, and through Jesus Christ as agent of creation and redemption. Various positions are taken on a number of peripheral assumptions. The central assumption deals with the *Christian* in Christian psychology while the peripheral assumptions may reflect Christian *psychologies*. The peripheral assumptions deal with such issues as the mind-brain relation, the nature-nurture controversy, the priority of general or special revelation, the extent of the pervasiveness of sin, and determinism and free will; they may distinguish one integration from another. Integrationists take a position on each, however implicit or explicit, but peripheral assumptions remain secondary and subservient to the supernatural one.

The third level of analysis is that of theoretical proposition and hypothesis. The fourth and final level constitutes data. While conflict between psychology and theology may exist at these levels, it is not as pronounced as at the first two levels.

Examples of integration

Conflict between psychology and theology is most prominent at the world-view and special assumption levels. The credo of the secular psychologist is: "I believe in the efficacy of empiricism, the divinity of determinism, the reality of relativism, the revelation of reductionism, and the necessity of naturalism" (adapted from Collins, 1977). Collins (1977) spent considerable time and effort addressing the issues of world-view and special assumptions. He found the traditional behavioral assumptions of empiricism, determinism, relativism, reductionism, and naturalism problematic in an integration of psychology and theology. Since these do not correspond well with traditional theological tenets, he suggested the faulty assumptive foundations be rebuilt. He proposed an expanded empiricism that allows God to reveal himself through sense impression and other means. Expanded empiricism permits more subjectivity in observation and knowledge than does the more radical version of scientism (Bufford, 1981).

In lieu of the traditional behavioral assumption of determinism, Collins substituted freedom and determinism. His solution was a soft determinism where the laws of the universe limit the number of alternatives, yet within those alternatives the individual is free to choose the course of action. The alternatives are not equally attractive or probable, because heredity and past environmental influences affect their relative likelihood. Among direct influences on behavior the supernatural work of the Holy Spirit and angels must be included.

As a replacement for unlimited relativism Collins upheld a biblical absolutism, in which the individual searches the Scriptures for absolutes. Absolutes as general principles guide behavior and increase knowledge. Where the Bible appears to be silent, value judgments are deduced from biblical principles.

A modified reductionism is also proposed, permitting the individual to gain further information about nature, but not asserting that nature itself can be reduced to "nothing but" basic elements. Christian supernaturalism is inserted in the place of naturalism. There is a sovereign God who created the natural order, and his laws account for the orderliness of nature. However, God is a transcendent being, not bound to the created order.

While the work of Collins was at the world-view level, Koteskey (1980, 1983) addressed the general theoretical level. The integrative mechanism he employed is a variant of Schaffer's (1968) view that God is personal and infinite. Humans are like God in having personality (soul, spirit, etc.), but a chasm exists between God, the Creator and created mankind relative to infiniteness. Thus the personal dimension emphasizes the ways in which humans mirror God's image and are different from animals, while the infinite aspects point to human-divine differences and a commonality with animals. In this way perspectives and ideas from structuralism, gestalt psychology, and humanistic psychology illustrate likenesses between the divine and human. Behaviorism and functionalism point to the similarities of humans and animals, while psychoanalysis marks how unlike God humans are.

Koteskey's (1983) position is not that psychology and theology need to be integrated, but that theology (i.e., Schaffer's discussion of the personal and infinite dimensions) should serve to integrate a fragmented secular psychology. The content areas in psychology are ordered into his pattern. For example, physiological studies in structure, motivation, emotion, sensation, and conditioning describe similarities between humans and animals. Godlikeness is seen in the areas of perception, cognition, and cognitive aspects of motivation, emotion, and social relationships. Psychiatric disorders can be ordered similarly. Organic mental disorders, appearing in childhood or adolescence, somatoform disorders, phobic disorders, psychosexual disorders, and anxiety disorders are at the animal end of the continuum. Personality disorders, paranoid disorders, schizophrenic disorders, narcissism, and affective disorders are failures to achieve human potential at the Godlike end of the continuum.

At the general theoretical level Bufford (1981) examined behavioral psychology and its relation to Scripture. His basic position is that there is little in behavioral psychology and its practice (i.e., methodological behaviorism as a way of knowing and changing) to contradict current biblical understanding. However, when behavioral psychology takes a more radical view (i.e., radical or metaphysical behaviorism), the naturalistic and reductionistic premises pose problems at the philosophic level for a classical theologian. This tension is due in large measure to Platonic dualism, with an exaggeration of naturalism by Enlightenment scientists and a corresponding exaggeration of supernaturalism by theologians of the Middle Ages. Neither exaggeration is consistent with the biblical record.

Bufford conceptualized causation of events in an intriguing way. The two causes, divine and natural, could either be present or absent. When these are combined into a 2×2 matrix, 4 possible types of causation emerge. When both divine and natural causes are absent, there is chaos. When divine cause is absent but natural cause is present, a naturalistic explanation is given. In the event that a supernatural cause is present and the natural cause is absent, there is said to exist a supernatural explanation or miracle (e.g., creation *ex nihilo*). Providential explanation is the divine employing natural mechanisms as sources of causality. The Christian scientist or psychologist must endorse the providential explanation, since chaos and miracles are not predictable nor are they recurring events. Natural explanations must also be ruled out on the basis of the assumption of divine causation.

Providential explanations have an impact on how human freedom is construed. In the behavioral literature freedom is not so much an attribute of human nature as a behavior. It is not the absence of control, but it is absence of *effective* (most often aversive) control. An individual acts free when he removes himself from an aversive control situation. In this way freedom is predictable in that an observer could predict an individual's behavior without causing it, simply by foreknowing the nature of freedom. God can foreknow an individual's freeing actions without causing the action.

Human freedom is a constrained or limited freedom, wherein the limits are determined by divine intervention or providential process. The individual is free to choose only from those options known. Only God as a sovereign, infinite being has "free will in the sense of unhampered or uncaused choice" (Bufford, 1981, p. 54). Bufford contends that the behavioral view expressed above is consistent with the Westminister Confession of Faith.

Several writers have attempted to present Christian perspectives on specific propositions or hypotheses. Both Custance (1980) and Jones (1981) argue that there is biblical and scientific support for a dualistic solution to the mind-brain problem. Their hypothesis is a modernization of Cartesian interactionism. Citing the works of the neurosurgeon Penfield, the physiologist Eccles, the brain researcher Sperry, and the philosopher Popper, they assert that consciousness cannot be equated with brain state and that full humanness, in the biblical perspective, is described only when physical and mental dimensions of the person are recognized. Furthermore, human dignity has its fullest meaning when the physical and spiritual (i.e., mental) dimensions are viewed as God's creation. However, Myers (1978) reviewed the same literature and holds a monistic (i.e., holistic) view of human nature in which mental conditions (e.g., thoughts, feelings, and beliefs) are identical to brain states.

At the data level of analysis Myers (1978, 1980) has reported a remarkable parallel between experimental studies in social psychology and biblical concepts. It seems that pride (i.e., undue concern for self) is manifested in a number of social-psychological processes of self-serving biases. From a theological point of view pride would distort the way the individual responds to experience in the world. Similar processes are reported in laboratory experiments. Persons attribute positive consequences to their own good action but blame environmental forces such as fate or task difficulty for bad behavior or outcomes. The individual asserts that he had freedom and responsibility when the outcomes of acts are good, but avoids personal freedom and responsibility when outcomes or behaviors are bad. Self-serving biases induce individuals to change attitudes and values to be consistent with behavior, because attitudes are derived from behavior. Self-serving biases are present in the way one makes causal attributions in altering memory to fit one's basic beliefs, in overreliance on anecdotal evidence, in overestimating the accuracy of one's own perception, and in "I knew it all along" after-the-fact analysis.

In addition to the theoretical and conceptual works of the type cited above, there is a plethora of applied works from Christian perspectives. These address a multitude of topics such as self-esteem, child rearing and discipline, pesonality development, husband-wife relations, and counseling.

Christian psychology, or the movement to integrate psychology and theology, meets all the criteria to be considered a school or system. Its general perspective and theoretical assumptions have been articulated. It is an explicit institutional goal in graduate psychology programs at Fuller School of Psychology (Fuller Theological Seminary), Rosemead School of Professional Psychology (Biola University), Psychological Studies Institute (affiliated with Georgia State University), and Wheaton College. Professional organizations recognize and emphasize aspects of integration and interface of psychology and religion: the Christian Association for Psychological Studies, American Scientific Affiliation, and Psychologists Interested in Religious Issues (Division 36 of the American Psychological Association). Several professional journals publish integration works—for example, *Journal of Psychology and Theology, Journal of Psychology and Christianity, Journal of the American Scientific Affiliation.* Integration is an important activity in a number of Christian liberal arts colleges. The integration of psychology and theology has also had an impact on seminaries, and is seen in recent rises in pastoral psychology and pastoral counseling programs.

References

Bufford, R. K. *The human reflex: Behavioral psychology in biblical perspective.* San Francisco: Harper & Row, 1981.

Carter, J. D., & Narramore, B. *The integration of psychology and theology.* Grand Rapids: Zondervan, 1979.

Collins, G. R. *The rebuilding of psychology.* Wheaton, Ill.: Tyndale House, 1977.

Custance, A. C. *The mysterious matter of mind.* Grand Rapids: Zondervan, 1980.

Ellison, C. W. Christianity and psychology: Contradictory or complementary? *Journal of the American Scientific Affiliation,* 1972, 24, 131–134.

Jeeves, M. A. *Psychology and Christianity.* Downers Grove, Ill.: Inter-Varsity Press, 1976.

Jones, D. G. *Our fragile brains.* Downers Grove, Ill.: Inter-Varsity Press, 1981.

Kantor, J. R. *The scientific evolution of psychology* (Vol. 2). Chicago: Principia Press, 1963.

Koteskey, R. L. *Psychology from a Christian perspective.* Nashville: Abingdon, 1980.

Koteskey, R. L. *General psychology for Christian counselors.* Nashville: Abingdon, 1983.

Larzalere, R. E. The task ahead: Six levels of integration of Christianity and psychology. *Journal of Psychology and Theology,* 1980, 8, 3–11.

Myers, D. G. *The human puzzle.* San Francisco: Harper & Row, 1978.

Myers, D. G. *The inflated self.* New York: Seabury, 1980.

Oates, W. E. *The psychology of religion.* Waco, Tex.: Word, 1973.

Roback, A. A. *History of psychology and psychiatry.* New York: Philosophical Library, 1961.

Schaeffer, F. A. *The God who is there.* Downers Grove, Ill.: Inter-Varsity Press, 1968.

Timpe, R. L. Assumptions and parameters for developing Christian psychological systems. *Journal of Psychology and Theology,* 1980, 8, 230–239.

Vitz, P. C. *Psychology as religion.* Grand Rapids: Eerdmans, 1977.

41

Christian Counseling and Psychotherapy
David G. Benner

O ne of the more visible products of attempts to integrate psychology and Christian theology has been the development of a number of systems of counseling and psychotherapy qualifying themselves with the adjective *Christian*. While many have viewed these developments with enthusiasm, some have argued that it is ridiculous to describe psychotherapy as Christian. To do so, they feel, suggests that there is a unique procedure that a Christian should employ for every action. If it is appropriate to talk about Christian psychotherapy, then why not Christian plumbing or Christian penmanship? However, the focus of psychotherapy is obviously much closer to that of Christianity than is the case in activities such as plumbing or penmanship. Also, the value-laden nature of the therapy process necessarily makes it either more or less Christian.

A more serious criticism is raised by Bobgan and Bobgan (1979), who view psychotherapy and Christianity as fundamentally incompatible. Contrasting the psychological way to health with the spiritual way, these authors assert that psychotherapy is not a neutral set of scientific techniques but rather a religious system, and a false one at that. The attempt to "Christianize" psychotherapy is therefore seen as a further erosion of the spiritual ministry of the church.

While agreeing that psychotherapy cannot be seen as a value-free set of techniques, a good many Christian mental health professionals and lay persons have seen that this is precisely why it is imperative that Christians subject their theories and practice of therapy to rigorous biblical evaluation. Others have gone further than this, arguing that since existing secular theories of therapy are built upon non-Christian presuppositions, a truly Christian approach must begin (and in some cases end) with the biblical view of persons. Concepts and techniques are then drawn from secular systems if they are found to be compatible with the new foundation.

Current Approaches

One factor that makes it difficult to overview and classify current Christian approaches to therapy is the often unclear line of differentiation between pastoral counseling and other forms of Christian therapy. Hiltner and Coltson (1961) demonstrated that the context of pastoral counseling (usually a church) and the symbols and expectations attached to the role of the clergy all serve to make it somewhat different from therapy offered outside an explicitly pastoral context. However, as pastoral counselors have sometimes moved physically out of the church to secular centers of pastoral psychotherapy, and as some psychotherapists have made a more explicit and visible identification with Christianity and its values, the differences are often less apparent. Since pastoral counseling is dealt with in a separate article, the primary focus here will be nonpastoral therapy.

In a recent summary of the major current approaches to Christian therapy Collins (1980) identifies 17 systems, including 4 that are explicitly pastoral, which he suggests to be distinctively Christian. While these vary tremendously in their sophistication, for the most part they are quite simplistic and fall far short of being a comprehensive system or model of therapy.

Ford and Urban (1963) suggest that a system of therapy needs to include a theory of personality development, a theory of psychopathology, a statement of the goals of therapy, and the conditions and techniques for producing behavior change. These ideals of a comprehensive system are met imperfectly by most, if not all, models of psychotherapy. For example, Gestalt therapy and reality therapy are usually seen to be deficient in terms of their assumptions about both normal and abnormal personality development. Existential therapy has most commonly been judged to be weak in terms of its therapeutic techniques.

The current approaches to Christian counseling are no more adequate in terms of these criteria. In fact, in the majority of cases they are much less comprehensive. For example, relationship counseling (Carlson, 1980) includes assumptions only about the conditions for change, ignoring personality development, psychotherapy, and goals of therapy. Similarly growth counseling (Clinebell, 1979), love therapy (Morris, 1974), and integrity therapy (Drakeford, 1967) all give only very minimal treatment to the processes of normal or abnormal personality development, focusing on goals and techniques of therapy. Only biblical counseling as developed by Crabb (1977) explicitly sets forth a model of personality development and psychopathology and then relates goals and techniques of therapy to this foundation. In this regard it stands as probably the most comprehensive of the existing Christian approaches. However, in comparison to psychoanalysis, client-centered (person-centered) therapy, or behavior therapy, it still must be seen as simplistic and far from a comprehensive model.

To be fair, however, it is important to realize that it was probably not the intention of these authors to present their ideas as a comprehensive system of counseling but rather as an *approach* to counseling. For example, Carlson (1980) states that his intent is to present a style of counseling that is based on Jesus' style of relating. He goes on to assert that "there is no recognized set of techniques that are exclusively Christian" (p. 32) and that there is "no agreed-upon focus of change" (p. 33). His focus, therefore, is on a style of relating, which he feels is the point where a counselor or therapist is most able to be explicitly Christian.

There is one additional point that should be noted in evaluating existing Christian approaches to counseling. With the exception of biblical counseling and nouthetic counseling none of the other approaches have been explicitly developed from Christian theology. Rather, they are adapted forms of existing secular theories which the authors argue are consistent with Christian truth. Thus, we find transactional analysis (Malony, 1980), reality therapy (Morris, 1974), and family systems therapy (Larsen, 1980) at the basis of approaches to therapy which are argued by respective advocates as being basically compatible with biblical theology.

This leads to the question of how these approaches differ from others that are not called Christian. Is Christian psychotherapy anything more than a Christian doing psychotherapy? Vanderploeg (1981) argues that "there is no difference between Christian and non-Christian therapy. The goals are the same, . . . the means are the same. . . . The difference lies not within therapy but within the therapists themselves. One group is Christian and the other is not" (p. 303). Those who have disagreed with this position and have argued for an approach to psychotherapy that is uniquely Christian have usually done so on the basis of either uniqueness in theory or uniqueness in role and/or task. These two major arguments will be considered separately.

The Bible and Personality Theory

For a number of authors the answer to the question of what makes a particular approach to counseling Christian has been quite simple and direct. They assert that Christian counseling is based on the biblical model of personality. In other words, they assume that Scripture contains a unique anthropology and theory of psychotherapy. Adams (1977) argues that the Bible is the only textbook needed for the Christian to learn all that is needed for counseling. He asserts that "if a principle is new to or different from those that are advocated in Scriptures, it is wrong; if it is not, it is unnecessary" (p. 183).

Others (Carter, 1980; Crabb, 1977) have avoided the assumption that nothing useful can be learned about counseling apart from the Scriptures but have retained the expectation that Scripture does contain a unique personality theory and implicit model of counseling. The striking thing, however, is that seldom do these people agree as to just what Scripture suggests to be this unique model. This is reminiscent of Berkouwer's (1962) assertion that the failures to find a system of personality or psychology in Scripture "have only made clear that because of the great variety of concepts used in the Bible, it is not possible to synthesize them into a systematic Biblical anthropology in which the structure and composition of man would be made clear. . . . It is obviously not the intention of the divine revelation to give us exact information about man in himself and thus to anticipate what later scientific research on man offers" (p. 199).

Although the Scriptures should not, therefore, be expected to provide a comprehensive theory of personality or psychotherapy, they obviously do contain a view of persons that is most essential to the individual wishing to provide Christian therapy. In fact, whatever else Christian counseling is, surely it must be based on and informed by these biblical perspectives on human nature. Three biblical themes seem particularly relevant: the unity of personality, creation in the image of God, and the reality of sin.

Psychospiritual unity

Historically, attempts to understand what Scripture teaches about human personality have often begun with a discussion of the so-called parts of persons (heart, soul, mind, etc.). In fact, one long-standing debate in biblical anthropology has been over whether man is best seen as a dichotomy (body-soul) or trichotomy (body-soul-spirit). Significantly, this debate is now receding into history, as the consensus of many theologians has increasingly been that the primary biblical emphasis is on the unity of personality. The suggestion is that while Scripture does present a number of characteristics of persons, these were never intended to be interpreted as components or parts. Always they are to be seen as perspectives on the whole.

The implication of this is that man does not *have* a spirit, man *is* spirit. Similarly, man does not have a soul or a body, but *is* soul and *is* body. Further, this means that since we do not have spiritual or psychological parts to our personality, neither do we have problems that are purely spiritual or purely psychological. All problems occur within the common substrate of psychospiritual processes and affect the totality of a person's functioning. The Christian therapist must therefore resist the temptation to artificially separate problems and people into psychological and spiritual parts. Similarly, the Christian therapist cannot ignore a problem just because it has a superficial religious or spiritual appearance.

Created in God's image

The second aspect of the biblical view of persons that needs to be considered is the concept of the *imago Dei*. Although Scripture directly discusses the fact of our creation in God's image in only a few passages, theologians have usually given it a central place in their doctrine of man. Vanderploeg (1981) has similarly argued that it must be seen to be foundational to any understanding of psychotherapy. The fact that we were created in God's image establishes human beings as essentially relational, called to relationship with God and with each other. Viewing the major goal of psychotherapy as helping individuals deal with and enhance their relationships, Vanderploeg then argues that this represents helping people expand and explore the *imago Dei* within them.

The doctrine of the *imago Dei* also helps us understand man's religious nature. Hart (1977) has arued that because we were created in the image of God, our whole life is intended to mirror God. We were created to serve God and to lose ourselves in joyous fellowship with him. By his gift of free will he allows us to choose whether we will, in fact, serve him or not. However, we will serve someone or something, and that is the heart of our religiosity. Religion therefore defines mankind. It is not something added on to an otherwise complete being. It describes our essential meaning, our need to be self-transcendent and to lose ourselves in service to God and others.

The reality of sin

While the fact of our creation in God's image validates the good and noble aspects of human functioning, the Christian view of persons must be balanced by the reality of sin. More than just a tendency to fail to meet our personal expectations or those held of us by others, sin has traditionally been viewed by Christian theology as active rebellion against God and his holy law. This rebellion results in alienation from God, self, and others. These consequences of sin are therefore ultimately, although not necessarily personally or directly, at the root of all our problems.

This reality informs a Christian approach to counseling. If sin is real, then guilt may not always be neurotic. Sometimes it will be real, and forgiveness and repentance will then be necessary. Pattison (1969) states that "the task of the psychotherapist, then, is not to assuage guilt feelings, although that is often a necessary preamble to successful therapy. Rather, the therapist seeks to help the patient see himself and his relationships with others in the light of how the patient violates the relationships to which he is committed. . . . Patients would quite willingly settle for pacification of their superego, but they are reluctant to undergo the pain of changing their pattern of relationships so that they no longer need to feel guilty" (pp. 106–107).

When combined with other equally important biblical themes such as grace, the incarnation, and life after death, the concepts discussed above should be at the foundation of any theory of personality that calls itself Christian. However, they are far from adequate as a complete personality theory. While we therefore may conclude that the Scriptures should not be expected to yield a comprehensive system of therapy, it is clear that they contain perspectives on persons that ought to be foundational for Christian therapy.

Roles and Tasks

The second possible basis for the uniqueness of Christian therapy is the role and tasks of the Christian therapist. In his sociological analysis of psychiatry and religion, Klausner (1964) suggests four different ideological positions based on the differentiation of the task and role in counseling or psychotherapy: reductionist, dualist, alternativist, and specialist. Reductionists maintain that there is only one role and one task. This is because there is only one type of personal problem and only one type of person equipped to address it. Material reductionists view this problem in scientific, psychological terms and see the person trained in this system as the only one equipped to handle such problems. Spiritual reductionists view the problem in spiritual or religious terms and see the minister as the only one equipped to handle such problems.

Dualists believe that there are both psychological and spiritual problems. However, they also believe that one qualified person can address both these types of problems. Alternativists are opposite to the dualists, claiming only one basic type of problem but allowing for the two separate roles in the treatment of this problem. Mental health professionals and clergy are viewed as equally valid, functionally equivalent alternative roles, both groups being appropriately involved in the treatment of the one basic problem experienced by people. Finally, specialists argue that there are two discrete tasks and therefore there must be two roles. Ministers and therapists are, respectively, spiritual specialists and psychological specialists, each dealing with one of the two basic types of problems.

All four of these positions are represented in the contemporary Christian counseling literature. The spiritual reductionist position is probably best represented by Adams (1977) and Bobgan and Bobgan (1979). These authors argue that nonorganic psychological problems are really mislabeled spiritual problems. The one person equipped to provide help for such problems is the Christian who draws his mandate, goals, and techniques from the Bible and from this source alone. While this position has been well received by many conservative Protestant pastors, most Christian mental health professionals have viewed it as providing an inadequate account of psychological functioning and a limited understanding of the role of the therapist.

This assumption of one basic type of problem is shared by the alternativists. Benner (1979) represents this position, arguing that all emotional or psychological problems are at core both spiritual and psychological. Because of the fundamental unity of personality, depression is as much an issue of spiritual significance as guilt is a matter of psychological significance. The challenge is for the Christian therapist to view people as spiritual beings regardless of their religiosity and to be sensitive to spiritual dimensions of their functioning. The challenge to the minister is to similarly view a person as a psychospiritual unity and to resist the tendency to either reduce psychological problems to spiritual problems or to ignore psychological problems since these are beyond their competence. This is not to suggest that all ministers or psychotherapists will be adequately equipped to handle the broad range of problems encountered in pastoral counseling and in psychotherapy, but rather to encourage both groups to view problems within the matrix of psychospiritual unity and to respond accordingly.

The alternativist position is attractive to many because it seems to combine something of the simplicity of the reductionist model with a more adequate understanding of psychological processes. Its major weakness lies in its difficulty in explaining what often appear to be differing levels of psychological and spiritual health within a person. If psychospiritual processes are as unified as argued, the parallels in psychological and spiritual functioning should be even more pronounced than those often seen.

The dualist position is perhaps the most popular in contemporary Christian therapy. Tournier (1963) has been a very influential representative of this position. Minirth (1977) is perhaps an even better representative, arguing that Christian therapy must be responsive to the unique problems of body, soul, and spirit. The first step is therefore the differential diagnosis of the problems of each sphere. Each type of problem is then treated by appropriate and unique methods. Advocates of this position view it as a psychology of the whole person in that the therapist is prepared to respond to both spiritual and psychological problems. Critics view it as more a total treatment approach than a whole-person approach in that the person is not viewed as a whole but rather as the sum of a number of different parts.

A related criticism questions the possibility of differential diagnosis and treatment of spiritual and psychological problems. When is depression a psychological problem and when is it a spiritual problem? Perhaps more difficult to resolve are the technical questions associated with the different tasks required for work with explicitly religious issues versus nonreligious issues. For example, Pattison (1966) asks when the therapist should treat religious questions as grist for the therapeutic mill and when he or she should enter into either a Socratic dialogue or perhaps an explicit instructional role. Also, what are the effects of such movement between roles on transference and countertransference? These questions do not as yet seem adequately answered.

The specialist model has been argued by Pattison (1966), who suggests that different roles are appropriate for the unique tasks of the therapist and minister. The role of the minister, who works as a definer of social and moral values and behavior, is best served by a close social-emotional relationship with the parishioner. In contrast, the task of changing personality argues for the therapist to remove himself from a direct involvement in the patient's social value system and maintain more personal and emotional distance.

The problem with this position is that the distinction which it makes between the goals of therapists and ministers may be exaggerated. Perhaps personality change and changes in social values and behavior are not as discrete as presented. However, if the goals are as represented, Pattison's conclusion as to the role that best supports each set of goals appears helpful.

Goals

What goals should then guide Christian therapy? Ward (1977) suggests that the ultimate goal of Christian therapy must always be to assist the client in becoming more like Jesus Christ. Arbuckle (1975) claims that the desire of the Christian to convert and to change others to his own personal faith appears to be contradictory to general counseling philosophy, which values client self-determination. But are these incompatible? First, we must realize that therapy is never value free and that all therapists either implicitly or explicitly communicate their values and personal religion. Therefore, the question is not whether the therapist has certain personal values or goals but how these influence the therapy process. A therapist who uses the therapy relationship to force his or her beliefs on another person is obviously behaving in an unprofessional manner. Christ clearly had the goal of bringing people into relationship with the Father, but his relating to individuals was never characterized by coercion. He clearly was willing to allow people their right of self-determination.

This suggests that while the Christian therapist will have the ultimate spiritual welfare and growth of the client as a part of his concern and goals, he will be willing to work with less ultimate concerns if this is most therapeutically appropriate. Again, Christ's own behavior illustrates this. His frequent healings of individuals apart from an explicit verbal proclamation of the gospel show his concern to meet people at their point of need. His ministry was not always in ultimate dimensions, even though he never lost sight of those ultimate concerns.

Ellens (1980) points out how easy it is for Christian therapists to substitute private philosophy for demandingly sound psychotherapeutic practice. He states that "the practice of the helping professions which is preoccupied with the final step of wholeness, spiritual maturity, will usually short circuit the therapeutic process and play the religious dynamic of the patient or therapist straight into the typical religious patient's psychopathology" (p. 4).

The goals of the Christian therapist will also be guided by the picture of the whole mature person that is presented as the goal of Christian growth in Scripture. Thus, for example, the Christian therapist would seek to encourage the development of interdependence, this in contrast to the autonomy and independence valued in many therapeutic approaches. Other aspects of Christian maturity are also readily translatable into therapeutic goals for the Christian counselor. The Christian therapist will be likely, therefore, to share many of the goals of his secular counterpart. However, the goals that direct Christian therapy should grow out of the overall Christian view of persons discussed earlier.

Techniques

Is Christian therapy unique by virtue of employment of certain techniques? Are there uniquely Christian or non-Christian techniques? Adams (1977) answers these questions affirmatively and, assuming techniques to be dependent on their presuppositional base, has judged the techniques of secular therapies to be inappropriate for the Christian therapist. The relationship between most techniques and the theory with which they are primarily associated seems, however, to be very loose indeed. One has only to note the very diverse theoretical orientations laying claim to the same techniques to see this point.

Most techniques seem to be neither Christian nor non-Christian. Therefore, they should be judged not on the basis of who first described them but rather their function. Do they support the therapeutic goals? Also, they should be evaluated for their consistency with the overall theoretical framework guiding the therapy. The Christian therapist will thus be cautious of pragmatic eclecticism as the sole guide to which techniques to employ.

Some Christian therapists do employ explicitly religious resources such as prayer, Scripture reading, or even laying on of hands. While any of these interventions may well be appropriate under some circumstances, the responsible therapist would want to understand clearly the significance of using them for the client and the therapy process.

Summary

Christian therapy is clearly not a monolithic development. Little consensus exists on such basic questions as the role and task of the therapist and even the question of whether Scripture should be expected to yield a definitive model for Christian counseling. A recent survey of the membership of the Christian Association for Psychological Studies (Cole & DeVries, 1981) indicated that 48% of the Christian mental health professionals responding do not expect Scripture to yield a unified biblical model of counseling. The same percentage do expect such a development. Also, 87% see an eclectic approach as most faithful to Scripture, which they see as consistent with a great diversity of styles of counseling.

If Christian therapy is not simply the application of some biblical theory of personality and therapy, what then is it? This chapter has suggested that it is an approach to therapy offered by a Christian who bases his or her understanding of persons on the Bible and allows this understanding to shape all aspects of theory and practice. This suggests an ongoing process rather than a finished product. Seen thus, the Christian therapist is not one who practices a certain type of therapy but one who views himself in God's service in and through his profession and who sees his primary allegiance and accountability to his God, and only secondarily to his profession or discipline.

References

Adams, J. E. *Lectures in counseling.* Nutley, NJ.: Presbyterian and Reformed Publishing, 1977.

Arbuckle, D. S. *Counseling and psychotherapy.* Boston: Allyn & Bacon, 1975.

Benner, D. G. What God hath joined: The psychospiritual unity of personality. *The Bulletin of the Christian Association for Psychological Studies,* 1979, 5(2), 7–11.

Berkouwer, G. C. *Man: The image of God.* Grand Rapids: Eerdmans, 1962.

Bobgan, M., & Bobgan, D. *The psychological way/the spiritual way.* Minneapolis: Bethany Fellowship, 1979.

Carlson, D. Relationship counseling. In G. R. Collins (Ed.), *Helping people grow.* Santa Ana, Calif.: Vision House, 1980.

Carter, J. D. Towards a biblical model of counseling. *Journal of Psychology and Theology,* 1980, 8, 45–52.

Clinebell, H. *Growth counseling: Hope-centered methods of actualizing human wholeness.* Nashville: Abingdon, 1979.

Cole, D. T., & DeVries, M. The search for identity. *The Bulletin of the Christian Association for Psychological Studies,* 1981, 7(3), 21–27.

Collins, G. R. (Ed.). *Helping people grow.* Santa Ana, Calif.: Vision House, 1980.

Crabb, L. J., Jr. *Effective biblical counseling.* Grand Rapids: Zondervan, 1977.

Drakeford, J. W. *Integrity therapy.* Nashville: Broadman, 1967.

Ellens, J. H. Biblical themes in psychological theory and practice. *The Bulletin of the Christian Association for Psychological Studies*, 1980, 6(2), 2–6.

Furd, D. H., & Urban, H. B. *Systems of psychotherapy.* New York: Wiley, 1963.

Hart, H. Anthropology. In A. DeGraaff (Ed.). *Views of man and psychology in Christian perspective.* Toronto: Institute for Christian Studies, 1977.

Hiltner, S., & Coltson, L. G. *The context of pastoral counseling.* New York: Abingdon, 1961.

Klausner, S. Z. *Psychiatry and religion.* New York: Free Press, 1964.

Larsen. J. A. Family counseling. In G. R. Collins (Ed.). *Helping people grow.* Santa Ana, Calif.: Vision House, 1980.

Malony, H.N. Transactional analysis. In G. R. Collins (Ed.), *Helping people grow.* Santa Ana, Calif.: Vision House, 1980.

Minirth, F. B. *Christian psychiatry.* Old Tappan, N.J.: Revell, 1977.

Morris, P. D. *Love therapy.* Wheaton, Ill.: Tyndale House, 1974.

Pattison, E. M. Social and psychological aspects of religion in psychotherapy. *Insight: Quarterly Review of Religion and Mental Health*, 1966, 5(2), 27–35.

Pattison, E. M. Morality, guilt, and forgiveness in psychotherapy. In E. M. Pattison (Ed.), *Clinical psychiatry and religion.* Boston: Little, Brown, 1969.

Tournier, P. *The strong and the weak.* Philadelphia: Westminster, 1963.

Vanderploeg, R. D. Imago dei as foundational to psychotherapy: Integration versus segregation. *Journal of Psychology and Theology*, 1981, 9, 299–304.

Ward, W. O. *The Bible in counseling.* Chicago: Moody Press, 1977.

42

Christian Growth
Richard E. Butman

Of keen interest to developmental psychologists of late has been the issue of adult growth and maturation. Traditionally developmental psychology has focused almost exclusively on child and adolescent growth and maturation, with limited attention given to adulthood and old age. Increasingly, however, developmental theorists are interested in life span development, with some seriously studying the implications of human development for the maturation of faith and the quest for human meaning. There is a need for careful reflection on the relationship between spiritual and psychological maturity and the processes of growth in each. Recent efforts by Malony (1978, 1983), Carter (1974a, 1974b), Oakland (1974), and Nouwen (1972) are examples of such integrative thinking.

Mature Religion

A major work by Strunk (1965) has attempted to define mature religion, a task that is needed in order to give a sense of perspective to the maturation of faith and reason. He sees religion as a dynamic

276

organization of cognitive-affected-conative factors, suggesting that the characteristics of mature religion be analyzed in terms of beliefs, feelings, and actions. Mature religious beliefs are characterized by: 1) lack of contamination by childish wishes; 2) deep involvement in the world in terms of one's attitudes; 3) a high awareness of one's convictions; 4) the conviction of the existence of a Being greater than oneself; and 5) comprehensiveness and articulation in a manner that serves well in the search for meaning. Religious feelings that are mature, according to Strunk, are characterized by profound experiences of mystical oneness resulting in feelings of wonder and awe, elation and freedom. Mature religious actions are characterized by: 1) good integration with the religious factors of the psyche; 2) the presence of love as a comprehensive action with productiveness, humility, and responsibility as natural signs of this love; and 3) a dynamic balance between commitment and tentativeness. Strunk believes that in the analysis of mature religion one will find these factors dynamically organized both horizontally and in depth, yielding a religious motive of master proportion. He argues that individuals will not be "mature" or "immature" but will fall on a continuum somewhere between.

According to Strunk, the questions the Christian helper should be asking are: 1) What am I doing personally to foster my own religious growth and development? 2) What am I doing personally to foster that maturation process in the persons with whom I work? 3) How are the religious organizations and systems of which I am a part facilitating development on a corporate level?

Faith Development

Fowler (1981) has written a seminal work on the stages of development through which the faith aspect of a human life may pass. He is a stage theorist, seeing moral/faith development as progressing through invariant and sequential stages. Fowler is careful to distinguish between religion and faith in discussions of Christian growth and development. Faith should not be confused with creed (i.e., the listing of one's theological beliefs in a creedal statement should not be equated with a confession of faith). Faith is answering the basic question, "On what do you set your heart?" Making certain theological assertions part of the furniture of the mind is not the same as faith. Rather, Fowler sees faith as an active mode of being and committing which has a strong relational component of trust in or loyalty to someone or something else. Such a faith, in its more mature form, becomes imaginative in that it allows the person to see everyday life in relationship to the issues of ultimate meaning and in the broader context. Faith, then, is dynamic, evolving, and relational, not static and cognitive.

Building on a theoretical foundation of Erikson, Piaget, and Kohlberg, Fowler presents a six-stage model of faith development which clearly reflects these significant psychosocial, cognitive, and moral theorists. Stage 1, *intuitive-projective*, is the fantasy-filled, imitative phase in which the child can be powefully and permanently influenced by other models and their visible faith. Stage 2, *mythic-literal*, is the stage in which the individual begins to make personal the beliefs, observances, and stories that symbolize belonging to his or her community support system. That is followed by stage 3, *synthetic-conventional*, which provides a coherent orientation in the midst of a more complex and diverse range of involvements. It synthesizes values and information; it provides a basis for identity and outlook. Also, it is a conformist stage in that it is acutely tuned to the expectations and judgments of others and does not yet have enough independence to construct and maintain an autonomous perspective.

Stage 4, *individuative-reflective*, is marked by a double development. The self, previously sustained in its identity and faith by a network of significant others, now claims an identity no longer built by the compositive of one's roles or meanings to others. Fowler suggests that "self (identity) and outlook (world view) are differentiated from those of others and become acknowledged factors in the reactions, interpretations and judgments one makes on the actions of self and others" (p. 182). Stage 5, *conjunctive*, involves the integration of much that was suppressed or unrecognized in the interest of stage 4's self-certainty. Faith in this stage reunites symbolic power with conceptual meaning. Stage 6, *universalizing*, is a disciplined making real and tangible of the "imperatives of absolute love and justice of which stage 5 has partial apprehensions. The self at stage 6 engages in spending and being spent for the transformation of present reality in the direction of transcendent actuality" (p. 200). In any of these stages faith development can be facilitated or retarded by the quality of the communities of faith of which one is a part. These potentially nurturing bodies hold great importance for the believer in terms of assisting him or her in the working out of faith.

Fowler has a high view of persons, one that places the quest for meaning at the core of human existence. He also makes a valuable contribution to the discussion of faith development by offering an important perspective on the critical distinction between faith and creed. Much of the research by conservative Christians in the past decades has been crippled by potentially static and overly cognitive notions of faith. Although we must be careful not to see all of faith development in terms of invariant sequential stages or to use a stage model to categorize persons in a legalistic manner, the idea of developmental milestones is invaluable in the study of faith growth and maturation, since it forces us to reflect on those factors that might facilitate or retard the process of deepening one's commitments. Finally, Fowler's model is longitudinal in its outlook, which encourages us to study the maturation process in a participant-observer manner, a study approach increasingly being advocated by integrative thinkers (e.g., Farnsworth, 1981; Van Leeuwen, 1982).

Psychospiritual Wholeness

Summarizing the existing literature on spiritual and psychological health, the following qualities would seem to characterize the psychospiritually whole person: a strong religious faith commitment expressed both individually and corporately; the ability to resist conformity pressures, especially in uncertain situations; a small circle of close, intimate friends; a deep appreciation of God's handiwork; the ability to generate novel solutions to problems (i.e., creativity); self-acceptance and openness toward others; the desire and the ability to confront others openly, directly, and honestly; a good balance between the rational and the emotional; involvement in helping those less fortunate than oneself; interdependence; good decision-making ability; a tolerance for ambiguity in life; the ability to see through the petty conflicts of life; a high level of moral development; and a belief that one's actions make a difference and that one is not simply the victim of forces beyond one's control.

Probably no one meets all these criteria all the time. Certainly we are limited by our own finiteness, fallenness, and humanness. Spiritual maturity, not unlike psychological normality, is a matter of one's batting average. While we can reasonably expect that a deeply internalized faith commitment will enhance a person's psychological well-being, we cannot expect Christians ever to become fully self-actualized and/or sanctified (McLemore, 1982). The doctrine of sin implies the utter impossibility of such perfection. Persons bring to their Christianity their own "raw material." Without a reliable standard to measure anyone's faith except our own, we should be careful not to judge others. Rather, our energies should be geared toward creating opportunities and settings in which spiritual growth and development can be maximized and regression can be minimized. The skillful administration of grace by nurturing Christian communities with a clear sense of direction with regard to faith development will truly be an important part of the process.

References

Carter, J. D. Maturity: Psychological and biblical. *Journal of Psychology and Theology*, 1974, 2, 89–96. (a)

Carter, J. D. Personality and Christian maturity: A process congruity model. *Journal of Psychology and Theology*, 1974, 2, 190–201. (b)

Farmsworth, K. E. *Integrating psychology and theology*. Washington, D.C.: University Press of America, 1981.

Fowler, J. *Stages of faith*. San Franciso: Harper & Row, 1981.

Malony, H. N. *Understanding your faith*. Nashville: Abingdon, 1978.

Malony, H. N. (Ed.). *Wholeness and holiness*. Grand Rapids: Baker, 1983.

McLemore, C. W. *The scandal of psychotherapy*. Wheaton, Ill.: Tyndale House, 1982.

Nouwen, H. J. M. *The wounded healer*. Garden City, N.Y.: Doubleday, 1972.

Oakland, J. A. Self-actualization and sanctification. *Journal of Psychology and Theology*, 1974, 2, 202–209.

Strunk, O. *Mature religion*. New York: Abingdon, 1965.

Van Leeuwen, M. S. *The sorcerer's apprentice: A Christian look at the changing face of psychology*. Downers Grove, Ill.: Inter-Varsity Press, 1982.

43

Demonic Influence and Psychopathology
Henry A. Virkler

Belief in demons and demonic possession has been a world-wide phenomenon from earliest recorded history. Incantations, various forms of demonic phenomena, and exorcisms abound in archaeological discoveries from Sumer, Babylonia, Egypt, and Assyria. The religions of India, China, and Japan contain elements of demonism, as do the animistic religions of Africa and South America (Hitt, 1973).

Throughout the Old Testament, Moses and other prophets repeatedly warned against involvement in demonically energized activities such as divination, sorcery, and idol worship. At the time of Jesus belief in demons was widespread among the Jews. From the New Testament record it is clear that Jesus and the New Testament writers regarded demons as personal, fallen, spiritual beings, stronger than men but weaker than God. Demons were viewed as being able to oppress and possess human beings.

Jesus and the New Testament writers were more conservative than surrounding pagan cultures in that they did not ascribe all physical and mental illness to demonic causation. The scriptural writers repeatedly distinguished the state of being demon-possessed from that of illness. In at least 17 places in the Gospels and Acts this distinction is made (e.g., Matt. 4:24; 8:16).

Furthermore, Jesus and New Testament writers underscored the difference between demonically caused and nondemonically caused illness in their discussion of healing. Both kinds of illnesses were healed, but by different means. Demonically caused illnesses were healed by casting the demon out of the person, whereas nondemonically caused illnesses were never healed by exorcism or binding of demons.

The church throughout most of its history has maintained these same views—that is, that demons are real and do inflict physical and mental illness, but that not all illness is of demonic causation. In the early church converts from pagan and Jewish backgrounds were usually exorcised before baptism, and throughout the Middle Ages exorcism was included in the rite of infant baptism. There has been an office of exorcist in the Roman Catholic Church until the present day. However, there has also been a place for physicians who heal natural illnesses by natural means.

In recent years some Christian theologians have attempted to demythologize the New Testament characterization of demons and possession, claiming that either Christ was a product of the prescientific thinking of his day or else he accommodated himself to it. It is difficult to reconcile such theories with orthodox views of Christology or the inspiration of Scripture. If Christ's teachings on demons were erroneous, then his teachings in other areas may also be in error. If Christ knew that people were not demon-possessed but knowingly accommodated his teachings to what he knew to be false, he could not serve as a sinless atonement for humanity. If God inspired an erroneous Scripture, than either his omniscience or his truthfulness is jeopardized. The only view that leaves the orthodox doctrines of Christology and inspiration intact is to believe that demons exist and that they do at times tempt, oppress, or possess people.

Levels of Demonic Involvement

For heuristic purposes we may consider four levels of demonic involvement in human temptation. These levels represent a continuum ranging from no demonic involvement to significant involvement. They should not be taken to refer to discrete categories.

No involvement

Scripture makes it clear that temptations may come from our sinful nature without the necessity of demonic intervention. Jeremiah 17:9 says, "The heart is deceitful above all things and beyond cure." Jesus said, "From within, out of men's hearts, come evil thoughts, sexual immorality, theft, murder, adultery, greed, malice, deceit, lewdness, envy, slander, arrogance and folly. All these evils come from inside and make a man unclean" (Mark 7:21–23). And James 1:14–15 states that "each one is tempted when, by his own evil desire, he is dragged away and enticed. Then, after desire has conceived, it gives birth to sin; and sin, when it is full-grown, gives birth to death."

Temptation

Scripture speaks of a second category of temptation that is demonic in its origin. Christ was tempted directly by Satan (Matt. 4:1–11). Satan apparently tempted Ananias to lie (Acts 5:3); he incited David to take a census in Israel in a way that was displeasing to God (1 Chron. 21:1). An evil spirit also is spoken of as somehow involved in the treachery of the men of Shechem against Abimelech (Judg. 9:23). Finally, Paul reminds believers that they battle against evil supernatural forces, and thus must be fully equipped (Eph. 6:10–18).

It seems likely that in many cases yielding to one's sinful human impulses provides an opening for demonic temptation. For example, David's pride in the growing strength of Israel probably made him more easily susceptible to Satan's temptation to take a census for the wrong reasons. Judas's love of money made him susceptible to Satan's temptation to betray Jesus. Scripture repeatedly affirms that the practice of yielding to sin make one less and less able to resist its temptations (e.g., John 8:34). This suggests that yielding to sinful temptations arising from one's own nature makes one increasingly susceptible to demonic temptation as well.

Oppression

A more intense level of demonic involvement in human life is variously referred to in the literature as demonic influence, demonic oppression, demonic subjection, or demonic obsession. Within this category demons exert considerable influence over a person's life short of actual possession (Unger, 1971, p. 113). Oppression may range from a simple form of occult subjection that may go unnoticed for years until a particular event uncovers it, to a moderately intense form of oppression where a negative reaction occurs toward any form of Christian counseling, to a state where the person is continually surrounded and oppressed by the powers of darkness (Koch, 1971, p. 32). Since demonic temptation, oppression, and possession form a continuum rather than discrete categories, extreme forms of oppression share much in common with possession.

The tragic end of King Saul's life illustrates well the phenomenon of demonic oppression. Saul began to lose favor with God following his intrusion into the priest's office (1 Sam. 13:8–15) and then in his deliberate disobedience in the war with the Amalekites (1 Sam 15:1–9). Saul apparently continued his disobedience toward God until God removed the Holy Spirit from him and an evil spirit came to tempt him episodically for the rest of his life (1 Sam. 16:14).

Unger (1971, p. 114) summarizes the biblical data regarding manifestations of demonic oppression as blindness and hardness of heart toward the gospel (2 Cor. 4:4), apostasy and doctrinal corruption (1 Tim. 4:1), and indulging in sinful, defiling behavior (2 Peter 2:1–12). This is roughly paralleled by Lechler's (1971) description of symptoms he has seen in his European psychiatric experience with cases of oppression. Wilson (1976, pp. 226–228) reviews three contemporary cases from his American practice which also seem to fit the characteristics of oppression.

People usually seem to become demonically oppressed in one of two ways—either through personal, continued involvement in sin, or through family involvement in the occult (Koch, 1971). In the latter type of situation the oppressed person himself may not have been involved in the occult but may have had a spell put on him by a relative or acquaintance.

While the above discussion has focused on the psychological and spiritual aspects of oppression. Scripture mentions briefly that demonic oppression sometimes results in physical illness also (Luke 13:10–16).

Possession

Some Christians have objected to the translation of *daimonizomai* as demon-possessed, preferring instead the word *demonized*. Lexically the word means "to have a demon, to be possessed by a demon, or to be exercised by or under the control of a demon. It is never used to refer to someone who is demonically tempted or oppressed." Thus there seems to be no clear lexical objection to the use of "demon-possessed" to translate *daimonizomai*.

In several instances where demon possession is described in the biblical record, no specific symptoms are mentioned. Identifiable symptoms that are noted include the possessed individual manifesting supernormal strength; going about naked; being unable to speak, hear, or see; experiencing self-destructive convulsions with attendant symptoms such as rigidity, foaming at the mouth, and bruxism; and saying things that evidence a supernatural knowledge. In some cases the symptoms caused by the demon seem to be continuously present. In other instances the manifestation of the demon's presence seems to be episodic.

While some have questioned whether demon possession continues today, large numbers of missionaries who work in countries where demonic (idol) worship is prevalent testify that demon possession continues to exist there with symptoms quite similar to the biblical characterizations (Nevius, 1968; Peters, 1976; Tippett, 1976).

Possession occurs through idol worship, occult involvement, spells cast by another person, or by receiving healing through sorcery (Koch, 1971). Possession is sometimes by a single demon and sometimes by multiple demons.

There is continued debate among Christians about whether believers can be possessed or not. A number of accounts from experienced missionaries assert that this does occur. It is particularly noteworthy that the highly respected biblical scholar Merrill Unger, who in 1952 had written in *Biblical Demonology* that true believers cannot be demon-possessed, says that he has received so many letters from missionaries all over the world documenting this kind of occurrence that he now believes that it does happen (1971, p. 117). The common means by which this seems to happen is through believers arrogantly attacking demons or through continued practice of sin.

Demonic Influence and Mental Illness

Differentiation of demon possession from mental illness is immediately beset by several problems. The foremost of these is that the symptoms arising from psychopathology and demonization overlap to a considerable extent; nearly every symptom thought to be an indicator of demon possession is also found in psychopathology of nondemonic origin. The same phenomenon is found in the biblical record: blindness sometimes had a demonic etiology (Matt 12:22) and at other times only a natural base (Mark 8:22–25). Deafness and dumbness were likewise found to have sometimes a natural and sometimes a demonic base.

Second, diagnosis is always forced to contend with the problem of role enactment. People continuously fulfill a variety of roles in which they behave as they consciously and unconsciously believe persons in these roles should act. There is strong evidence to suggest that the role a person adopts modifies his or her perception of reality in ways consistent with that role. Thus, a person who experiences unusual mental events and begins to believe that he is demon-possessed may begin to act in ways that are consistent with demon possession without actually being demonically possessed. If such a person receives feedback from his environment that his perception of being possessed is correct, his experience is further reinforced.

A third complicating problem in differential diagnosis is that demon possession does not occur on a blank personality. Psychopathological states and demonic possession may coexist within the same person, with a consequent blending and overlapping of the symptoms resulting from each state (Jackson, 1976, p. 263).

Fourth, we have no guarantee that the relative descriptions of demonically caused symptomatology found in Scripture were intended to be normative examples of possession across time and cultures. All that the narrative accounts of demonization found in the Gospels and Acts claim is that they are accurate descriptions of demonization of that time, not normative descriptions of demonization that can be used for all successive generations. Hermeneutically it is more correct to accept the biblical descriptions as suggestive criteria for diagnosis than as normative criteria.

Fifth, most Christian workers faced with diagnosis will be well trained in psychology *or* theology, but rarely in both. We tend to underestimate the contribution of a field that we do not understand well. Thus psychologists and psychiatrists, heavily influenced by the antisupernaturalistic bias of their secular training, may tend to underdiagnose demonic oppression and possession. Conversely, theologically trained workers may underdiagnose mental illness originating in the natural realm. Mallory states that "there seems to be a tendency in this [deliverance] literature, to attribute to demons what is not understood by the author's limited knowledge of mental illness" (McAll, 1976, p. 322).

There are a number of reasons why proper diagnosis is important. Many Christians have observed the damaging effects that occur when a person in the midst of a brief reactive psychosis or suffering from severe depression has been told that he is demon-possessed. In addition to the stress that produced the actual psychological disorder, the person now has the added guilt and anxiety that demons have taken up residence in his body.

There are at least three unhealthy aspects to the practice of considering sins that arise primarily from our own human natures to be the result of demonic forces. First, it tends to remove the responsibility of recognizing and confessing one's own sinfulness. Scripture clearly teaches that God will not allow believers to be tempted beyond what they are able to withstand, meaning that when we do sin, we are responsible for that action. As Montgomery (1976) rather bluntly states: "The devil made me do it is not an acceptable theological stance, but rather a demonic form of escapism to avoid confrontation with personal sin within" (p. 22).

Second, to view ourselves as a battleground upon which forces of good and evil alternately rampage without volitional control robs us of a sense of potency. We may fail to make needed changes in our lives because we believe such changes are beyond our control. Further, by suppressing and repressing our own urges, viewing them as demonic by-products rather than as parts of ourselves, we are building an unhealthy personality structure. Large portions of our selves remain dissociated rather than integrated.

Accurate differential diagnosis is important in order that truly demonically oppressed or possessed people can receive appropriate treatment. Traditional psychotherapeutic and chemotherapeutic methods have no demonstrated efficacy in the treatment of possession. Diagnosis can proceed in a manner similar to the way other medical or psychological diagnoses are made. This includes taking a history, analyzing the constellation of presenting symptoms, observing epiphenomena or related activity within the person's social system, and evaluating the person's response to treatment.

History taking would focus on the person's spiritual history and involvement with the occult, and on immediate precursors of the present situation. Many who write in this area emphasize that even casual interactions with occult practices may result in long-standing effects. In addition it seems to be important to investigate family involvement in the occult back as far as three or four generations. Evidence of occult involvement in the past does not prove that the present problem is demonic but increases the probability that it may be so. An analysis of the immediate precursors to the present situation may be helpful in differentiating role-enactment behaviors from genuine possession.

Some writers have concluded that diagnosis of demon possession on the basis of symptom analysis is indeterminate, since each individual symptom found in demon possession is also found in some kind of mental illness. Such a conclusion seems needlessly pessimistic. In most diseases it is the complex of symptoms, rather than any individual symptom, that is the basis of a diagnostic decision. Thus while various mental illnesses share one or two symptoms in common with demon possession, there are none that share the entire symptom complex.

The symptom complex may be described in terms of physical symptoms, psychological symptoms, and spiritual symptoms. Physical symptoms often include 1) preternatural (more than natural) strength, 2) change in facial demeanor (usually to one of intense hatred and evil), 3) change in voice tone and pitch (usually the voice deepens and becomes harsher or takes on a mocking tone), 4) epileptic-like convulsions with attendant symptoms, and 5) anesthesia to pain.

Psychological symptoms may include 1) clairvoyance (seeing things that could not be seen through normal means), 2) telepathy (communication from one mind to another by other than normal means), 3) the ability to predict the future, 4) the ability to speak in languages not known by the possessed person, 5) clouding of consciousness while in the trance state, and 6) amnesia for things which happened while in the trance state.

Spiritual changes may include 1) significant change in moral character (a previously modest person will dance naked), 2) becoming verbally or physically aggressive or falling into a trance if someone prays, and 3) an inability to say Jesus' name reverently or to affirm that he is God's son in the flesh (1 John 4:1–2).

An important epiphenomenon of diagnostic significance in demon possession is that possession is often accompanied by poltergeist ("noisy ghost") phenomena. These may include such things as unexplainable noises, furniture or household goods inexplicably overturned, pungent orders, and showerings of damp earth.

If the preceding criteria do not yield a diagnosis, the person's response to treatment may also be used. If standard psychotherapy and chemotherapy do not produce expected results, it would be possible to conduct a trial ceremony to bind or exorcise any demons who might be involved. If it was believed that it might be clinically disadvantageous to involve the client in the process, it is possible to conduct such a ceremony without the client's knowledge or presence (McAll, 1976).

Two classes of mental illness that some have viewed as having overlapping symptomatology with demon possession are the disorders of multiple personality and undifferentiated schizophrenia. In multiple personalities and demon possession there are voice changes, abrupt personality changes, and frequently amnesia for some of the other personalities and their behavior. However, in multiple personalities there are usually not epileptic-like convulsions, anesthesia to pain, clairvoyance, telepathy, ability to predict the future, ability to speak in languages not learned by at least one of the personalities, or the spiritual changes that usually occur with demon possession. In addition, the various personalities identify themselves as human personalities rather than demons.

In undifferentiated schizophrenia there are also some similarities to demon possession. The person may speak with words or syntax that is not part of his native language. He may claim to be someone other than who he is normally known to be. He may occasionally possess unusual strength. There may be changes in his voice tone, and pitch and facial expressions. He may claim to have unusual telepathic powers. There may sometimes be clouding of consciousness, and he may sit as if in a trance for long periods of time. Personal hygiene often deteriorates, and occasionally such persons will even walk about naked.

However, there are significant differences between the person with undifferentiated schizophrenia and the demon-possessed person, even within the above-mentioned similarities. There is a vast qualitative difference between the word salad and neologisms of the schizophrenic, and the sometimes eloquent speaking in foreign languages of the demon-possessed person. Within the demon-possessed person we usually find two or more well-organized, goal-directed personalities, each episodically taking control of the body they inhabit. The delusion of the schizophrenic in which he believes himself to be someplace he is not is easily seen by others to be patently false and a product of his own distorted perceptions. The schizophrenic may claim to have clairvoyance or telepathy, but his claims usually prove groundless. In the case of the demon-possessed person, the demon actually has supernatural access to such information and the clairvoyance and telepathy may be genuine.

The person with schizophrenia may or may not be a believer, but even if he is not, he generally will not demonstrate the radical negativism toward prayer that characterizes the demon-possessed person. Furthermore, poltergeist phenomena happen with the demon-possessed person but not the schizophrenic. The schizophrenic will often respond to antipsychotic medication, whereas the demon-possessed person does not. The schizophrenic person may respond to exorcism with a symptomatic remission, but the psychotic symptoms generally return in a short period of time.

Treatment

In cases of actual demon possession pagan and church history reveal three basic classes of exorcism. One means of exorcism used at various times and within various cultures has been physically beating the possessed person. The theory behind this practice was that if one were to inflict enough pain on the body which the demon was possessing, the demon would choose to leave. A second class of exorcism methods involves the use of magic formulas. Such formulas have been used from the time of the ancient Assyro-Babylonian cultures (or before) until the present day (Norvell, 1974).

Jesus presents a definite break with both of these methods. He needed neither scourging nor magic rituals. His exorcism method was powerful, direct, and brief. Frequently Jesus exorcised demons with a single word, "Go." At other times he used a slightly longer command, "Come out of him." Jesus' longest recorded exorcism was: "You deaf and dumb spirit, I command you, come out of him and never enter him again" (Mark 9:25). Jesus commanded his followers to continue the ministry of exorcism and empowered them to do so. Their instruction was to cast out demons in his name.

There is no instruction given that Christian exorcists must force the demon to name himself so that they might exorcise him by name. Furthermore, the biblical record suggests that exorcism can be done without the presence or cooperation of the person possessed (Mark 7:25–30). It does, however, admonish those involved in deliverance ministry to have a firm faith in Jesus' power to exorcise the demon and to prepare for exorcism by prayer. Scriptures also warn that it is dangerous for unbelievers to attempt to exorcise demons in Jesus' name (Acts 19:13–16).

A similar list of suggestions has been made by those Christians who have been actively involved in deliverance ministry in the twentieth century. The following recommendations represent the consensus of the authors listed in the references: 1) Remember that the power to exorcise demons lies in Jesus' name, not in a prescribed procedure or ritual. 2) Faith in Jesus' ability to exorcise demons is essential. Prayer beforehand is important preparation. 3) Self-examination and godly living is essential. More than one would-be exorcist has been embarrassed by a demon publicly revealing his private sins. 4) Exorcism should be done by a group of believers whenever possible. 5) Exorcism can be performed without the presence or cooperation of the possessed person. When the possessed person is able to be involved, it strengthens the process for him or her to let the demon know that he or she wants the demon to leave. 6) The possessed person should make a full confession of sins, pray a prayer of renunciation, and make a clean break with sin by burning occult books, breaking mediumistic contacts or friendships, and so on. 7) More than one demon may possess a person simultaneously. It is important that all demons be cast out before the exorcism process is discontinued. 8) Relapses can occur after exorcism. On more than one occasion demons have reported that they have been enabled to re-enter a believer's life because of lapses into pre-Christian ways of living. Therefore the exorcised persons should fill their lives with Bible reading and the Holy Spirit. 9) A follow-up support group of two or more people who can meet regularly for prayer and fellowship is recommended.

References

Hitt, R. *Demons, the Bible and you.* Newtown, Pa.: Timothy Books, 1973.

Jackson, B. Reflections on the demonic: A psychiatric perspective. In J. W. Montgomery (Ed.), *Demon possession.* Minneapolis: Bethany Fellowship, 1976.

Koch, K. (Ed.). *Occult bondage and deliverance.* Grand Rapids: Kregel Publications, 1971.

Lechler, A. What is the demonic. In K. Koch (Ed.), *Occult bondage and deliverance.* Grand Rapids: Kregel Publications, 1971.

McAll, R. K. Taste and see. In J. W. Montgomery (Ed.), *Demon possession.* Minneapolis: Bethany Fellowship, 1976.

Montgomery, J. W. *Demon possession.* Minneapolis: Bethany Fellowship, 1976.

Nevius, J. L. *Demon possession* (8th ed.). Grand Rapids: Kregel Publications, 1968.

Norvell, A. *Exorcism.* West Nyack, N.Y.: Parker Publishing, 1974.

Peters, G. W. Demonism on the mission fields. In J. W. Montgomery (Ed.), *Demon possession.* Minneapolis: Bethany Fellowship, 1976.

Tippett, A. R. Spirit possession as it relates to culture and religion. In J. W. Montgomery (Ed.), *Demon possession.* Minneapolis: Bethany Fellowship, 1976.

Unger, M. F. *Demons in the world today.* Wheaton, Ill.: Tyndale House, 1971.

Wilson, W. P. Hysteria and demons, depression and oppression, good and evil. In J. W. Montgomery (Ed.), *Demon possession.* Minneapolis: Bethany Fellowship, 1976.

44

Forgiveness
Jeffrey M. Brandsma

$\mathbf{E}$ven though it has been a continuing problem throughout history, modern psychological literature does not offer much discussion of the concept of forgiveness. Yet it is crucially important in interpersonal and intrapsychic functioning. Moreover, it is one of the key ideas bridging psychology and theology.

One possible exception in the psychology literature is Mowrer (1972), who has written extensively on the subjects of guilt, confession, and restitution. He is opposed to privatism, the idea that sin can be remitted through private prayer, sacraments, or psychotherapy. In his view there must be overt action with significant others involving self-disclosure in order for these processes to be completed. In contrast to this interpersonal emphasis the view developed in this chapter is that forgiveness has both intrapsychic and interpersonal elements and that these will vary in each case.

To deal with forgiveness conceptually it is necessary to first describe the context in which it occurs. The situation is one wherein a person experiences a violation of his or her sense of fairness—that is, in a context of an implicit need or an explicit agreement one person is wronged by omission or commission. What was expected (or needed) was not forthcoming. These actions or lack thereof can be inadvertent or completely conscious on the part of the violator; the effect on the violatee can be consequential or trivial. In the extreme case the violator will take no action to undo any of his violations.

In the situation described the one who is wronged experiences both frustration and loss. The loss is experienced as a diminishment of the self in terms of esteem, possessions, a dream, or one's sense of adequacy. An important concomitant of this dysphoria is that the person is brought closer to awareness of various needs, some of the most important of which are survival, dependency, vulnerability, and adequacy. The psyche responds quickly and automatically to protect itself by generating anger at the violator, thus externalizing the problem.

The Anger Defense and Its Consequences

Anger has both positive and negative possibilities. On the positive side it generates energy and a sense of power; it protects the self and initiates strivings that may be used to master or constructively change the situation. Anger creates distance and boundaries between people, and thus defines one's autonomy and values. In an angry situation it usually becomes clearer what one stands against and thus what one stands for. On the negative side excessive energy can be channeled into the generation of many nonconstructive fantasies, and often an emotional commitment is made to "do justice" or "get even, if it is the last thing I do." This feels quite appropriate in the heat of the moment, but as time goes on this decision and the dedication of a portion of one's energy to it tends to become preconscious and overgeneralized. From then on it produces much bitterness and unfocused hostility. The effects of the experience on personality will differ with the age of the person engaged in this process as well as with the number of past similar experiences. In general, the younger the person and the more past similar experiences, the more insidious and pervasive the effects will be.

In a state of threat and anger the self tends to become rigid in relationships and exercise hidden agendas. Generalized trust in others decreases, and a pattern of not giving until one first gets, and of being hypersensitive to this, emerges. Thus, a self-perpetuating process in relationships is begun.

Perhaps because restitution is often not possible, desirable, or even necessary, the wronged person often never becomes aware of what would be appropriate restitution or does not think through possible resolutions. As emotional generalization and overdetermined secondary gain occur, the situation soon develops wherein it seems that there could never be enough done, or the right amount at the right time to undo the wrong. With no awareness, no request, and no restitution forthcoming, interpersonal contact is broken, and one is likely to begin retribution in passive or active ways. Soon this is sensed as hostile by the violator, and an escalation (continued or new omissions or commissions) may occur in responses from the original violator. This provides the interactional basis for a vendetta or feud, a game without end.

In such a dyadic state there soon comes to exist a willful, competitive conspiracy between both parties to nurture their anger and wounds in order to pay back greater than they have received, even though the ostensible purpose may be to get even. In transactional analysis terms both persons then devote much of their energy to collecting anger stamps, organizing them into books, and waiting to cash them in when the external environment allows or when the internal pressure grows too great.

Basically there can be one of three responses to violation: retribution, love, or ignoring the act. The last option may involve forgiveness if ignoring the wrong is not used as a strategy to punish the other person by indifference—for example, by not responding to a spouse's needs. A loving response does, however, involve forgiveness, and it is to that process that we now turn our attention.

The Process of Forgiveness

To forgive, a person must re-experience the hurt caused by the violator in a different context, one that allows less threat and more availability of resources like cognition and empathy. One basis for forgiveness is an awareness of ownership of a need in the situation of violation. If we didn't want anything from anyone, they couldn't hurt us, we wouldn't get angry, and they wouldn't need forgiving. Thus one's own need is critical in the depth of the hurt, and thus the hurt is not attributed quite so much to the other person's behavior, no matter how despicable. To ascertain this truth often requires a humbling of the self to admit a dependency or to give up a defensively held grandiose view of the self. Re-experiencing a hurt in the context of a therapeutic relationship while owning one's needs usually heals and broadens the self, even if it is a humbling experience.

A second basis for forgiveness is to abandon the egocentric position of seeing others only in terms of one's own needs. A broader appreciation of another's motives, needs, and reasons for acting helps one to be more magnanimous. For example, one could depersonalize the violation not as a defense, but as a perception of reality—"It's not you personally; he does it to everybody." Another example: "Father, forgive them, for they know not what they do." It is helpful in this regard if the person who is wronged can understand in some way that the violator was trying to protect or enhance his or her interests or self, albeit in a misguided fashion. Some might label this as being more objective, but it is not that. It is taking a more empathic and subjective view of the other's behavior, but at the same time detaching oneself personally from the other and the consequences. A broader view of parents as people, for example, often helps children, when older, to forgive their parents' mistakes.

Often it is useful to look at the empirical basis for one's expectation that another "should" have acted in a different way. If no expectation is explicit or contractual, it again points to one's own needs projected onto the situation. If there were an explicit contract, one could become assertive and request an appropriate resolution or retribution. When one has laid this groundwork, he or she is more nearly in a position to give up anger. This is the point of having no emotional push toward retribution. To come to this position often requires support, because in admitting one's need and putting aside the anger defense, one is again becoming vulnerable to hurt.

Outcomes of Forgiveness

Even if a person is able to give up his anger and its distilled bitterness, if he judges the probability of the violator's changing in a positive direction to be slight he may decide to continue to avoid the violator. In this case the outcome is a basic affective neutrality toward the violator. Included in successful avoidance and neutrality is also a commitment not to look for retributive opportunities or to take advantage of those that might present themselves.

With others, spouses in particular, the situation will demand contact and the person will need things from the other. Here forgiveness implies a commitment to risk again the possibility of being hurt. However, this does not have to imply complete vulnerability; it probably will mean a more discriminating trust and vulnerability and perhaps an agreement to work together with the other to see that the violation does not occur again. An example would be one spouse agreeing to be more sensitive to the other's needs so that the other does not have to get into entangling relationships outside the marriage.

Certain persons may have difficulty forgiving because they think that to forgive is to condone an action. This false deduction is probably a consequence of refusing to give up self-protective anger. This often leads them to demand that the other person change before being forgiven, thus giving them a guarantee that they will not be hurt again.

The closely related problem of forgiving oneself is similar. It requires an expanded awareness of one's motives and impact on others, repentance, and, if possible, restitution. It is often the "end of innocence" wherein one must accept a humbler view of the self and a more complicated view of reality. Rigidly high standards for self must be lowered or tempered even as rigidly high standards for others must often be lowered in forgiving them.

Theological Perspective

A theological perspective adds a necessary and unique set of dimensions to any understanding of forgiveness. It helps in dealing with the extreme cases where forgiveness seems humanly impossible—that is, those who consciously wrong others and remain unrepentant.

Unlike the recent psychological literature the Bible does provide extensive discussion of forgiveness. In stories and examples and particularly in the life, work, and teachings of Jesus we find principles of forgiveness set forth. In Christian theology *agapé* love is the ultimate principle of the universe. By *agapé* is meant a love of persons and an existential commitment to their whole being. Christian values provide an imperative to forgive and, if possible, to reestablish a loving relationship, even if this involves a struggle.

An added and crucial corollary to this imperative is that a person does not in any sense deserve to be forgiven. Man has been corrupted by his heritage, pride, willfulness, and alienated relationship from God. He has chosen to disregard his relationship to his Maker and his fellows. There is no human way to undo this ontological condition of estrangement, and God's standards continue to be unfaltering. This situation was irreconcilable until God acted in a historical context to forgive through and indicate his forgiveness in the Christ events. The incarnation and resurrection remain great mysteries, but one clear meaning of God's action is quite evident—we are indeed forgiven.

The Old Testament indicates that vengeance belongs to God ("I will repay"), but the New Testament indicates that the slate of violations is wiped clean for the individual who will accept his provision. This is achieved through no inherent goodness of our own, but rather through God's action in coming to us. An unconditional loving action produces reconciliation and breaks though estrangement. It is a great gift wrapped in a humiliating judgment. Justification occurs through personal acceptance of this fact, which then leads to a life stance that responds to and becomes an instrument of this love. We have been surprised by undeserved love; if this can be experienced in some human fashion, perhaps then, in some feeble way, we can pass this grace on in our forgiving of others. We are unable to do this on our own. However, to the extent that we can participate in God's love, an experience transcending our self and selfishness, to that extent we can pass on forgiveness to others, trusting God to help us with our vulnerabilities.

Therapeutic Applications

In therapy directed toward intrapsychic forgiveness, it is important to remember that forgiveness must occur on at least two broad levels: the anger defense and the narcissistic insult to the self. Appropriate therapy must resolve both levels or the problem will soon return.

Forgiveness points to an emotional change away from anger and implies both behavioral and cognitive elements. More specifically, forgiveness implies behaviorally that the person has a low probability of emitting retributive behaviors. Cognitively it implies that the person will learn to accept what happened without continuing to obsess over retributive fantasies.

Once the problem is framed and agreed upon, the therapist can work to help the client understand his own individual needs and projections in the troubling situation. If successful, this may result in a re-experiencing of the hurt and anger in a context of exploration. The therapist might ask the client to specify what exactly he wanted or didn't want, how it affected him, and what (if anything) could be done by either party to undo the violation. Often useful is homework in which the client makes a list of all his "angers"—that is, the violations of the other. The list can be discussed to see which are forgivable and which are not, and why.

A good intermediate goal is neutrality. One can work toward emotional desensitization. This is usually accomplished by some sort of rehashing of the situation and an altered understanding of the other's actions. Thus, for example, alternative explanations might be suggested that would account for the behavior but not frame it as a premeditated personal attack. Forgiveness may then be achieved after this first goal of neutrality, or partial forgiveness, is reached.

In the case where there has been an explicit contract between the parties, a counselor can work toward having the wronged person assert himself to claim some form of restitution. Role playing can be done in the office and later, with some modification, in reality. An important aspect of office work would be the therapist prophylactically engineering the situation wherein the client asserts himself clearly and then does *not* get what he asks for. This is very difficult for the client, and many feelings need to be discussed throughout the process, particularly at the point of frustration. However, as a result of working through this frustration, a personal strengthening and constructive resolve is likely to occur.

A natural outcome after a violation of some magnitude is to avoid contact with the violator. This is often an excellent strategy (the notable exception being a spouse) *if* the time is used to work on forgiveness rather than retribution. The therapist's role during this crisis would be to clarify the avoidance, interpret its utility and function, and perhaps comment on its desirability. This might involve working toward making it a flexible, more cognitively controlled coping device, not a rigid permanent solution.

Usually at several points in this process the focus can shift to forgiving one's self for such things as being so stupid, having unacknowledged needs, misreading a situation, making bad decisions, and so on. This of necessity involves a reworking of one's self-image into one that is less prideful, more human, and more in tune with a broader internal and external reality. Indeed, this process of self-forgiveness is basic to the process of forgiving another and to the whole process of living. The tears that are shed in this kind of therapy are for the injured self, which must be forgiven and healed as well.

As an ideal, the therapist should help the client in this process to participate in the activity of God and the personality of Christ. This is to say that the client does not condone wrongdoing, still has high standards, and knows that the other does not deserve forgiveness. However, in spite of this, he is still able to maintain an ongoing attitude of forgiveness and to seek rapprochement with himself and others in the future because of the model of and implicit imperative contained in God's forgiveness. What the client and therapist often cannot accomplish on their own they can still strive for with the help of God's Spirit. And the business of reconciliation, of returning good for ill, goes on.

References

Brandsma, J. M. Forgiveness: A dynamic, theological, and therapeutic analysis. *Pastoral Psychology*, 1982, *31*(1), 40–50.

Mowrer, O. H. Conscience and the unconscious. In R. C. Johnson, P. R. Dokecki, & O. H. Mowrer (Eds.), *Conscience, contract, and social reality*. New York: Holt, Rinehart & Winston, 1972.

45

Divine Guidance
Joseph E. Talley

Divine guidance presupposes what has been traditionally called the will of God. Being guided implies a destination, tangible or intangible, and divine guidance implies the revelation of some part of the divine intention. To state specifically how divine guidance works would be presumptuous of any psychologist. However, discussion of some of the psychological complications associated with divine guidance is appropriate, as it represents an aspect of religious life open to psychological examination.

The concept of divine guidance is biblically based. Many passages of Scripture support this—for example, Ps. 32:8, "I will instruct you and train you in the way you shall go; I shall counsel you with my eye on you." Once we acknowledge that divine guidance exists, we must face the problematic questions of when and why this guidance is sought and how it is recognized as divine guidance. This is a move toward the psychological realm.

Such guidance shows itself in Scripture surely, but what of problems such as vocational and marital choice? Here many persons engage in prayer, in listening for a divinely inspired thought or feeling, or in looking for a sign—some event that is interpreted as having a special meaning. As one listens to inner thoughts and feelings, how can one single out a God-given directive? Packer (1973) warns Christians against a reliance on inner promptings and advocates depending on Scripture. Nevertheless, inner promptings still influence how we interpret Scripture, and many personal questions are not directly answered biblically.

Misattribution of Inner Promptings

It is important to realize that the mind is full of many promptings that come from different sources. Christian tradition has often dichotomized inner "voices" into the voice of the "flesh" and the voice of the "spirit." Oversimplifying the problem in this manner may lead to worse confusion. If these two voices, also seen as God versus the devil, are believed to be the only ones, then all voices that are not in some obvious way "fleshly" may be presumed to be of God.

An example would be the young person who prays for guidance about vocational choice and subsequently has the idea of becoming a missionary. This idea may be accepted uncritically as divine guidance, without giving consideration to the fact that the person's parents are missionaries and that they are hoping their child will make the same choice. In short, the importance of internalized parental voices often is ignored or even unrecognized, since such voices may sound similar to how we imagine divine guidance might sound.

Until internalized parental voices can be recognized as such and separated from the individual's self, the analyzing and observing ego, there is always doubt as to the true source of what is attributed to divine guidance. Until this separation is accomplished, divine leading toward almost anything not thought correct by the parents' convention would be assumed incorrect or even a demonic temptation. Thus, in this situation one is not truly open to God's leading. This separation is an aspect of "being born again," as it dethrones the parents as gods (or as devils) and allows God to now be Father.

Parental internalizations comprise the superego. This includes the ego ideal, that which we strive to be, and the conscience, the internal threat of punishment for not acting in accord with the ego ideal. Parental voices may often be identified as divine directives because they often carry this threat with them. It is a "do this, or else" thought. However, if it is God guiding, the feeling should be one of peace. Although the recognition of possible negative consequences for not following through may be present, fear should soon be quelled. In Scripture, particularly in the opening chapters of the Gospel of Luke, when the Spirit of God reveals something the receiver is initially afraid but is told not to fear. The anxiety then subsides.

Personality Types and Their Vulnerabilities

When and why does one seek divine guidance? Since any action is influenced by a variety of motives, it is not productive to ask if we seek divine guidance to serve God or to satisfy ourselves. It is likely that in seeking divine guidance we are motivated both to serve God and to fulfill certain psychological needs. Some of these needs, such as wanting to see ourselves as "good" people, may be relatively benign. However, other needs reflect more pathological personality traits that can contaminate the whole process of seeking divine guidance.

In such situations the needs of the individual so predominate that what is thought to be a desire for guidance is often a wish to indulge a hidden pathological need. In the extreme, such needs are associated with personality disorders. However, most people have tendencies in the direction of at least one of these disorders. Therefore, each person should identify his or her own tendencies or vulnerabilities in the hope that knowing the self better will allow for a more mature discernment of divine guidance. Otherwise one risks confusing one's own wishes with divine guidance.

Histrionic personality

The histrionic personality is characterized by overly intense, reactive behavior. Such persons are prone to exaggeration and often act out a role, such as the victim, without being aware of it. They crave stimulation and excitement and tend to be impressionable and easily influenced. Being suggestible, they show an initial positive response to any strong authority figure who might be able to provide a magical solution to their problems. The individual with a significant histrionic tendency might search for divine guidance in the hopes of avoiding the normal frustrations encountered in life and would use the search for guidance or its results to gain attention. Any search for divine guidance that seems to draw attention to the self must therefore be carefully examined to see whether it reflects underlying histrionic qualities rather than a search for God's will.

Narcissistic personality

The traits of the narcissistic personality can also negatively influence the search for divine guidance in that grandiosity, preoccupation with attention and admiration, and characteristic responses to threats to self-esteem may result in utilizing a relationship with God to feel more important than others. When narcissism predominates, the person feels an inflated sense of self-esteem. This is due to an identification with God to the point that one might see the self as merged with God and above the human experience. The power, strength, and goodness of God are wished for by a self that senses a lack of these qualities. Since everyone has some narcissism, one must suspect the temptation to interpret divine guidance in a way that makes one more special or important than others.

Dependent personality

The excessively dependent person allows others to assume responsibility for major areas of his or her life. Such persons lack self-confidence and the ability to function independently. They leave major decisions to others. Overly dependent persons may want God to decide daily minutia for them (e.g., what to wear that day). The overly dependent person hopes that divine guidance will enable him to avoid being a thinking, responsible adult with the option of choice regarding his actions. It is hard to believe that God would not have us accept responsibility for utilizing our own judgment at times. Perhaps God even sometimes withholds guidance in order to encourage appropriate self-confidence, independence, and adult growth.

Compulsive personality

Traits of the compulsive personality include excessive perfectionism, the insistence that things be done in his or her own way, and indecisiveness. In seeking divine guidance a person with compulsive traits might insist on guidance that conforms to a human notion of perfection, which may well not be identical to God's perfection. The compulsive would also be inclined to conclude that a leading in one direction must mean no subsequent changes. This definition of divine guidance is quite narrow and not necessarily God's view, but the compulsive clings to it out of fear of losing control of the situation.

The issue of indecisiveness is related to the importance of knowing the various voices of the mind. The more compulsive one is, the more doubting, obsessing, and ruminating there will be as to whether a prompting is indeed divine guidance. There will be a reluctance to follow a leading without some proof that this course will lead to good things. God has never promised to show all aspects of a path, but the compulsive person resists taking the first step without being able to see the whole path. Obviously such persons greatly limit the divine guidance they might receive by maintaining such stringent requirements.

Faith and Wisdom

Thus, the paradox emerges that we are to ultimately follow God's leading on faith without guarantees or proofs, while at the same time we must attempt to discern which of the voices we hear is the divine voice guiding us. It is essential that we know ourselves, the instruments through which divine guidance is received, well enough to have confidence that what we interpret as divine guidance comes from outside the personality itself. Recognizing internalized parental voices and being aware of various motives of the personality for seeking divine guidance help us identify and interpret divine guidance more accurately.

Reference

Packer, J. I. *Knowing God*. Downers Grove, Ill.: Inter-Varsity Press, 1973.

46

Hope
James R. Beck

Hope is a desire accompanied by the expectation that the desire will be obtained. It is partly cognitive (it is a thought), partly emotional (it involves anticipation and other positive affects), and partly volitional (it contains belief). Hope has traditionally had spiritual or religious connotations. For this reason hope has not been a major focus of psychological study in spite of its obvious emotional components. It has, however, been very present in literature and is a prominent concept in the Bible.

In Scripture hope is a major theme in both Testaments. The psalmists often spoke of hope as a major resource for coping with defeat, discouragement, and danger (e.g., Pss. 119:116; 146:5). The hope of the Old Testament was but a foreshadow of the hope found in Jesus Christ (Col. 1:27; 1 Tim. 1:1). Hope is prominent in Acts and the Epistles and is described as a central element of the Christian's resources.

Theologically hope serves the function of linking the believer to the future promised by Christ. As the follower of Christ experiences a new spiritual life, there is a keen awareness that the earthly enjoyments of faith in Christ are incomplete. What has begun on earth will continue into eternity. Hope links the believer's present with a glorious future.

Biblical anthropology does not give an exhaustive commentary on the psychological value of hope to men and women. Psalm 22:9 reads in the Authorized Version, "Thou didst make me hope when I was upon my mother's breasts." At first glance the verse appears to suggest that hope is innate or is a part of human experience reaching back into infancy. More recent translations suggest that the more probable interpretation is that the Lord caused the psalmist to trust as an infant, thus referring to the mother-child bonding phenomenon. However, the Bible emphasizes the strategic role of hope in the human personality. Faith seems to answer the human need for spiritual meaning, love relates to the intrapersonal and interpersonal needs of humans to relate to self and others, and hope reflects the motivational needs of humans to find meaning and purpose in the future. Hope is clearly portrayed as a significant motivator of human endeavor (Titus 2:11–14; 1 John 3:3). Hope longs for the resurrection body (Jeeves, 1976).

Psychology has indirectly studied the concept of hope from three different vantage points: 1) the role of hope in human motivation theory; 2) the importance of hope in human personality (as inferred from the absence of hope in certain pathologies); and 3) the curative power of hope in the recovery of severely disturbed persons.

Several important personality theories emphasize the significance of purpose as an ingredient in the human system. Hall and Lindzey (1957) describe purposive or teleological qualities as those which are goal seeking and future oriented. The classical analytic theories of Freud, Jung, and Adler all emphasize purpose, as do Fromm and Sullivan. In fact, so many contemporary theorists emphasize the purposive side of human personality that Hall and Lindzey suggest this aspect of personality is almost taken for granted and is no longer an issue of debate in psychology, as it was in the early twentieth century. Purpose is related to hope in that both are future oriented and both assume the attainment of some longed-for desires.

Hopelessness, or the lack of hope, is a prominent feature of the various depressive syndromes and of suicidal persons. Beck (1967) notes that hopelessness is a clinical feature of moderate and severe depressions and is present in about one-half of mild cases. Furthermore, Beck states, "In our studies we found that suicidal wishes had a higher correlation with hopelessness than with any other symptom of depression" (p. 58). It seems reasonable to conclude that if hopelessness is so highly associated with the desire to kill oneself, then the presence of hope in the human psyche must be vitalizing and central to survival.

The final avenue of psychological investigation into hope, exemplified by Stotland (1969), confirms the above deduction. Stotland views hope as a mediating variable that helps explain data regarding the recovery of hospitalized schizophrenics and depressives. When optimism and hopefulness are conveyed by the staff and the milieu, he concludes, people recover.

References

Beck, A. T. *Depression: Causes and treatment.* Philadelphia: University of Pennsylvania Press, 1967.

Hall, C. S., & Lindzey, G. *Theories of personality.* New York: Wiley, 1957.

Jeeves, M. A. *Psychology and Christianity: The view both ways.* Downers Grove, Ill.: Inter-Varsity Press, 1976.

Stotland, E. *The psychology of hope.* San Francisco: Jossey-Bass, 1969.

47

Inner Healing
H. Newton Malony

As described by its advocates, inner healing is a process wherein the Holy Spirit restores health to the deepest aspects of life by dealing with the root cause of hurts and pain. Basically it involves a twofold procedure in which 1) the power of evil is broken and the heritage of wholeness that belongs to the Christian is reclaimed, and 2) memories of the past are healed through prayer.

Forms of Healing

According to McNutt (1974), one of the leading figures in the field, inner healing is one of four forms of healing and is directed primarily toward the healing of memories. He concludes that there are three major types of sickness: sickness of the spirit caused by personal sin; sickness of the emotions caused by psychological hurts from the past; and the sickness of the body caused by physical disease or accidents. Prayer can be directed toward any one of these. The prayer of repentance asks forgiveness for sin; the prayer for bodily healing is directed toward physical healing; and the prayer for inner healing is concerned with healing the effects of painful memories. There is a fourth kind of prayer mentioned by McNutt: the prayer for deliverance from demon oppression, or exorcism, in which symptoms of each of the other three sicknesses can appear.

Betty and Ed Tapscott, other leaders in this movement, agree with McNutt's model but do not include exorcism as one of the primary forms of healing (Tapscott, 1975). They suggest that "breaking the power of Satan" is the first step in any healing but feel that this is accomplished through spiritual healing, which means coming to know Jesus as personal Savior. This involves confession of sin, renunciation of occult power, being willing to forgive in the same manner that one has been forgiven, being honest, and being humble. Spiritual healing is the foundation for inner healing of the mind and physical healing of the body.

The other side of breaking the power of Satan is reclaiming one's Christian inheritance, according to the Tapscotts. This means reaffirming what was true in creation and what has been provided in salvation; namely, that God wants people to be whole and has given many spiritual riches to his followers if they will but claim them. These acts of renouncing evil and reaffirming faith in God's goodness become the basis for inner healing, which is accomplished by prayer for the healing of memories. They are also the foundation for physical healing, which occurs through prayer for God to make the body whole again.

Most, if not all, inner healers agree that the several types of sickness and their remediation often occur together. Therefore, even though they emphasize one form of healing (e.g., inner healing), they are aware of, and utilize, the other types as well.

Of special interest is their attitude toward secular healers such as physicians and psychologists. After noting that millions of dollars are spent each year going to physicians, psychologists, and psychiatrists, one writer suggests that divine healing is the best. The old adage, "Doctors treat but Jesus heals," is offered as an unquestioned truth. Removing symptoms (which doctors do) is not the same as healing the cause (which Jesus does through inner healing). This same writer praises God for Christian psychologists but concludes that "inner healing is psychotherapy, plus God!" Another writer puts it thus: "Psychiatrists bring a degree of healing by probing into the past and bringing understanding of our weak and vulnerable spots and our angry and fearful reactions, but only the Holy Spirit can move into these areas and remove the scars" (Stapleton, 1976, p. x).

Among contemporary inner healers only McNutt accords an equal place to secular healers such as physicians and psychiatrists. He states that he always prefers to work as a team with them rather than by himself. But even he qualifies this approbation by saying that whereas in the 1950s he, like so many priests, discounted his own abilities to heal and referred most psychologically disturbed persons to professionals, he has come to believe that psychiatry does not always help and that prayer for the healing of memories is often the treatment of choice (McNutt, 1974).

Techniques

Prayer for the healing of memories is the core of inner healing. Memories are the residues of experience. Practically everyone has memories from the past from which he or she needs release, even if these are only minor hurts or childlike fears. Others have memories of being unwanted or neglected, of evil deeds or unexpected accidents, or even of events that happened while they were still in their mothers' wombs. Breaking the power of unresolved and oppressive memories is a prime component of inner healing.

This understanding is the major diagnostic model for the prayer that releases persons from the tyranny of the past. It is presumed that the fears, guilts, lethargies, and depressions that result from oppressive memories are against the will of God and, as such, are susceptible to being remedied by him if the person is willing. Of particular import to inner healers has been Hugh Missildine's *Your Inner Child of the Past* (1963). Inner healers feel that they are talking sound psychology because many models of psychopathology put similar emphasis on past experience. They see themselves as legitimate, even though they insist that they do not pretend to be psychologists.

Although there is a basic similarity in approach among those who practice this form of healing, there are some distinctions. The specific approaches of three prominent practitioners—the Tapscotts, Francis McNutt, and Ruth Carter Stapleton—will be examined here.

The Tapscotts

The Tapscotts feel that memories can be healed by the individual himself as well as by the ministrations of another who has the power of healing. They encourage the person to begin with a prayer for the forgiveness of sins and a reaffirmation of Jesus as personal Savior. They suggest that the person next renounce all the forces of evil or Satan that have become a part of his life, asking the Holy Spirit to reveal these forces. At this point the person is to trust the Holy Spirit to bring to mind the images and memories that are handicapping. Even though no release is apparent, the person is to vocally renounce the power of these memories and images. Then he is to ask Jesus to fill the void that is left if the memories should leave. Jesus is asked to give his peace, his joy, and his love.

It is important to note that up to this point persons will quite likely have experienced no healing. Instead they are restating their faith and asking for God's power in their lives. Then they are requested to visualize Jesus walking hand in hand with them back through every moment of their lives. As the Holy Spirit lifts up memories of unpleasant situations, they are to take Jesus into these events. Jesus will redeem the painful memories, set the person free from them, and heal the past. The person is asked to thank God in advance for the miracle that will be worked through inner healing.

The Tapscotts provide printed prayers to be used with or by persons at every stage of the process. Although they do not say so, they seem to imply that these are once-for-all events. However, they recognize the possibility that the release from such experiences might fade, and they prescribe a set of acts designed to keep the inner person healed. These include daily prayer and Bible reading, conscious praise, regular commitment to the Lord, dedication of one's home to God, standing firm against Satan, becoming part of a spirit-filled fellowship, finding a prayer partner, and constantly forgiving others.

Francis McNutt

McNutt begins with the assumption that the basic need of life is for love; if we are ever denied it at any time in our lives, our ability to love and trust others may be seriously affected. The wounds resulting from loss of love fester and handicap us. The first step in inner healing is for Jesus to heal these wounds. The second step is for Jesus to give us the love we want and thus to fill the empty spaces once they have been healed and drained of the poison of past hurts and resentment. Whenever the person becomes aware of fears, anxieties, resentments, hates, or inhibitions, that is the time to seek inner healing.

Before the prayer for healing is offered, two questions are explored with the person. First, when can you remember first feeling this way? Second, what was happening that caused you to feel this way? If the person cannot remember an incident, then God is asked to reveal it. After the time and place of the hurt has been identified, a prayer for the healing of the hurt is offered. In as imaginative and childlike manner as possible, the healer prays that Jesus will go back into the experience and heal the person of the wound that resulted from it. McNutt states, "Jesus, as Lord of time, is able to do what we cannot. . . . The most I was ever able to do as a counselor was to help the person bring to the foreground of consciousness the things that were buried in the past, so that he could consciously cope with them in the present. Now I am discovering that the Lord can heal these wounds . . . and can bring the counseling process to its completion in a deep healing" (1974, p. 187).

After the memories have been healed, the person prays to God to fill the void in his life with love. Because of the basic need for love, full healing cannot occur until the person is given what he has been missing, namely love. McNutt notes that this part of inner healing is often more difficult than the healing of the wounds of the past. The person is so accustomed to being without love that he does not know how to receive it. If the person says he does not feel the love of God, Jesus is asked to speak to the person at the depth of his soul and to call him by name. Since the nature of the wounds is known to the healer, he or she prays that God will provide the specific kind of love that the person did not have. Again, the prayer is very childlike and imaginative.

Ruth Carter Stapleton

Of note is Stapleton's emphasis on inner healing as a process, not a one-time event. Her accounts are replete with long-term relationships in which the person returns to the healer again and again. In only a few cases does she report immediate results. Further, she places an emphasis on the fact that inner healing is something more than sound doctrine or even insight into traumatic events. She suggests that most people act as though they want help when they do not really want to change.

Stapleton suggests that the desire to be whole often comes as a result of some inspirational experience with an evangelist or healer. After this the motivation toward healing changes and becomes the basis on which inner healing can occur. She postulates an "inner child" that lives in most of us and has an insatiable need for approval and love. This inner child needs to be "revealed and healed." Although she agrees with other healers that there are real past traumas that need to be faced and healed, there are in many people fantasized hurts grounded in the child within us. Thus, she seems to have an implicit model of evil which must be faced or revealed in the healing process. Finally, she emphasizes group experiences of inner healing much more than do others. Members of the group were often used in role play of other members' situations and much mutual insight occurred.

Stapleton's term for the process of inner healing is *faith imagination therapy*. In this process she recommends that persons visualize as vividly as possible Jesus coming into the experiences that have been identified as troublesome. They are encouraged to allow Jesus to respond to the situation and to take over their own behavior. She contends that forgiveness lies at the heart of all inner healing, and she encourages persons to use each situation as an opportunity to forgive and build. As Jesus dominates the visualization, persons are encouraged to allow themselves to develop into the persons God intended them to be.

Although Stapleton relies heavily on intuitive insights given her by the Holy Spirit, she leaves to the person the task of filling in the details of the visualization. In this process of faith imagination with Jesus at the center, healing deep inside the person occurs. The final step in the process is when the individual ceases being too proud or too self-depreciatory to begin some kind of ministry of service to others. As noted, for Stapleton this process is one that requires prolonged contact over an extended period of time.

Relationship to Guided Imagery

The psychotherapeutic technique most similar to the procedures in inner healing is that of guided imagery (Leuner, 1969). Stapleton is in accord with many practitioners of this technique in asserting that faith imagination is a way of inducing positive changes deep within the mind. According to Leuner guided imagery attempts to replace regressive and defensive mental habits with more mature, adaptive ego functioning. The core method in both guided imagery and faith imagination is that of suggestion. Several aspects of these procedures should be noted.

Initially the role of the therapist or healer is definitely an active one. Although many inner healers listen long and empathically (as would many psychotherapists using guided imagery), when they begin to treat the person they become very active. They are not client centered in their approach or their presumptions. They act on a great deal of intuition, and once they intuit a dynamic, they assertively lead the individual in a fantasy designed to induce healing.

However, it would seem that neither inner healers nor therapists employing guided imagery exert quite the control that hypnotists do, although their methods are similar. Neither faith imaginations nor guided fantasies are hypnotic suggestions. They have more fluidity to them. In many hypnotic situations the hypnotist provides most, if not all, the details. In inner healing and guided imagery the individual is encouraged to imagine the action and elaborate the basic situation in fantasy.

There is yet another similarity in the two methods that should be noted. They both use archetypal personages in their fantasies. Guided imagery as a psychotherapeutic technique usually relies on Jungian understandings of psychic structure and dream analysis. For example, roads are life lines, mountains are ambitions or problems, crossroads are decision points, caves are suppressed memories or fears, witches are denied impulses, and old men are inner wisdoms. Inner healers confine themselves to two figures in the Trinity—the Holy Spirit and Jesus Christ. They encourage the individual to allow the Holy Spirit to reveal the incidents that provoked trauma and to allow "Jesus" to be present in the reliving of those events and to heal them.

One could say that the inner healer's Jesus is most like the "old man" of guided imagery. However, there is a radical difference. The guided imagists assume that the old man is the source of inner wisdom, which was there all along but which had been denied due to the pressures of living and to defenses against trauma. The inner healers make a different assumption. Although they rely heavily on reclaiming the inheritance of the image of God in creation, they emphasize much more the gifts of salvation that have been made available through the cross of Christ. Furthermore, Jesus is not inner wisdom but transcendent personal power. He exists outside the person and is much more than denied power. He brings insight and healing that are unavailable to personal resources no matter how suppressed. He is a person, not simply an insight.

Finally, there is a common presumption among inner healers and guided imagists that something more than insight is needed for healing to occur. Both groups are action therapists in the sense that they agree that re-experiencing is the prime means of psychological change. In this they resemble both gestalt therapists and psychoanalysts, although their presumptions of the dynamic processes involved are somewhat different. Gestalt therapists are more inclined to induce the re-experience of past processes, such as feelings, while psychoanalysts are committed to a spontaneous working through of the transference with the therapist.

Guided imagists and inner healers deal with total events, although the former typically induce standard classical fantasies while the latter encourage reliving of actual personal situations. Yet in both, the participation of the person in present experiencing is the vital component of healing. However, it should be said that here again the inner healers assume that inner resources will not, in and of themselves, accomplish the task. What is needed is the presence and power of the living Christ, who will do for the person what he could not do for himself—namely, heal the memories and heal the person so that he can live anew.

Critique

Several critiques of inner healing have been given. The most recent is that of Alsdurf and Malony (1980), who have analyzed a number of the assumptions underlying the work of Stapleton. Although inner healers differ in some crucial ways, the Alsdurf and Malony critique seems to apply to all in general.

Initially Stapleton is accused of engaging in a simplified psychotherapy, although she denied this. In fact, she claimed that her approach is not counseling in the sense that this word is used among mental health professionals. Yet it is hard to deny that she was indeed engaged in such when one examines her accounts of her work. She met with persons in periodic sessions over extended periods of time. She led group meetings that included sharing, role playing, guided fantasies, and interpersonal catharsis. In spite of her denial she seemed to evidence a cavalier reliance on serious psychodynamic theorizing and an overreliance on semipopular authors such as Missildine.

While her basic presumption that Jesus can heal quickly and deeply allowed her to expect miracles, she used many standard psychotherapeutic methods without acknowledging them. Furthermore, she seemed naively free from the caution that most psychotherapists have in approaching some problems optimistically while recognizing great difficulties inherent in others. Again, her too easy acceptance of one model, Missildine, caused her to assume an almost photographic memory of the past while practically reifying a psychic structure, the inner child of the past, that most theorists would find problematical.

Perhaps the basic problem is that while Stapleton provided fairly intensive psychotherapy, she did not seem to acknowledge the manner in which students of psychopathology have come to understand these issues. To deny this reality is to remain free from self-criticism while evoking the discount of those who know better. This is not to say that her (and other inner healers') basic belief in the power of Jesus to heal needs to be subjected to such analysis by secular theory. It does not. It is to say that this tradition of healing would be strengthened if inner healers could be better informed about how human beings function and what causes them to be as they are.

Another critique, which may be more attributable to Stapleton than to other inner healers, is that she lacks a thorough doctrine of sin. In some comments made to secular groups of therapists, it seems as if she were willing to identify her approach too simplistically with holistic healers who may be operating under Eastern presumptions that do not acknowledge man's basic propensity toward evil. Thus, while using Christian terminology she may be implicitly utilizing basic assumptions more like secular therapists who have concluded that humans have the resources for self-healing. It should be noted that McNutt and the Tapscotts put great emphasis on the importance of the forgiveness of sin in their methods and that Stapleton denies any such omissions when confronted with this critique. However, her words in certain settings belie this denial and denote a possible naive reliance on a methodology that seems to bypass the need for the individual to face personal evil in an effort to affirm the power of Jesus to heal hurts resulting from traumatic past events.

All in all, however, inner healing should be looked upon as a unique and powerful form of therapy currently held in wide respect by a large part of the Christian world. Christian psychotherapists should study it deeply and attempt to learn from its bold use of Christian resources in the helping process.

References

Alsdurf, J. M., & Malony, H. N. A critique of Ruth Carter Stapleton's ministry of "inner healing." *Journal of Psychology and Theology*, 1980, *8*(3), 173–184.

Leuner, H. Guided affective imagery. *American Journal of Psychotherapy*, 1969, *23*, 4–22.

McNutt, F. *Healing*. Notre Dame, Ind.: Ave Marie Press, 1974.

Missildine, W. H. *Your inner child of the past*. New York: Simon & Schuster, 1963.

Stapleton, R. C. *The gift of inner healing*. Waco, Tex.: Word Books, 1976.

Tapscott, B. *Inner healing through healing of memories*. Houston: Tapscott, 1975.

48

Jesus Christ
William T. Weyerhauser

Although he wrote no books on psychology, or any other subject for that matter, Jesus Christ must be counted among the eminent contributors to psychology, his contribution being through his life and teaching. Whatever one may believe about Jesus, it is safe to say that no one, upon a serious reading of the Gospels, can fail to acknowledge his role as a profound teacher. Jesus' role as a teacher derived its power and authority, in part, from the fact that he lived out what he taught. He *was* his teaching. Those who were convinced of the truth of his teaching were grasped by his presence and by the fact that his teaching was simply a verbal expression of the truth manifested by his presence. He not only spoke of love, he was loving. He not only spoke of forgiveness, he was forgiving.

Since his teachings were congruent with the truth of his being, it can be said that they had ontological validity. With respect to human nature, if a statement has ontological validity it expresses a truth about the essence of human nature. As Christians we affirm that as Jesus expressed the truth of his being in his life and teaching, he also manifested what is true for us. Jesus said, "I am the way, and the truth,

316

and the life; no one comes to the Father, but by me" (John 14:6). His truth is our truth. For us to know God means that we have to grapple with the meaning and relevance of Jesus' truth for ourselves.

If we believe that Jesus' teachings are ontologically valid, then we also imply their psychological validity. This is to say that Jesus teaches a way of life that facilitates mental and emotional health, and brings about wholeness within. Jesus calls each one to align with a way of being which brings one inwardly in touch with the deepest possibilities within the self, to be all that one can be. If psychology ignores this way and its potential for those who have mentally and emotionally lost their way, it does so to its own detriment. One might even argue that Jesus's teachings set the agenda for psychology, for he addressed those concerns that are most fundamental to human nature. It is one these concerns that psychology needs to focus on in order to contribute to the development of wholeness within persons.

What did Jesus emphasize about human nature that has implications for psychology? What really was the good news? Jesus proclaimed that one is not bound by, or limited by, that which his senses would tell him is reality. The world perceived by the senses is not the real world. The view that sees man as constituted essentially of matter, as beginning with the birth of his body and ending with the death of his body, is not only inaccurate but terribly limiting. Jesus asserted repeatedly in many different ways that there exists an inner dimension to man that is incorporeal. He called this dimension the spirit, and it is in the spirit that the real source of one's personhood and the truth of his being reside. This is the light within that must shine rather than stay hidden. The light within is a much more reliable guide to illuminate one's way than a code of expectations that comes from without, such as human traditions and laws.

This inwardness, the realm of spirit, is the kingdom of God; it is there for persons to inherit if they but seek it. At the time of Jesus the Jews were looking for a Messiah who would restore the kingdom of Israel and reign as God's representative on earth. The Jews anticipated an earthly kingdom with a political leader sent by God. Jesus turned this anticipation inward. The kingdom of God is not external and will not come as a political institution. Rather it is within. Man's connection with God is that of spirit to Spirit.

Since the kingdom of God is within, we are not separated from each other, as our three-dimensional frame of reference suggests, but at the level of being we are one. We are united and together with each other in God. Separation then becomes an illusion, a transitory phenomenon. The truth is that we are in union in spirit though we persist in our illusion of separation. Jesus directed his teachings toward enabling one to discover the nature of his being, his union at the level of being with others and with God, and the nature of his illusions.

From a psychological standpoint the inheritance of the kingdom of God may be viewed as the process of self-discovery. If self and spirit are the same, then the therapeutic process of self-discovery becomes a spiritual quest. On the one hand, the nature of each person's quest is different because each person is unique. On the other hand, since each is essentially spirit, there are challenges or tasks that each quest shares.

Jesus' teachings are most relevant for psychology because he addressed those challenges that are common to everyone's quest. For example, the process of self-discovery has to involve at some point the severing of dependency ties to parents. Jesus addressed this challenge when he said: "Do not think that I have come to bring peace on earth; I have not come to bring peace but a sword. For I have come to set a man against his father, and a daughter against her mother, and a daughter-in-law against her mother-in-law; and a man's foes will be those of his own household. He who loves father or mother more than me is not worthy of me; and he who loves son or daughter more than me is not worthy of me" (Matt. 10:34–37). Jesus did not mean that he had come to foster domestic strife but rather that the process of following him, the quest for the discovery of the truth of one's own being, inevitably involves a revision of the nature of one's parental relationships. This can cause strife, but strife is certainly not the primary goal.

What is it that Jesus taught that is most germane to the tasks we all face in the process of self-discovery? Jesus said that the two most important commandments are, "You shall love the Lord your God with all your heart, and with all your soul, and with all your mind. . . . And . . . you shall love your neighbor as yourself" (Matt. 22:37–39). These commandments put the challenge to be loving at the heart of self-discovery. A close look at the first commandment suggests it can be taken as an exhortation and as a statement of fact. As an exhortation it is a directive. As a statment of fact the first commandment contains the truth that what one has as one's central concern one *will* love with all one's heart, soul, and mind. "Where your treasure is, there will your heart be also" (Matt. 6:21) is another way of saying this. If the pursuit of money has become one's central concern, then that is what will grasp one totally. If another person has become one's central concern, then that relational involvement will grasp one totally. This fact underlines how important it is that one's central concern allow for the fullest and most meaningful growth of oneself. To love anything short of that which calls forth the fullest expression of one's being only violates one's being. Love of God is the only central concern that does not violate one's being.

Too often love of God implies an objectification of God, as though God is out there somewhere and it is one's duty to love him and worship him. Once God is objectified, what becomes emphasized is one's separation from him. As long as one believes there is a separation that must be bridged, he precludes the bridgement. One's belief sustains the separation. To love God without objectifying God is to commit oneself to love. For "God is love." To love God is to love loving. To love loving is to make loving God one's central concern.

To take on the challenge to be loving does not violate one's being. In fact it draws the fullest possible expression of one's being out of oneself. To be loving also requires one to love one's own being. One cannot reject or hate oneself and love another, for since a person relates through himself to another and since his self is the channel for love, self-rejection sabotages his efforts to love. He cannot relate around himself to another. One relates through one's self-hate, and ends up projecting this on the other in such a way that the other comes to be seen as an attacker.

The relationship between love of self and love of another leads to the second commandment, "You shall love your neighbor as yourself." This can also be seen as a statment of fact as well as an exhortation. As an exhortation it is a directive. As a statement of fact it asserts that you *will* love your neighbor as yourself. If you love yourself, you will love your neighbor. If you do not love yourself, you cannot love your neighbor. So love of self becomes the basis for love of neighbor.

This may sound egocentric. However, egocentricity and self-love are antithetical. Egocentricity is self-protectiveness, not self-love. Egocentricity seeks to resolve feelings of insecurity with the erection of defenses around the self. Then these defenses come to be taken for the self and one loses sight of his true self.

Self-love is self-affirming and seeks the nondefensive expression of being. Self-love emerges in the struggle to be loving, for in this effort one has to cull away the inner obstacles to self-love. As one lovingly engages in this culling process, he is brought closer and closer to the beauty of his own being. This is a gradual and lengthy process and requires an ongoing rigorous self-examination to bring to awareness the nature of one's defenses and the myriad ways one substitutes a reliance on them for being true to oneself.

How does one learn to love? This is not a question that can be addressed prescriptively. One cannot really tell another how to love, one can only suggest he go and try it. Jesus did show what it means to love by loving those around him. How did Jesus love? He remained consistently true to himself in all his interactions with others. He insisted on his freedom to be true to his own being and granted the other the freedom to be true to his being. He shared his vision of himself unreservedly and so awoke those around him to their own beings.

Forgiveness as a manifestation of love is crucial to the process of self-discovery. In the struggle to forgive one discovers himself, because in forgiveness he shifts his focus from blaming another for having wronged him back to himself. In blame one can only see another's fault. One loses sight of himself in the challenge to be himself in truth. In blame one says, "I cannot be until you acknowledge the wrong you did to me." As Finch asserts: "How little do we appreciate the fact that what gets the focus of our attention, gets us. The feat of holding some grudge actually has the effect of the grudge holding us. Being unwilling to let go of yesterday retards us. The self becomes stifled in a mode of existence that does not exist" (Malony, 1980, pp. 253–254).

Forgiveness is particularly relevant in working through the blame one holds toward one's parents. As long as one blames one's parents for their failures to care, one continues to hold one's parents responsible for one's being. It is as if one says to one's parents, "You have been bad parents and until you become good parents, on my terms, I cannot be myself." If one cannot be oneself, one cannot love oneself. So the blame one sustains toward one's parents impedes one's self-discovery. Forgiveness is the only antidote. In forgiveness one releases any claim one has on the other to be good on one's own terms.

Forgiveness is not simply an intellectual process. It may necessitate that one experience intense rage in order to allow one to existentially discover the basis for one's blame. Forgiveness, if genuine, is a process of working through one's feelings to a release of a grudge one is holding against the other. The challenge to forgive is ongoing. Any time one turns away from forgiveness, one locks oneself into a grudge and imprisons oneself therein.

The effort to be loving in all love's manifestations facilitates the emergence of authentic selfhood. To live in this effort is to take Jesus' teachings seriously. If psychology ignores what Jesus taught by way of modeling and by way of instructing, it ignores what is crucial to the accomplishment of the clinical task—that of facilitating the development of personhood.

Reference

Malony, H. N. (Ed.), *A Christian existential psychology: The contributions of John G. Finch*. Washington, D.C.: University Press of America, 1980.

49

Personhood

C. Stephen Evans

Both in ordinary and philosophical usage persons are usually contrasted with mere things. Thus, to say of some human being that she is a person is to emphasize the differences between the human and subhuman orders, and to inquire about the nature of personhood is to inquire about the nature of those differences.

It was probably Kant who most shaped the meaning of the word *person* with his insistence that persons and only persons are ends in themselves, who should never be treated solely as means. Thus, to speak of human beings as persons is, among other things, to speak of them as morally significant beings, the potential bearers of rights and obligations. This moral sense of personhood must be distinguished from the related legal sense, in which infants may not be considered full persons while corporations are. The term *self* often does much of the same work as the term *person*, and some philosophical discussions use the terms interchangeably.

Though there is general rough agreement on the characteristics that distinguish human persons from nonpersons, different thinkers have at various times regarded different characteristics as being most fundamental. Medieval thinkers emphasized rationality as the essential characteristic of persons, following Boethius, who defined a person as an individual substance of a rational nature. In the modern classical period John Locke, while not ignoring rationality, emphasized the quality of self-awareness over time as decisive for personhood, including particularly memory. More recent thinkers have tended to emphasize activity, seeing persons as responsible agents whose decisions reflect values or caring concerns (Macmurray, 1957). These different views should be regarded as complementary perspectives rather than as rivals, since all these characteristics are significant elements of personhood.

Although the term *person* is usually employed to differentiate human persons from the subpersonal order, some thinkers have attempted to reduce or eliminate these differences. The view that human persons are not really unique or qualitatively different from the rest of the natural order is generally called reductionism, since the aim is to eliminate the special status human persons seem to enjoy by reducing them to the status of other animals. Early behaviorism, as developed by Watson (1930), was an avowedly reductionistic program. Skinner's (1971) radical behaviorism continues this reductionistic program, as is evidenced by the title of his popular book, *Beyond Freedom and Dignity*. More recent social behaviorists have, however, modifed behaviorism considerably in a nonreductionistic direction.

Historically most thinkers who have defended the uniqueness of the person have been dualists who have held that the self or soul is not a material entity and must be distinguished from the body. Not surprisingly, therefore, most reductionists have been materialists who have identified the person with the body.

Not all materialists are reductionists, however. Some recent thinkers have attempted to avoid both dualism and reductionism. Strawson (1959) developed a view of the person as a unique kind of entity, which must be described in two different ways. To properly describe human persons we must employ both material predicates and personal predicates. Since personal predicates are not reducible to material predicates, Strawson's view should not be regarded as reductionistic.

Most contemporary discussions of personhood have been problem oriented and have tended to focus on one of three areas: 1) the problem of consciousness, or the relationship of mind to body; 2) the problem of the identity of the person over time; and 3) the nature of personal actions. The latter area encompasses the traditional debate over freedom and determinism.

The Mind-Body Problem

Two facts about human persons seem obvious. First, persons have bodies. Second, persons are conscious. The mind-body problem concerns the relationship of these two facts and their relative significance for answering the question as to what kind of entity human persons really are.

Classical positions on the mind-body problem fall naturally into two groups: monistic positions and dualistic positions. Dualistic views regard the mind or soul (roughly equivalent terms), the seat of consciousness, as a distinct nonphysical substance. In this view a human person is a composite of this nonmaterial substance and the body. Some dualists prefer to identify the person exclusively with the soul. Not all dualists agree on the relationship between the soul and the body. Most, like Descartes, have been interactionists who hold that body and soul can reciprocally control and influence each other. Thus, dualism is compatible with the obvious ways in which consciousness is affected by and even dependent on the brain and central nervous system. Other dualists have been parallelists, who have denied interaction between soul and body because of the difficulty in explaining interaction between two radically different substances.

Monistic views, which deny that a human person is or has two distinct substances, are an even more varied lot. Idealists or panpsychists believe that the person is a purely spiritual entity, interpreting the body as being in some sense spiritual. Materialists reject the existence of any nonphysical substance; in this view a person is identical with his body. Neutral monists teach that a person is one substance that has both mental and physical characteristics.

Epiphenomenalism is a special case that does not fit easily into any other category. The epiphenomenalist views consciousness as a by-product of the body. Thus the mind is distinct from the body, as dualists affirm, but completely a function of the body, as materialists affirm.

Materialists differ among themselves as to how to describe and explain the mental aspects of persons. Metaphysical or philosophical behaviorism (to be distinguished from methodological behaviorism) holds that the mind consists of certain types of behavior as well as tendencies to engage in behaviors. Central state materialism, or the mind-brain identity theory, holds that conscious events are not just conditioned by, but are strictly identitical with, neurophysiological events in the brain and central nervous system. Eliminative materialism takes the bull by the horns and boldly denies that mind or consciousness really exists. On this view a scientific description of the workings of the brain and central nervous system could in principle, if not in practice, replace our mentalistic language altogether.

Christians do not all hold to the same position on the mind-body problem. Traditionally most Christians have been dualists, and many still are. Some contemporary Christian thinkers have attempted to develop dualistic views that do justice to the unity of the person and body and do not devalue the body in Platonic fashion. In general anyone who believes in an "intermediate state" after death, in which a person continues to exist prior to the resurrection, is committed to dualism. Other Christians today are more drawn to forms of neutral monism or nonreductionistic materialism, which make life after death depend completely on a bodily resurrection (Reichenback, 1978).

Personal Identity over Time

Over the course of a lifetime persons change enormously, both intellectually and physically. In what sense, then, can a person be said to be the *same* person at one point in time that he was at some earlier point in time? Unless some good answer to this question can be given, it would seem wrong to punish or reward a person for some past action. Surely one is not generally responsible for actions performed by a different person. The choice of criteria for personal identity also has a crucial bearing on the possibility of life after death, for these criteria simply express our beliefs about how much and in what ways a person can change and still remain the same person. For example, could a person leave his body and still remain the same person? Could he receive a new body?

Several different views of personal identity have been defended. One of the most prominent is the memory theory, which was put forward by Locke. In this view a person is identical with a past person if he has memories of that person's actions and experiences. One major difficulty with this theory is that to remember myself doing some past action *presupposes* that I am identical with that person rather than accounts for that identity. A second theory proposes bodily continuity as the criterion of personal identity. This position obviously rules out any possibility of life after the death of the body.

Dualists who believe that the self is a conscious soul which, though embodied, is not identical with its body handle this issue differently. From the dualistic perspective, since the self is a metaphysical reality, a resurrected person can be the same person, even though the body is new, so long as the new body is possessed by the same self or soul. Christians who are nondualists must argue that bodily similarities and memory experiences would be sufficient to regard a resurrected person as the same individual.

Theory of Action

Correlated with the distinction between persons and mere things is the distinction between actions and mere events. If a rock rolls down a hillside and crushes a car, it makes sense to ask what caused the event. However, if a person pushes a rock down a hillside onto a car, it makes sense to ask who did it as well, and to inquire about the meaning of the action. In the case of the action it is not obvious that the action is caused in the way in which mere events are caused, for most human beings believe that at least some of their actions are freely chosen. Making sense of this distinction between actions and mere events has generated a great deal of discussion, which is still largely unresolved. Among the most debated issues is the relation between reasons for action and causes. Unlike most cases of causal explanation, giving a reason for an act does not seem to render the act inevitable but rather to make the act intelligible. One can know the reason for an act without knowing any relevant causal law. Reasons also serve to justify as well as explain actions in a way that ordinary causal explanations do not. Despite these differences between reasons and ordinary causes, reasons do seem to serve as motives, and it is widely held that they must therefore serve as causes in some sense.

Closely related to this dispute about action is the traditional debate over freedom and determinism. Three classical positions on this issue continue to have adherents. The determinist insists that all human actions have antecedent conditions that necessitate their occurrence and that freedom of the will is an illusion grounded in ignorance of the causal factors. The libertarian, or advocate of free will, claims that at least some human actions, usually those involving rational reflection or moral effort, are not completely determined by their antecedent conditions. This position is easily caricatured. The libertarian admits that not all human behavior is free and that even free choices are limited by the past, but he insists, however mysterious it may seem, that human persons are not completely a product of their past.

The compatibilist believes that freedom and determinism must both be accepted. This is possible if freedom is defined as acting in accordance with one's own wants or preferences, yet those preferences are seen as causally determined. On this view a free action is one that is shaped by the person's internal wants and is not compelled or coerced by some external factor. Libertarians object to this on the grounds that the compatibilist view reduces to determinism. Libertarians claim that since the compatibilist admits that our wants are ultimately caused by external factors, this implies that even in the case of uncoerced acts the ultimate responsibility for an action always rests outside the individual. To the libertarian a person can be held morally responsible for an action only if he could have done otherwise, even given his past history.

The debates about personhood have a particular significance to Christians. Not only do Christians believe that human beings have an eternal destiny, they believe that God himself, the ultimate reality and ground of everything else real, is a person. Many twentieth-century theists have termed their whole philosophy *personalism*. For the theist, to explore the nature of personhood is to plumb the depths of the whole of reality, and the unique characteristics that demarcate human persons from other creatures must be seen as forming the image of God in man, an image that has been defaced but not obliterated.

References

Macmurray, J. *The self as agent.* New York: Harper & Row, 1957.

Reichenbach, B. *Is man the phoenix?* Grand Rapids: Christian University Press, 1978.

Skinner, B. F. *Beyond freedom and dignity.* New York: Knopf, 1971.

Strawson, P. F. *Individuals: An essay in descriptive metaphysics.* London: Methuen, 1959.

Watson, J. B. *Behaviorism* (3rd ed.). Chicago: University of Chicago Press, 1930.

Additional Readings

Allport, G. W. *Becoming.* New Haven: Yale University Press, 1955.

Berofsky, B. (Ed.). *Free will and determinism.* New York: Harper & Row, 1966.

Bertocci, P. A. *The person God is.* New York: Humanities Press, 1970.

Borst, C. V. (Ed.). *The mind-brain identity theory.* New York: St. Martin's Press, 1970.

Evans, C. S. *Preserving the person.* Downers Grove, Ill.: Inter-Varsity Press, 1977.

Penelhum, T. Personal identity. In P. Edwards (Ed.), *The encyclopedia of philosophy.* New York: Macmillan, 1967.

Ryle, G. *The concept of mind.* New York: Hutchinson's University Library, 1949.

Shaffer, J. *Philosophy of mind.* Englewood Cliffs, N.J.: Prentice-Hall, 1968.

50

Psychological Consequences of Sin
William G. Bixler

A biblical understanding of the psychological consequences of sin must begin with the fall and its disastrous effects for all of creation. The first three chapters of Genesis hold that all pain, suffering, and disorder stem, not from God's good intentions, but from the disobedience of Adam and Eve. In this sense it is right and proper to assert that all psychological disorder is the result of sin. However, this assertion must be qualified by the equally biblical notion that persons suffer psychologically not only because they are sinners and follow in Adam's train, but because they are victimized by a world infected by sin.

The third and fourth chapters of Genesis provide a vivid illustration of this. Adam and Eve commit the primal sin and are then made to suffer the consequences of their own actions as pain in childbirth and toiling by the sweat of one's brow. However, the next section of the narrative tells the story of the murder of Abel by his brother, Cain. The text makes it clear that Abel is killed because of his brother's jealous wrath and not because he had offended God. Abel is innocent of wrongdoing, and thus becomes the victim of the sin of his brother.

The Scriptures are replete with this dual understanding of the consequences of sin, consequences that stem from one's own evil and consequences brought about by the evil of others. A major biblical theme is God's recognition and condemnation of the victimizing capacity of sin. As Berkouwer (1971) notes, "Nowhere does the Scripture take an easy view of our sin on the false presumption that it is merely a sin against our fellowman. The anger of the Lord rests on that man who sheds an innocent man's blood. An unimaginable guilt may show its ugliness in human affairs: but just as unimaginable is the judgment against the man who spurns his neighbor and does injury to his fellowman who was made in the image of God" (p. 243). Injury to one's neighbor may take the form of actual physical abuse; however, the injury that can be inflicted on a person's mind and emotions is often more subtle and more damaging.

Another form of psychological damage can be attributed to the effects of the fall on the natural world. Paul alludes to this when he describes the entire creation as being subject to futility and enslaved to corruption so that it "groans and suffers" (Rom. 8:20–22). In essence the physical universe is injured and, in turn, can injure its inhabitants in such diverse ways as disease, flood, and famine. These distortions, or "injuries," of the physical creation are the result of sin, the first sin, and thus those who suffer psychological trauma due to these distortions may said to be suffering, albeit indirectly, the psychological consequences of sin.

That these physical distortions can cause psychological trauma is beyond dispute. A great number of diseases and physical maladies may seriously disrupt the psychological functioning of an afflicted person. For example, brain lesions or tumors may cause symptoms ranging from depression to hallucinations to gross sexual misconduct. Hypothyroidism (underactivity of the thyroid gland) may cause delusions, hallucinations, apathy, and slowness of thought. Involuntary crying or laughing may occur with the onset of multiple sclerosis, while hypoglycemia (low blood sugar) may precipitate full-blown anxiety attacks (Bockar, 1975). Also, there is a good deal of recent research suggesting that certain mental disorders such as schizophrenia and bipolar disorder may have genetic components.

Both natural and man-made disasters leave victims not only physically battered but psychologically paralyzed. The effects of a disaster such as an earthquake on victims can include hysterical reactions, phobic reactions, nightmares, anxiety, social withdrawal, and concentration loss, among other symptoms.

There is also the psychological victimization of persons by their fellow human beings. Paul's solemn warning to fathers to avoid provoking their children to anger "lest they become discouraged" (Col. 3:21) carries with it an implicit recognition that psychological damage can result from poor parenting.

The psychological damage to young children who have been physically or sexually abused is sometimes irreparable. Victims of rape and incest can develop depression, anxiety, dissociations, or other symptoms as a means of coping with the shame, frustration, fear, and rage associated with the traumatic experiences. These and other more subtle attacks on an individual's dignity and worth may precipitate emotional problems.

That extensive, and often permanent, psychological damage can be inflicted on persons by the sins of others cannot be denied. Thus, any counseling approach that wishes to take the concept of sin seriously must recognize that sin victimizes the innocent and that the psychological consequences of sin include the wounds and scars of the emotionally abused.

However, while affirming the biblical notion that sin victimizes, it must not be forgotten that the perpetrators of sin pay dearly, both spiritually and psychologically, for "missing the mark." To assume that sinning would have no psychological consequences would be to deny the holistic view of persons espoused by the Bible. "Scripture constantly makes it clear that sin is not something which corrupts relatively or partially, but a corruption which fully affects the radix, the root, of man's existence, and therefore man himself" (Berkouwer, 1962, p. 140).

The belief that persons suffer mental torment for their sins was until recently a belief firmly rooted in Western culture and reflected in the great literature—for example, Shakespeare's Lady MacBeth. It is ironic that what was one of the most important themes in Western literature is now denied by many behavioral scientists who are attempting to understand the nature of human personality and existence while ignoring the insights of a Shakespeare or Dostoevski.

It should be noted that not all psychologists deny the existence of sin or the consequences stemming from sinning. Menninger (1973) attempts to salvage the concept of sin from the dustbin of the current era. He documents how our society has chosen to ignore or destroy the notion of sin and the price that has been paid for doing so.

Sin and guilt cannot be separated biblically or psychologically; thus it is guilt that most profoundly affects the psyche of those who sin. This idea has had an ardent spokesman in Mowrer (1961; Mowrer & Veszelovszky, 1980), who holds that a certain degree of mental illness stems not from psychological guilt feelings but from real, actul guilt brought on by misdeeds—that is, sin. While his terminology, which includes words such as *guilt, confession,* and *expiation,* is not as theologically precise as one might hope, Mowrer has attempted to shed light on the role of conscience and morals in mental disorder.

One of Mowrer's students, Smrtic (1979), describes a number of cases of persons with psychological symptoms such as anxiety, suspiciousness, mania, and suicidal gestures which he believes stem directly from wrong behavior and unconfessed sin. An exhaustive list of psychological symptoms related to actual sin in the life of individuals is not possible, due to the unique psychological makeup of each person. However, suffice it to say that feelings of meaninglessness, isolation, anxiety, and guilt may stem from the emptiness of being alienated from God by willful disobedience.

Neither Mowrer nor Smrtic would argue that unconfessed guilt is the cause of all psychological disturbance. However, they have provided a much-needed counterpoint to the idea that all mental disorder is the result of victimization and that none of it is caused by the disturbed person himself.

Thus, it is apparent that psychological disorders may be rooted in the sin of victimization, the sinfulness of the distorted creation, or the personal sin of the disturbed individual. The biblical doctrine of the spiritual, mental, and psychological unity of the person allows for the possibility that all three causative factors could be operating simultaneously in one individual. In this situation a variety of interventions would need to be utilized. For example, confession and prayer, psychotherapy, and medication might all be needed to help a person overcome the debilitating effects of depression.

A truly biblical approach to counseling and psychotherapy recognizes that while sin is the root cause, a loving response to a suffering person would involve spiritual, psychological, and medical forms of treatment in concert. As Tournier (1962) has so perceptively noted, "Every psychological confession has religious significance, and every religious confession, whether ritual and sacramental or free, has its psychological effects. It is perhaps in this fact that we perceive most clearly the unity of the human being, and how impossible it is to dissociate the physical, psychological and religious aspects of his life" (p. 204).

References

Berkouwer, G. C. *Man: The image of God.* Grand Rapids: Eerdmans, 1962.

Berkouwer, G. C. *Sin.* Grand Rapids: Eerdmans, 1971.

Bockar, J. A. *Primer for the nonmedical psychotherapist.* New York: Spectrum, 1975.

Menninger, K. A. *Whatever became of sin?* New York: Hawthorn, 1973.

Mowrer, O. H. *The crisis in psychiatry and religion.* Princeton, N.J.: Van Nostrand, 1961.

Mowrer, O. H., & Veszelovszky, A. V. There indeed may be a "right way": Response to James D. Smrtic. *Psychotherapy: Theory, Research, and Practice,* 1980, *17,* 440–447.

Smrtic, J. D. Time to remove our theoretical blinders: Integrity therapy may be the right way. *Psychotherapy: Theory, Research, and Practice,* 1979, *16,* 185–189.

Tournier, P. *Guilt and grace.* New York: Harper & Row, 1962.

51

Religious Legalism
William G. Bixler

Religious legalism refers to a complex set of attitudes and beliefs organized around the conviction that certain laws must be obeyed in order to establish and maintain a relationship with God. These laws are usually considered divine in origin and therefore immutable. They may encompass any area of life, with no aspect of human activity considered too insignificant or private to warrant possible exemption from regulation.

A belief in a moral code is not, ipso facto, religious legalism. However, legalism results from such a belief when strict obedience to the code is conceived as being the sole or primary means of gaining and keeping the favor of the Deity. Legalism thrives on a distorted sense of obligation.

The theological roots of modern-day religious legalism may be traced to the intertestamental period, when a fundamental change occurred in the role of Old Testament law for the Jews. The concept of the covenant as the condition of membership in the people of God was replaced by that of obedience to the law. This obedience became the basis of God's verdict of pleasure or displeasure toward the individual. The sole mediator between God and man became the Torah, and all relationships between God and man, Israel, or the world became subordinated to the Torah. Most importantly, justification, righteousness, and life in the world to come were thought to be secured by obeying the law (Ladd, 1957).

This attitude was prevalent during the time of Christ and influenced the biblical precursors of twentieth-century legalism: Pharisaism, Judaizing theology, and gnosticism.

Pharisaism attempted to represent the true people of God by obeying the law, and in doing so hoped to prepare the way for the Messiah. The Pharisees observed all the legal prescriptions of Scripture in fine detail; they also held to the authority of the halakah, the body of legal descriptions that interpreted the law. The regulations increased in number and complexity to the point of pedantry. For example, because food could not be cooked on the Sabbath, a debate arose between two groups as to whether water alone or both water and cooked food could be placed on a previously heated stove without committing a violation (Muller, 1976). The regulations became so difficult to obey that they proved a stumbling block to those who could not keep them all, and who thus felt they were outside the kingdom of God. Christ spoke to that tragic situation in his scathing denunciation of Pharisaical legalism (Matt. 23:4).

A variant of this form of legalism was introduced into the churches in Galatia, prompting Paul to write his famous letter on Christian liberty to the congregations in that province. The Judaizers, as they became known, infiltrated the churches, claiming that full salvation was impossible apart from observance of Jewish law and ritual. They were especially adamant that gentile Christians be circumcised, since this was the symbol of membership in the New Israel. Paul's theological and emotional antipathy toward this form of legalism is quite evident in his sarcastic suggestion that those who argue for the necessity of circumcision should take the next logical step and castrate themselves (Gal. 5:12).

Paul also had to combat legalism in the form of incipient gnosticism at Colossae. This syncretistic heresy taught that the goal of life for gnostic adherents was to obtain true knowledge (gnosis), which would eventually allow them to leave the prison of the body and merge with the composite whole. Apparently a number of Colossian Christians were seeking heavenly visions as part of their rite of passage into a knowledge of the divine mysteries. They were informed that such visions could come about only by a rigorous discipline of asceticism and self-denial. Abstinence from food and drink, observance of initiatory and purifactory rites, and possibly a life of celibacy and mortification of the human body (Col. 2:21,23) were all prescribed as part of the regimen necessary to obtain fullness of life (Martin, 1978).

While each of these ancient forerunners of present-day legalism differed from the other in certain respects, all three attempted to legislate certain behavior as the primary means of obtaining "salvation"—whether that was defined as hastening the advent of the Messiah, gaining membership in the New Israel, or seeking the eventual release of the soul from the confines of the body.

These forms of legalism did not die off; rather, they merely altered their appearance and continued to plague the church throughout the centuries. A study of church history would suggest that too often religious legalism has been the norm rather than the exception. American evangelicalism continues to wrestle with legalistic tendencies within its ranks, partly due to its Puritan roots and fundamentalist legacy. The Puritans, for example, at one time decreed that one could dress a baby on the Sabbath but not kiss it; they also allowed that a man could comb his hair on that day but not shave his beard (Brinsmead, 1981b). Fundamentalism, while usually not as extreme, continues in a similar legalistic framework with its absolutizing prohibitions of many activities that do not have sufficient scriptural warrant.

An examination of the phenomenon of religious legalism reveals some striking similarities to obsessive-compulsive disorder (which includes characteristics of both obsessional neurosis and obsessional personality disorder, while recognizing that the former is usually more dysfunctional).

Religious legalism often infects the practitioner with a sense of moral superiority and a concomitant critical, condemning attitude toward those who do not conform to the same standards of conduct. This type of attitude is graphically illustrated in the biblical story of the Pharisee who stood in the temple thanking God that he was not like the terrible sinners around him. Christ warns that this type of self-exaltation can prevent a person from being justified before God (Luke 18:10–14). Similarly the obsessive-compulsive individual claims moral superiority and will often show an air of condescension to those around him. The manifestation of moral superiority most often hides feelings of inferiority and self-hatred that are then projected onto those who are deemed inferior. Just as the legalist must obey all the laws perfectly, so too the obsessive-compulsive person strives for perfection, avoiding tasks that might cause him to fail. Failure for the obsessional is equivalent to breaking the law for the legalist. Absolute perfection is the minimum acceptable standard for both.

Both types of persons have great difficulty with the gray areas of life. The legalist wishes to legislate every area of life and thus tends to concentrate on behavioral and religious minutiae. The obsessive-compulsive is characterized by aversion to ambiguity and a tendency to put all of life into neat, black-and-white categories.

Anxiety and fear are primary motivators for both the legalist and the obsessive-compulsive. The practitioner of legalism is driven to obedience by an overwhelming fear that God will punish or reject him if he does not obey perfectly. The person caught in obsessive-compulsiveness is driven to obey rules, obsessions, and compulsions by the unceasing threat of internal punishment meted out by the perfectionistic and hypercritical superego. Although the rules of conduct may differ for both types of person, they serve a similar function of assuring that catastrophe, whether spiritual or psychological, may be averted as long as the laws are obeyed or the compulsions followed.

Legalism is caused by biblical and doctrinal distortions and misunderstandings. Obsessive-compulsiveness can be traced in theory to a basic anxiety (Horney, 1950), defined as a feeling of profound insecurity, apprehensiveness, and helplessness in a world conceived as potentially hostile. Thus, they are not the same phenomenon. However, the affinities between the two are such that they can exist hand-in-glove with each other. The intertwining of legalism and obsessive-compulsiveness creates a hybrid that is very resistant to alteration through counseling or psychotherapy.

Counseling of the legalist/obsessive-compulsive must be grounded in the therapeutic triad of empathy, genuineness, and unconditional acceptance on the part of the therapist. The importance of acceptance cannot be overstated. By accepting the client just as he or she is, the therapist models, although imperfectly, a loving, accepting Christ whose love is not contingent on one's being perfect, since he died for us while we were yet sinners (Rom. 5:8). At the same time this unconditional acceptance will help mitigate the destructiveness of the critical, perfectionistic superego.

An examination of the cognitive elements of the disorder will decrease their power over the person as he or she learns to look at the world, the self, and God in a new light. Individuals with this type of problem usually have very negative concepts of God stemming from doctrinal distortions and/or an equation of the heavenly Father with the person's punitive, rigid earthly father. Helping a person to gain insight into these aspects of the problem can prove both spiritually and emotionally liberating.

Lastly, the Reformation principle of *sola fide*, justification by faith alone apart from works or obedience to the law, can provide an antidote to the poison of legalism/obsessive-compulsiveness. Bruce (1977) notes that Paul's statement that Christ is the end of the law (Rom. 10:4) means that since Christ has come law has no place whatsoever in one's approach to God. "According to Paul," he adds, "the believer is *not* under the law as a rule of life—unless one thinks of the law of love, and that is a completely different kind of law, fulfilled not by obedience to a code but by the outworking of an inward power" (p. 192).

The New Testament does not make appeal for proper behavior on the basis of Old Testament rules. Christians' behavior throughout the New Testament is shaped and colored by what Christ has done. The law of Christ demands that believers forgive as they have been forgiven (Col. 3:13), accept one another as Christ has accepted them (Rom. 15:7), and place the same value on people that the blood of Christ places on them (Brinsmead, 1981a).

As Luther observed, no good work helps justify or save an unbeliever. Thus the person who wishes to do good works should begin not with the doing of works but with believing, which alone makes a person good; for nothing makes a person good except faith, or evil except unbelief.

Only faith in Christ can liberate the legalist/obsessive-compulsive from the twin tyrannies of the law and the superego. As he comes to experience the freedom and forgiveness in Jesus Christ, he begins to see that laws and compulsions are unnecessary and can be replaced by "works done out of spontaneous love in obedience to God" (Luther, 1943, p. 295).

References

Brinsmead, R. D. Jesus and the law. *Verdict*, 1981, *4*(4), 6–70. (a)

Brinsmead, R. D. Sabbatarianism re-examined. *Verdict*, 1981, *4*(6), 5–30. (b)

Bruce, F. F. *Paul, apostle of the heart set free*. Grand Rapids: Eerdmans, 1977.

Horney, K. *Neurosis and human growth*. New York: Norton, 1950.

Ladd. G. E. *A theology of the New Testament*. Grand Rapids: Eerdmans, 1974.

Luther, M. The freedom of a Christian. In M. Luther, *Three Treatises*. Philadelphia: Muhlenberg Press, 1943.

Martin, R. P. *New Testament foundations: A guide for Christian students* (Vol. 2). Grand Rapids: Eerdmans, 1978.

Muller, D. Pharisee. In C. Brown (Ed.), *Dictionary of New Testament theology* (Vol. 2). Grand Rapids: Eerdmans, 1976.

Additional Readings

Salzman, L. *Treatment of the obsessive personality*. New York: Aronson, 1980.

Shapiro, D. *Neurotic styles*. New York: Basic Books, 1965.

52

Worship
J. Harold Ellens

An Anglo-Saxon term implying esteem, gratitude, and praise for someone who has demonstrated worthiness for such respect and adoration, *worship* is derived from the Old English *worthship*, referring to the worthiness of the object of worship. The Latin word most used in reference to worship in the medieval church was *leiturgia*, from which we get *liturgy*. Liturgy is a strategy or pattern for action toward a chosen goal. The pattern or strategy is derived from the goal to be achieved. Thus, in liturgy form comes from the nature and shape of the content of the action. This is true in worship and in daily work. We may refer to the liturgy of work or of worship, but standard usage today is confined mainly to worship.

Christian worship is not mainly a program for teaching Christian truth, nor an emotional pep rally where one can get one's spiritual batteries charged. Worship is the celebration of the historical facts that God was uniquely in Jesus of Nazareth, reconciling the world to himself, and that God has always and continues to maintain and shepherd his creation in gracious providence and eternal love.

The celebration of worship arises from the individual and communal delight and relief of knowing those two historical facts. Worship is, therefore, the celebration of gratitude and hope. It is the act and experience of taking profound and grateful account of God's nature and behavior: he is for us, not against us. He is not a threat but our consolation. The psychological principle undergirding worship's redemptive value is that people who can be grateful can be healthy and people who cannot be grateful cannot be healthy. The purpose of worship is to enhance spiritual wholeness, emotional health, and creative, holy life, while expressing gratitude to God. Experiencing and celebrating the joy and relief of God's grace in forgiveness and providence produces the fulfillment of that purpose.

History

Christian worship is normally communal, an act and experience of persons in congregation. The Judeo-Christian worship tradition began in an individualistic pattern. The patriarchs from Adam to Jacob often worshiped alone. That pattern persisted during the era of the judges, though communal worship had been developed. Israel worshiped as a nation during Moses' leadership. Shiloh was a place of national communal worship during the early years in Canaan and was prominent in Israel's life by the era of Samuel. After a struggle with persisting individualism and tribalism in worship, Israel came to a unified communal worship when David brought the ark of the covenant to Jerusalem. This communal liturgical experience gave rise to the psalms of David, sung in Israel's worship. Communal worship came to full bloom with the building of Solomon's temple.

The believing community was split by Jeroboam between worship at Dan and Beersheba, and after the exile between Samaria and Jerusalem. However, when Israel honored its communal worship ideal, assembling as congregation at the temple in Jerusalem, its life as a nation and as a worshiping community centered in the liturgy of the great day of atonement. After the exile this focus was sturdily maintained, while the rise of synagogues came into vogue in local communities. These were centers of religious instruction, not worship centers as such.

The history of the Christian movement and its worship is equally meaningful. Early Christians seem to have gathered rather spontaneously for worship (Acts 2). They worshiped with emphasis upon communal celebration, in a free-form style, though they continued to practice the Israelite rituals and met in the synagogues. By the second century there was no uniform universal Christian liturgy, but numerous strong liturgical movements. Professional clergy, sacraments, catechetical programs, and preaching lectionaries were already everywhere in use. The church as an institution was forming.

In the third century Hippolytus standardized the liturgy mainly on the form current in Justin's time. A considerable variety in forms of worship throughout the churches of Europe, Asia, and Africa persisted, nonetheless, until the official promulgation of the first Roman rite in the seventh century. The liturgies of the Eastern churches tended to be less stereotyped and even more celebrational than those of the Western, or Roman, church. After Gregory the liturgies of the West have varied little from the first Roman rite, except those of the Reformation churches. The Roman Catholic Church has simplified some elements for local convenience.

The liturgies of the Reformation churches were shaped by a radical reaction to the formalism of the Roman rite. This reaction took two directions. The mainstream of Anglican Catholicism under Henry VIII flows into contemporary Episcopal and Methodist usage and endeavors to preserve as much of the historic liturgy of Christendom as is theologically and practically possible in the present age in local usage. The mainstream of Reformed liturgy flows into contemporary Presbyterian, Reformed, Baptist, Congregational, and most fundamentalist and evangelical usage. It endeavors to dispense with as much of the Roman rite as it can without losing distinctive Christian character and gospel-centered meaning. Lutheranism preserves some of both these mainstreams, adhering in significant degree to the cardinal elements of the Roman form while endeavoring to inspire it with the biblical and evangelical spontaneity and vitality sought by the Reformers.

Unfortunately large deficits persist in Protestant liturgies. In their attempt to avoid the formalism into which the Roman rite had fallen by the sixteenth century, they have tended to become mere contexts for preaching. That would have been appropriate to the teaching sessions of the early church's synagogues but not to worship in the third-century churches or in the liturgy of Gregory the Great. Protestantism has so significantly lost its sense of worship and liturgy as celebration that its people go "to sermon," not to worship. That is an excess deriving from the Reformation emphasis on the centrality of the Word at the expense of the sacraments. The result is a devaluing of the essential function of worship: the mediation to needy persons of the consolation of the gospel of grace, through the symbolic acts, elements, and sequences of the liturgy, for the psychological and spiritual healing of the congregation as individuals and as community.

Function and Structure

The function of worship is psychological and spiritual healing through the celebration of God's grace. Liturgy therefore must have the function of enacting the process of celebrating that grace. The psychospiritual dynamics of celebration involve symbolic elements such as bread and wine, the centrality of the pulpit, Bible, and the shape of the sanctuary; symbolic sequences such as opening greetings followed by God's law, congregational penitence, God's absolution, and eucharistic celebration of the gift of grace; psychospiritual growth in insight, anxiety reduction, relief from guilt, joy in God's peace, and comfort in Christian fellowship; and the reshaping of the worshipers' discipleship as they move from the sanctuary to renew the world.

The structure of liturgy should come from the demands of that function, as it did in the Old Testament temple rites and in the first Roman rite. The worshiper moves, in properly redemptive worship, from the world of work to the sanctuary, through the encounter with God to confession of sin, absolution, celebration of that absolution in the Eucharist, expressions and gifts of gratitude, sermonic guidance for the life of grace in the world of work, and finally the benediction. The psychospiritual process recapitulates our personal conversion processes. We move from the world to God. Then we move through the psychospiritual stages of greeting, guilt, grace, gratitude, and guidance. Then we move back to the world as renewed persons, renewing God's world. That is the healing and redeeming process worship is intended to be, was in Scripture, and endeavored to be in the historic Christian church.

Protestantism, particularly American fundamentalism and evangelicalism, unformly lacks this psychospiritual understanding of true worship. The focus on didactic sermons as the center of worship has turned Protestant worship into an essentially cognitive process, largely oriented on the left hemisphere of the brain. But worship should be more of a right hemisphere celebration, a response of the heart as celebration of God's unconditional, radical, and universal grace.

Additional Readings

Allinder, W. *Responses . . . to alterations in worship services . . . designed to enhance the use of the right hemisphere of the brain in worship.* Unpublished DMin Project, Drew University Theological School, 1983.

Ellens, J. H. *Psychology in worship.* New York: Harper & Row, 1983.

Springer, S. P., & Deutsch, G. *Left brain, right brain.* San Fransisco: W. H. Freeman, 1981.

Index